John Swett

School Elocution

A Manual of Vocal Training in High Schools, Normal Schools, and Academies

John Swett

School Elocution
A Manual of Vocal Training in High Schools, Normal Schools, and Academies

ISBN/EAN: 9783337157982

Printed in Europe, USA, Canada, Australia, Japan

Cover: Foto ©Thomas Meinert / pixelio.de

More available books at **www.hansebooks.com**

SCHOOL ELOCUTION

A MANUAL OF
VOCAL TRAINING IN HIGH SCHOOLS, NORMAL
SCHOOLS, AND ACADEMIES

BY

JOHN SWETT

PRINCIPAL OF THE SAN FRANCISCO GIRLS' HIGH AND NORMAL SCHOOL
EX-STATE SUPERINTENDENT OF PUBLIC INSTRUCTION, STATE OF
CALIFORNIA; AUTHOR OF "METHODS OF TEACHING"

NEW YORK
HARPER & BROTHERS, FRANKLIN SQUARE
1886

SCHOOL ELOCUTION

PREFACE.

This book is not an elaborate treatise, designed for special teachers of elocution, but a drill-book of essentials for use by teachers that do not make elocution a specialty. In most High and Normal schools, and in the advanced Grammar grades, the curriculum is so crowded that there is no time for the special training given by professional teachers of elocution to select classes of private pupils.

The time generally allotted to reading and elocution seldom exceeds that allowed for vocal music—perhaps one or two hours a week. Hence the successful training of large classes involves a great deal of concert drill; and this requires the use of a suitable manual of principles, directions, and drill exercises.

This treatise owes its existence to the difficulties met with in the management of a very large High school, including a postgraduate Normal department, in which an honest effort has been made to secure a fair degree of attention to school reading and elocution.

Fully realizing the limitations of teachers in similar schools, I have endeavored to keep within the bounds of what it is possible to accomplish without making elocution a hobby. The salient points of this hand-book are as follows

1. It includes only what it is possible to take up without material interference with the ordinary school curriculum.

2. It embraces only what pupils of average ability are capable of comprehending and mastering.

3. It includes a fair outfit of principles and practice for those who intend to become teachers.

4. It can be effectively used by teachers who are not specialists in elocution.

5. It contains clear and concise statements of principles and rules.

6. It is characterized by the copiousness and freshness of the illustrative drill-examples.

It was my good fortune, more than thirty years ago, to be a student under that most critical and scholarly elocutionist and Normal-school instructor, Professor William Russell; and it is natural that I should follow in the steps of my revered instructor. I am also indebted to many excellent manuals on elocution for principles and examples that constitute the common stock of matter on this subject.

I am under obligations to the publishers of the works of American authors for permission to make short extracts from their publications, and in particular, to Houghton, Mifflin & Co., for extracts from Longfellow, Whittier, Holmes, Lowell, and Emerson.

JOHN SWETT.

CONTENTS.

PART I. ORTHOPHONY AND ORTHOEPY.

I.	Introductory Hints and Directions	11
II.	Vowel Sounds	15
III.	Consonant Sounds	35
IV.	Classification of Elementary Sounds	39
V.	Orthoepy	45

PART II. PRINCIPLES IN ELOCUTION.

CHAPTER I. EMPHASIS, PAUSES, AND INFLECTIONS.

I.	Emphasis		57
II.	Pauses		64
	I.	Grammatical Pauses	65
	II.	Rhetorical Pauses	65
	III.	Rules for Rhetorical Pauses	69
	IV.	Emphatic Pauses	73
III.	Inflection		75
	I.	The Rising Inflection	82
	II.	The Falling Inflection	95
	III.	Inflection of the Parenthesis	109
	IV.	The Circumflex Inflection	111
	V.	The Monotone	119
	VI.	Examples of Pauses, Emphasis, and Inflection	128

CHAPTER II. FORCE AND STRESS.

I.	Force of Voice		141
	I.	Very Soft Force	144
	II.	Soft or Subdued Force	144
	III.	Moderate Force	147
	IV.	Loud Force	149
	V.	Very Loud or Declamatory Force	151
II.	Stress of Voice		155
	I.	Radical Stress	155
	II.	Median Stress	165
	III.	Vanishing Stress	172
	IV.	Thorough Stress	175
	V.	Compound Stress	180
	VI.	Intermittent Stress	181

CHAPTER III. MOVEMENT.

I. Moderate Movement	187
II. Fast Movement	189
III. Very Fast Movement	191
IV. Slow Movement	194
V. Very Slow Movement	195

CHAPTER IV. PITCH OF VOICE.

I. Introductory	199
II. Concert Drill	200
III. Faults	201
IV. Examples of Middle Pitch	201
V. Examples of High Pitch	203
VI. Examples of Low Pitch	209
VII. Examples of Very Low Pitch	211

CHAPTER V. QUALITY OF VOICE.

I. Pure Tone	216
II. The Orotund	220
III. Aspirated Quality	230
IV. Guttural Quality	237
V. The Falsetto	238
VI. The Semitone	239

CHAPTER VI. MODULATION AND STYLE OF EXPRESSION.

I. Modulation	245
II. The Reading of Poetry	248
III. Imitative Reading	255
IV. Exercises in Modulation	259
V. Dialect Reading and Personation	262

PART III. MISCELLANEOUS SELECTIONS.

SECTION I. PROSE SELECTIONS.

1. Elocutionary Training		277
2. Good Reading	*John S. Hart*	279
3. The Music of the Human Voice	*Prof. Wm. Russell*	280
4. The Art of Reading	*Dr. Rush*	281
5. On Learning by Heart	*Lushington*	283
6. School Libraries		286
7. Poems	*Oliver Wendell Holmes*	287

SCHOOL ELOCUTION. vii

8.	Scrooge and Marley	*Charles Dickens*	288
9.	Defense of Poetry	*William Ellery Channing*	293
10.	Falstaff	*Henry Giles*	296
11.	Wealth	*Ralph Waldo Emerson*	298
12.	The Astronomer's Vision		300
13.	Education	*Professor Huxley*	302
14.	Mathematics and Physics	*Herbert Spencer*	304

SECTION II. PROSE DECLAMATIONS.

1.	Character of True Eloquence	*Daniel Webster*	307
2.	National Greatness	*John Bright*	308
3.	The Passing of the Rubicon	*Knowles*	309
4.	Our Duties to Our Country	*Daniel Webster*	310
5.	The American War	*Lord Chatham*	311
6.	Freedom	*Col. E. D. Baker*	312
7.	The Voices of the Dead	*Orville Dewey*	313
8.	Grattan's Reply to Mr. Corry		314
9.	Supposed Speech of John Adams	*Daniel Webster*	315
10.	The Constitution and the Union	*Daniel Webster*	317
11.	The Constitution	*Daniel Webster*	317
12.	Duties of American Citizens	*Daniel Webster*	318
13.	Labor	*Orville Dewey*	319
14.	The Future of America	*Daniel Webster*	320
15.	Patriotism	*T. F. Meagher*	321
16.	The Fourth of July	*Daniel Webster*	322
17.	True Greatness	*Thomas Starr King*	323
18.	The Normans	*Frederick P. Tracy*	325
19.	Washington's Birthday	*Daniel Webster*	326
20.	Nations and Humanity	*Geo. W. Curtis*	327
21.	Character of Washington	*Phillips*	328
22.	Bunker Hill Monument	*Daniel Webster*	329
23.	The Birthday of Washington	*Rufus Choate*	331
24.	The National Clock	*Thomas Starr King*	332
25.	Free Schools	*Horace Mann*	333
26.	The Ballot	*E. H. Chapin*	334
27.	Educational Power		335
28.	Schools and Teachers		337
29.	Elements of the American Government	*Daniel Webster*	338

SECTION III. RECITATIONS AND READINGS: POETRY.

| 1. | The Crowded Street | *William Cullen Bryant* | 340 |
| 2. | The Builders | *H. W. Longfellow* | 341 |

3. Psalm of Life	H. W. Longfellow	342
4. Apostrophe to the Ocean	Lord Byron	344
5. Battle of Waterloo	Lord Byron	346
6. Santa Filomena	H. W. Longfellow	347
7. The Death Struggle	Sir Walter Scott	349
8. Sandalphon	H. W. Longfellow	350
9. The Old Continentals	McMasters	352
10. The Winds	William Cullen Bryant	354
11. The Day is Done	H. W. Longfellow	356
12. The Battlefield	William Cullen Bryant	357
13. Hymn to Mont Blanc	Coleridge	359
14. Morning Hymn	John Milton	362
15. Thanatopsis	William Cullen Bryant	363
16. Gray's Elegy		366
17. Daniel Webster	Oliver Wendell Holmes	371
18. St. Augustine's Ladder	H. W. Longfellow	373
19. Ring Out, Wild Bells	Tennyson	375
20. Summer Rain	James Russell Lowell	376
21. Hymn to the North Star	William Cullen Bryant	377
22. The American Flag	Drake	379
23. The Chambered Nautilus	Oliver Wendell Holmes	381
24. Kentucky Belle	Constance F. Woolson	382
25. The Charcoal Man	Trowbridge	389
26. Grandmother's Story of Bunker Hill	O. W. Holmes	391

PART I.

PART I.

ORTHOPHONY AND ORTHOEPY.

SECTION I.

INTRODUCTORY HINTS AND DIRECTIONS.

1. As correct pronunciation is an essential of good reading, it is important that pupils should acquire at the outset a thorough knowledge of the elementary sounds of the English language, and that they should be trained to a ready command of the organs of speech.

2. The melody of our mother-tongue depends in a great measure on the fullness and purity with which the vowel sounds are given. The most marked provincialisms in our country consist chiefly in the peculiar shades of sound given to certain vowels.

3. In high schools and normal schools, if anywhere, critical attention ought to be given to pronunciation. It is desirable that pupils should become familiar with the diacritical marks of the dictionary in order that they may be able to find, by themselves, the correct pronunciation of any word.

4. It is the object of the following lessons to train (1) the ear to the correct sound; (2) the voice to distinct enunciation; and (3) the eye to the use of diacritical marks.

I. Hints to Teachers.

1. In all short concert drill exercises, require pupils to *stand*, and to stand *erect*. Let the concert drill be preceded by a breathing exercise.

2. Insist upon it that pupils hold the book properly in the left hand, high enough to bring the head erect.

3. In the more difficult drill exercises, the teacher should first read the examples, requiring pupils to repeat in concert. To some extent, elocution must be taught by *imitation*.

4. The true economy of time in vocal culture, as in vocal music, *consists in training large numbers together*. The concert drill lessons may be given to two or three hundred pupils in the assembly hall as effectively as to a single class in the recitation room.

5. The concert drill in phonic spelling is designed to give pupils the full command of their vocal organs, and also to secure accurate articulation, enunciation, and pronunciation. At first, it may be desirable for the teacher to lead the class, giving every sound clearly, forcibly, and distinctly.

6. The grouped lists of words illustrating the vowel sounds should be pronounced distinctly and forcibly by the teacher, then by the class in concert, and finally, by individual pupils. The monosyllables in these lists should be spelled by sound, first by the teacher, next by the class in concert, and, finally, by individual pupils.

7. Insist upon it that pupils practice every lesson, after it has been read in school, at home, by themselves.

8. Impress upon pupils the fact that good reading, like vocal music, requires long-continued practice.

9. Insist upon it that pupils, when reading, shall raise their eyes from the book when approaching the end of a sentence, and repeat the last five or ten words looking directly at the teacher or the class.

II. Hints to Pupils.

1. Stand erect when you read, and hold the book in your left hand, high enough to bring the head erect.

2. By frequent inhalations, keep your lungs well filled with air.

3. Read loud enough to be easily heard by every member of your class. If possible, look over the advance lesson before the hour of class drill.

4. After the class drill at school, read each lesson by yourself at home. You can become a good reader only by patient and persevering practice.

5. If you have any marked faults in reading, you must endeavor to correct them by self-culture out of school.

6. Enter into the spirit of whatever you read, and read it so as to convey that spirit to those who listen.

7. Think about the meaning of what you read. Refer to the dictionary for the definition of any word you do not fully comprehend, or for the pronunciation of any word with which you are not familiar.

8. Listen attentively to the reading of your teacher, or of the best readers in the class, and try to imitate their style of reading.

9. Train yourself to the habit of raising your eyes from the book to look at the teacher or the class. It is a matter of politeness to look at those to whom you speak, or to whom you read. As you approach the end of a sentence, glance your eye along the words in advance of the tongue, and then complete the sentence without looking on the book. It is a good plan to practice this by yourself before a mirror.

10. Endeavor to become so familiar with the diacritical marks that you can find out, for yourself, from the dictionary, the pronunciation of any word without referring to the key, the table of sounds, or the teacher.

III. Preliminary Breathing Exercises.

Concert drill exercises in articulation and pronunciation should be preceded by short breathing exercises. These may be conducted in a great variety of ways, of which only a few are here indicated. The length of time in inhaling or exhaling may be regulated by the rise or fall of the teacher's hand.

1. Stand erect; feet firm; body braced; shoulders well back; arms akimbo.

2. Inhale slowly through the nostrils for five seconds; exhale slowly through the nostrils for five seconds. Repeat five times. Regulate the inhaling and exhaling by the rise and fall of the hand. In inhaling, fill the lower part of the lungs and do not elevate the shoulders.

3. Take a similar exercise, prolonging the time, first to ten seconds, next to fifteen seconds, and finally to twenty seconds.

4. Inhale; exhale slowly, giving, in a soft whisper, the sound of "Ah!" prolonged for five seconds; ten seconds; as long as possible.

5. Inhale; exhale slowly, giving the sound of long *o*, in pure tone, prolonged for five seconds; next for ten seconds; then for fifteen seconds; and finally, as long as possible.

6. Inhale; exhale slowly, giving for ten seconds the sound of long *e*; of Italian *a*; of long *oo*.

7. Inhale; repeat, in monotone, the long vowels, *a, e, i, o, u,* until the breath is exhausted.

8. Inhale; count, with one breath, to 10; next, to 20; then, to 30.

9. Repeat, in one breath, the letters of the alphabet.

10. Inhale slowly; exhale slowly, giving the sound of liquid *l* prolonged for five seconds; ten seconds; fifteen seconds; twenty seconds; next, the sound of *m*; of *n*; of *r*.

SECTION II.

VOWEL SOUNDS OR VOCALS.

I. Table of Diacritical Markings.

1. Phonic Marks of Vocals.

Macron. ‾	Breve. ˘	Circumflex. ^	Two dots. ¨	One dot. ˙	Wave or Tilde. ~
āle	ăt	âir	ärm, ạll	ȧsk, whạt	
ēve, thẹy	ĕnd	whêre			hẽr
īce, bȳ	ĭt, lȳnx		pïque		sĩr
ōld	ŏn	ôr	prọve	ṣon, wọlf	
mōōn	bŏŏk				
ūse	ŭp	ûrge	rụle	pụll	

II. Equivalent Vocals or Substitutes.

ạ = ŏ	whạt, nŏt	ȯ = ŭ	dȯne, sŭn		
ẹ = ā	thẹy, dāy	ọ, ụ = ōō	mọve, rụle, schōōl		
ĭ = ē	sĭr, hẽr	ọ, ụ = ŏŏ	wọlf, pụll, wŏŏl		
ê = â	thêre, câre	ȳ = ī	rhȳme, tīme		
ï = ē	pïque, wēak	y̆ = ĭ	hy̆mn, whĭm		
ô = ạ	ôr, ạll				

III. Markings of Subvocals and Aspirates.

ç, çh = s, sh	çent, çhaise	s̱ = z	is̱, ros̱e
ȼ, ȼh = k	ȼake, aȼhe	t̲h, *vocal*	t̲his, t̲hat
g̲, *hard*	g̲o, g̲et	n̲ = ng	in̲k, win̲k
ġ = j	ġem, aġe	x̱ = g̱z	ex̱ample

II. ILLUSTRATIONS OF VOCALS.

1. The long sound of a.

Marked with a macron, thus—ā. The equivalents of long *a* are also included. Avoid prolonging the vanishing *e* sound, thus—mā-eed for māde.

āge	dāy	breāk	greāt	gāuge
pāle	gāy	steāk	strāight	yeā
āid	māy	de̱ign	we̱ight	ne̱igh
pāid	wāy	re̱ign	fre̱ight	sle̱igh

WORDS OFTEN MISPRONOUNCED.

ā're a	rā'dix	prāi'rie	ā'pri cot
nā'ked	rā'tion	eñis'son	ap pa rā'tus
māy'or	pā'tron	glā'mour	mael'strom
mā'tron	pāst'ry	hein'ous	pā tri ŏt'ic
mā'cron	sā'chem	pā'tri ot	vā'ri e gat ed

II. Italian or open a.

Marked with two dots over it, thus—ä. Avoid the provincialism of hăf for hälf, lăf for läugh, etc.

ärt	eälf	pälm	äh!	gäunt	läunch
äre	hälf	psälm	bäh!	häunt	stäunch
ärm	hälves	sälve	päths	jäunt	läugh
älms	eälves	läth	äunt	täunt	quälms
bälm	bäth	gäpe	däunt	cräunch	zouäve
eälm	päth	wräth	fläunt	häunch	heärth

WORDS OFTEN MISPRONOUNCED.

däunt'less	jäun'dice	säun'ter	Col o rä'do
guä'vȧ	läun'dry	jäunt'y	Ne vä'dȧ
guä'no	läugh'ter	pi ä'no	Mon tä'nȧ
gäunt'let	llä'mȧ	so prä'no	Tu lä're
häunt'ed	plä'zȧ	fY nä'le	So lä'no

III. The broad sound of a.

Marked with two dots under it, thus—a̤. Avoid the two extremes: (1) That of giving a̤ the sound of short o, as ŏll for a̤wl, etc. (2) That of making a equal to two syllables, as a̤w'ŭl for a̤ll, ca̤w'ŭl for ca̤ll, etc.

ba̤ll	ca̤ught	cha̤lk	a̤l'der	faṳ'çet
ta̤ll	ôught	ta̤lk	a̤l'ways	ca̤l'dron
dra̤wl	brôught	sta̤lk	a̤u'ḡer	fa̤l'çhion
cra̤wl	thôught	ḡauze	caṳ'cus	pa̤l'try
spra̤wl	groa̤t	ba̤ul	ṣaṳ'çer	ôr'der

IV. The short sound of a.

Marked with a breve, thus—ă. Avoid giving short a, as in ăt, the sound of intermediate a, as in ȧsk, or of Italian a, as in älms. Say ănd, not ȧnd; ăn'swer, not än'swer, etc.

ănd	ăn'swer	păt'ent	ră'tion al
băde	băr'rel	păg'eant	răil'le ry
cătch	hăr'row	răth'er	săt'ir ist
plănt	măr'ry	nă'tion al	suăv'i ty
plăid	năr'row	păt'ron age	tăp'est ry

V. Sound of a as in câre.

Marked with a circumflex, thus—â. Avoid the two extremes: (1) That of giving it the sound of Italian a, as chär for châir, thär for thêre, etc. (2) That of long a, as eā'er for câre, thā'er for thêre, ā'er for âir, etc.

âir	sweâr	thêre	pâre	pâr'ent
dâre	squâre	whêre	pâir	fâir'y
râre	weâr	theîr	fâre	châr'y
fâir	hâre	hâir	lâir	seârce'ly
beâr	peâr	heîr	prâyer	seâr'çi ty

VI. Intermediate a, as in ȧsk.

Marked with a dot over it, thus—ȧ. This is a medium sound between Italian *a* and short *a*. Avoid the two extremes: (1) That of Italian *a*, as färst for fȧst, därnce for dȧnce, etc. (2) That of short *a*, as ăsk for ȧsk, dănce for dȧnce, ăf'ter for ȧf'ter, etc.

ȧsk	chȧnt	dȧnce	grȧft	lȧnce	quȧff
ȧnt	chȧff	dȧft	grȧnt	mȧss	rȧft
ȧft	chȧnce	drȧft	glȧnce	mȧst	rȧsp
bȧsk	cȧst	drȧught	gȧsp	mȧsk	shȧft
bȧsque	clȧss	fȧst	grȧsp	pȧss	stȧff
brȧss	crȧft	flȧsk	hȧsp	pȧst	slȧnt
blȧst	clȧsp	glȧss	hȧft	pȧnt	tȧsk
cȧsque	cȧsk	grȧss	lȧst	prȧnce	trȧnce

I. WORDS OFTEN MISPRONOUNCED.

In all these words be careful to give *a* its intermediate sound as in ȧsk, not the short sound as in ănd.

ȧf'ter	fȧst'er	mȧs'ter	pȧss'port
bȧs'ket	fȧst'est	mȧs'tiff	rȧft'er
cȧs'ket	glȧss'y	pȧs'time	slȧnt'ing
clȧss'es	grȧss'y	pȧs'tor	tȧsk'work
crȧft'y	lȧst'ing	plȧs'ter	vȧst'ness
crȧfts'man	mȧss'ive	pȧst'ure	wȧft'ed

II. WORDS OFTEN MISPRONOUNCED.

a slȧnt'	com mȧnd'	ad vȧn'tage
a mȧss'	dis mȧst'	ad vȧnce'ment
a lȧs'	de mȧnd'	com mȧnd'ment
a vȧst'	en hȧnce'	en chȧnt'ment
ad vȧnce	en chȧnt'	en hȧnce'ment
a bȧft'	per chȧnce'	re mȧnd'ed

SCHOOL ELOCUTION. 19

VII. Sound of a as in whạt.

Marked with a dot under it, thus—ạ. This sound is equivalent to short *o*, as in nŏt. The word *what* is pronounced hwŏt, not wŭt.

wạs	squạsh	squạb'ble	stal'wart
wạd	swạp	squạt'ter	wal-let
wạsp	swạn	squal'id	wal'low
yạcht	swạmp	squad'ron	wad'dle
squạb	swạb	quar'rel	wan'ton
squạd	wạnd	swal'low	wạs'sail

Call on the class for additional words.

VIII. The long sound of e.

Marked with a macron, thus—ē. Long *e* is one of the three vowel extremes, ä and ọ being the other two.

bē	thiēf	ēi'ther	ē'go tism
tree	niēce	nēi'ther	ē'qui poise
bēam	siēge	lēi'ṣure	lē'ni ent
elēan	sēize	lē'ver	a mē'na ble
ēar	deed	fē'brile	pre çēd'ence
ēaves	fiērce	fē'tiçh	rē'qui em

IX. The short sound of e.

Marked with a breve, thus—ĕ. Avoid yĭt for yĕt, āig for ĕgg, etc.

bĕg	fĕoff	lĕath'er	kĕt'tle	tĕp'id
lĕg	an'y	mĕaṣ'ure	mĕt'ric	tĕn'et
brĕad	mĕr'ry	plĕaṣ'ure	prĕf'ace	rĕs'in
sàid	bur'y	bĕs'tial	pĕt'rel	a gain'
says	hĕif'er	dĕe'ade	pĕr'uke	a gainst'
dĕaf	lĕop'ard	fĕt'id	sĕck'el	for gĕt'

X. Sound of e as in vẽrge.

Marked with a wave or tilde, thus—ẽ. This sound nearly coincides with the sound of *u* as in urge, but is not quite so broad and guttural. Avoid the error of sounding ẽ like āi, as āirth for ẽarth, etc. Give the *r* after ẽ its full sound.

ẽrr	sẽrve	ẽarth	ẽr′mine	sẽrv′ant
hẽr	vẽrse	ẽarn	ẽarn′est	vẽr′dict
hẽrd	vẽrge	lẽarn	mẽr′cy	hẽrb′age
fẽrn	vẽrb	hẽard	mẽr′chant	ẽarn′ings
pẽrt	wẽre	myrrh	pẽr′son	sẽr′mon
nẽrve	gẽrm	thĩrst	pẽr′fect	sẽr′vice

XI. Sound of e as in thêre.

Marked with a circumflex, thus—ê. This sound is identical with the sound of *a* as in câre.

thêre	âir	hâir	thêre′fore
whêre	êre	hêir	whêre′fore
thêir	ê′er	nê′er	whêre as′

XII. Sound of e as in th<u>e</u>y.

Marked with a macron under it, thus—<u>e</u>. This sound is identical with long *a*.

th<u>e</u>y	wh<u>e</u>y	w<u>e</u>ight	v<u>e</u>in	n<u>e</u>igh′bor
pr<u>e</u>y	wāy	fr<u>e</u>ight	vāin	h<u>e</u>in′ous
prāy	n<u>e</u>igh	strāight	d<u>e</u>ign	lā′bor

XIII. The long sound of i and y.

Marked with a macron, thus—ī, ȳ.

Īsle	dīe	līar	fīre	ho rī′zon
stȳle	eȳe	lȳre	buȳ′er	in quīr′y
fīre	tīes	bȳ	tī′ny	de rī′sive
lȳre	aȳes	rȳe	tȳ′rant	as pīr′ant

SCHOOL ELOCUTION.   21

XIV. The short sound of i and y.

Marked with a breve, thus—ĭ, y̆.

hĭm	lўnx	dĭs′trict	trĭb′une
hўmn	nўmph	sўn′od	sўr′up
wĭthe	sўlph	vĭne′yard	vĭe′ar
mўth	rhўthm	sўr′inge	pret′tў
pĭth	schĭşm	sўn′tax	wĭt′ty

XV. Sound of i as in fĩrst.

Marked with a wave or tilde, thus—ĩ. This sound is identical with the sound of *e* as in hẽr. Avoid giving the broader and more guttural sound of *u* as in ûrge. Be careful to give *r* its full sound.

fĩrst	bĩrch	sĩr	çĩr′cle	vĩr′tue
thĩrst	bĩrth	fĩr	çĩr′cuit	vĩr′gin
g̃irl	dĩrge	stĩr	çĩr′cus	stĩr′rup
mĩrth	vẽrge	ẽarn	g̃ĩr′dle	squĩr′rel
fĩrm	ẽarth	fẽrn	ĩrk′some	sĩr′loin
worm	myrrh	lẽarn	mẽr′çy	thĩr′ty
world	dẽarth	hẽr	ẽarth′ly	worth′y
work	bĩrd	pẽrch	ẽar′ly	çẽr′tain
worse	g̃ĩrd	hẽard	ẽarn′est	mĩrth′ful
worth	pẽarl	hẽarse	ẽarth′en	worth′less

XVI. Sound of i as in pïque.

Marked with two dots over it, thus—ï. This sound is equivalent to that of long *e* as in mē.

an tïque′	cui şïne′	ma chïne′	rou tïne′
bas tïle′	de brïs′	ma rïne′	ra vïne′
ea prïçe′	e lïte′	po lïçe′	re g̃ïme′
çhe nïlle′	en nuï′	pe tïte′	ton tïne′
çhe mïşe′	fa tïgue′	ob lïque′	u nïque′
cri tïque′	fas çïne′	pe lïsse′	phy şïque′

XVII. The long sound of o.

Marked with a macron, thus—ō. Avoid shortening or obscuring the sound of long *o* as in ōld, in such words as rōad, cōat, hōme, bōne, stōne, etc.

bōne	cōlt	jōlt	yōke	ōn'ly
stōne	cōmb	mōst	yōlk	ō'ral
bōth	dōlt	smōke	quōth	whōl'ly
brōke	fōlks	spōke	beau	clōse'ly
chōke	hōld	flōwn	shōw	lōne'ly
clōak	hōme	whōle	wōn't	trō'phy
crōak	rōam	mōre	dō n't	ō'pal
ōak	hōld	rōar	gōat	ō'dor

I. WORDS OFTEN MISPRONOUNCED.

Avoid the error of saying hôrse for hōarse, fôrce for fōrce.

bōat	cōax	door	cōarse	gōurd	blōw
cōat	lōad	floor	hōarse	mōurn	trōw
tōad	lōam	brooch	sōurce	tōll	glōw
tōast	ōath	pōur	fōrce	pōll	sew
rōad	ōats	pōrch	bōard	serōll	quōth
gōad	thrōat	bōrne	hōard	rōll	grōss

II. WORDS OFTEN MISPRONOUNCED.

In words like the following, avoid the error of giving long *o* the sound of *o* as in ôr'der; as bôr'der for bōard'er, fôr'ger for fōr'ger, pôr'trait for pōr'trait, etc. Give *o* its full, long sound.

bōard'er	pōr'ter	an chō'vy	de cō'rous
bōwl'der	pōr'tion	a rō'ma	dī plō'ma cy
bōw'sprit	pōr'trait	ab dō'men	dī plō'ma tist
pōul'try	fōr'ġer	co rō'na	op pō'nent
pōul'tice	stōr'age	con dō'lence	so nō'rous
shōul'der	mōurn'er	cog nō'men	fōr'ġer y

XVIII. The short sound of o.

Marked with a breve, thus—ŏ. The sound of short *o*, as in nŏt, is slightly modified by the different consonants with which it is combined. In words like cough, gone, loss, etc., the sound of short *o* is modified so that it tends towards a sound intermediate between short *o* and broad *a*. Avoid the common error of saying dawg or dorg for dŏg; gawd or gord for gŏd; also, that of gŭt for gŏt, etc.

ŏn	dŏḡ	ŏff	eŏst	mŏth	cŏugh
ŏf	fŏḡ	scŏff	lŏst	clŏth	trŏugh
ŏdd	lŏḡ	mŏss	frŏst	ŏft	lŏng
bŏx	gŏt	lŏss	slŏth	sŏft	strŏng
fŏx	gŏd	tŏss	brŏth	lŏft	gŏng
phlŏx	hŏd	crŏss	trŏth	ḡŏne	wrŏng

I. WORDS OFTEN MISPRONOUNCED.

In every word give *o* its clean-cut short sound.

cŏm'mȧ	dŏç'ĭle	flŏr'in	mŏn'ad
cŏm'mon	dŏn'key	hŏv'el	nŏm'ad
cŏm'et	fŏr'est	grŏv'el	ŏf'fiçe
cŏm'bat	fōre'head	hŏr'rid	ŏr'ange
cŏm'rade	frŏn'tier	jŏc'und	ŏff'set
cŏl'lar	fŏr'age	lŏft'y	ŏff'ing
cŏn'flict	gŏd'ly	sŏft'ly	dŏg'ma
cŏn'strue	slŏth'ful	ŏft'en	dŏc'tor

II. WORDS OFTEN MISPRONOUNCED.

bŏn'net	prŏç'ess	stŏl'id	dŏl' or ous
cŏf'fee	prŏg'ress	squal'id	hŏl'o caust
cŏf'fin	prŏj'ect	quar'rel	mŏn'o gram
cŏr'al	phŏn'ic	be trŏth'	mŏl'e cule
prŏd'uct	prŏv'ost	be lŏng'	ŏn'er ous
prŏd'uce	sŏn'net	ex tŏl'	ŏr'a cle

XIX. Sound of o as in dóne.

Marked with a dot over it, thus—ȯ. This sound is identical with short *u* as in sŭn.

nȯne	sȯme	a bȯve′	ȯven
dȯes	tȯngue	bȯm′bast	ȯn′ion
dȯth	rȯugh	bȯr′ough	ȯth′er
dȯst	cȯl′or	cȯv′er	plȯv′er
cȯme	cȯv′et	hȯv′er	cȯus′in
bȯmb	dȯz′en	hȯn′ey	slȯv′en
blȯod	cȯn′jure	mȯn′grel	wȯr′ry

XX. Sound of o as in mo̬ve.

Marked with two dots under it, thus—o̬. This sound is identical with that of o͞o in mo͞on, and of *u* after *r*, as in ru̬le. Avoid the provincialism of reducing the sound of o̬, o͞o, and u̬ to that of long *u* or *ew*, thus—dew for do̬, trew for tru̬e, tew for to̬, yew for you̬, skewl for scho͞ol, etc. The sound of o̬, o͞o, or u̬ is one of the extremes of the vowel scale, made correctly by projecting the lips free from the teeth.

mo̬ve	ho͞of	cro̬up	yo̬uth	ca no̬e′
pro̬ve	ro͞of	gro̬up	tru̬th	a do̬′
lo̬se	ro͞ot	so̬up	thro̬ugh	sham po͞o′
do̬	bo͞ot	who͞op	grew	bam bo͞o′
to̬	spo͞on	lo͞op	to͞ol	tat to͞o′
to͞o	so͞on	ro̬ute	gho̬ul	ap pro̬ve′
two̬	no͞on	sho͞ot	con to̬ur′	re pro͞of′
yo̬u	scho͞ol	wo̬und	ba ro̬uche′	be ho̬ve′
no͞ose	ru̬le	so͞on	car to̬uche′	gam bo̬ge′
lo͞ose	fo͞ol	mo͞on	ta bo͞o′	de to̬ur′
co͞ol	ru̬de	yo̬ur	ru̬l′er	who̬
go͞ose	ru̬se	sho̬e	mo̬ve′ment	who̬m
mo͞ose	cho͞ose	so͞othe	mo͞on′shine	who̬se
spo͞on	fru̬it	to̬ur	ob tru̬de′	ru̬′ral

XXI. Sound of o as in fôr.

Marked with a circumflex, thus—ô. This sound of *o* is identical with broad *a* as in all. It occurs before *r* in words of one syllable; in accented syllables when not followed by another *r*; and also in the derivatives of such words as nôrth, nôrthern, etc. Be careful to give *r* its full sound.

ôr	côrpse	côr′dial	gôr′ġeous	côr′ner
fôr	hôrse	bôr′der	môr′tal	côr′niçe
nôr	stôrm	fôr′mal	môr′sel	ôr′der
bôrn	thôrn	fôr′çeps	môrt′ġaġe	ôr′çhard

XXII. Sound of o as in wọlf.

Marked with a dot under it, thus—ọ. This sound is identical with that of short oo, as in bŏŏk, and that of *u* as in fụll.

wọlf	cọuld n't	wọrs′ted	bŏŏk	pụll
wọuld	wọuld n't	wọlf′ish	cŏŏk	họọd
cọuld	shọuld n't	gŏŏd′ness	hŏŏk	pụt
bọ′ṣom	wŏŏd′en	wọ′man	lŏŏk	pụsh

XXIII. The long sound of u.

Marked with a macron, thus—ū. This is a compound sound, formed of a slight sound of *y* joined with ōō long. After *d, t, l, n,* and *s*, it is somewhat difficult to introduce the *y* sound. Avoid the two extremes: (1) That of overdoing the *y* sound, so as to make dū′ty sound like jū′ty. (2) That of sounding *u* like oo long, as dōō′ty for dū′ty.

ūṣe	cūbe	dūe	lieū	sūit	pūre
fūṣe	cūre	sūe	view	deūce	lūre
mūṣe	tūbe	hūe	ewe	feūd	dūpe
mūte	tūne	flūe	new	slūice	dūne

I. WORDS OFTEN MISPRONOUNCED.

bū'gle	flū'id	mū'sic	hū'mid
beaū'ty	hū'man	pū'pil	nūi'sançe
eū'bie	jū'ry	pū'trid	neū'ter
dū'ty	lū'pĭne	stū'pid	sūit'or

II. WORDS OFTEN MISPRONOUNCED.

com mū'nĭ cate	com mū'ni ty	lū'na çy
con sti tū'tion	eū'mu la tive	lū'na tic
el o eū'tion	lū'min a ry	mū'ṣi cal
rev o lū'tion	lu gū'brĭ ous	čd'ū cate
in sti tū'tion	per pe tū'i ty	cal'eū lāte

XXIV. The short sound of u.

Marked with a breve, thus—ŭ. Avoid the vulgarism of saying ŏp for ŭp, ŏn'der for ŭn'der, etc. Say hŭr'ry, not hûr'ry; coŭr'age, not cûr'age.

bŭd	bŭr'row	ŭn'der	cŭr'ren cy
bŭff	fŭr'row	ŭp'per	sŏv'er eign
dŭmb	mŭr'rain	ŭt'ter	hŭr'ri cane
cŭr'ry	flŭr'ry	gŭt'ter	drŏm'e da ry

XXV. Sound of u as in rule.

Marked with two dots under it, thus—ṳ. This sound of *u*, when it follows the consonant *r*, is identical with that of *o* as in move, and *oo* in moon. Rule rhymes with fool, rude with mood, true with too, you with grew.

brṳte	rṳle	brṳiṣe	prṳ'dençe	rṳ'mor
frṳit	sehool	crṳiṣe	prṳ'dent	trṳ'ant
crṳde	trṳth	crṳ'el	prṳd'ish	trṳ'ly
rṳde	youth	ḡrṳ'el	rṳ'in	trṳf'fle
prṳde	trṳe	brṳ'tal	rṳ'ral	drṳ'id
prṳne	chew	brṳ'in	rṳth'less	do'ing

XXVI. Sound of u as in ûrge.

Marked with a circumflex, thus—û. This sound occurs in monosyllables before *r* not followed by a vowel; in accented syllables before *r* final, or *r* followed by one or more consonants different from itself, and in derivatives from any such words. It coincides with *e* as in vĕrge, *i* as in thĭrst, and *o* as in word, except that û is somewhat broader and more guttural.

bûrn	fûrl	spûrt	word	sûr'geon
bûrst	hûrl	spûrn	work	stûr'geon
cûr	hûrt	pûrge	worm	mûr'der
cûrl	pûrse	ûrn	world	mûr'mur
cûrse	nûrse	tûrn	worth	bûr'den

XXVII. Sound of u as in fu̱ll.

Marked with a dot under it thus—u̱. This sound is identical with that of *o* as in wo̱lf, and short *oo* as in bŏŏk.

bu̱ll	pu̱ss	bu̱l'lock	pu̱l'let
bu̱sh	pu̱ll	bu̱tch'er	pu̱l'ley
pu̱sh	fu̱ll	bu̱sh'es̱	pu̱l'pit
pu̱t	wo̱lf	bu̱l'rush	pu̱d'ding
wŏŏd	cŏŏk	bu̱l'let	pu̱t'ting

XXVIII. The diphthong oi as in oil.

The diphthongs *oi* and *oy* are equivalents. The sound of *oi* is a compound of a̱+ĭ.

oil	hoist	foist	joy	boil'er
boil	moist	poişe	troy	loi'ter
broil	joist	noişe	boy	roy'al
coil	toil	quoit	buoy	loy'al
coin	soil	point	toy	oint'ment
loin	roil	joint	oys'ter	voy'age

XXIX. The diphthongs ou and ow.

The diphthong *ou*, identical with *ow*, is a compound of ä + o̬. Open the mouth freely in giving the initial of this sound.

out	cow	ground	hour	bower
ounce	how	round	flour	power
our	now	sound	sour	lower
doubt	owl	clown	scour	shower
drought	fowl	drown	plow	tower
ġouġe	howl	frown	slough	dower

III. Exercises on Vocals.

I. HINTS AND SUGGESTIONS.

Concert drill exercises on the following table may be given as follows:

1. Preliminary breathing exercise.
2. Concert phonic spelling of the words under each vocal.
3. Concert pronunciation of words, with various degrees of force from the whisper to loud force, and with the rising, the falling, and the circumflex inflections.
4. If time will allow, require each pupil, singly, to take the drill indicated above.

II. TABLE OF VOCALS.

ā.—āle, sāil, pāy, thēy, vēin, gāuġe, brēak, ġāol.
ä.—äh! äre, hälf, läugh, heärth, guärd, äunt, älms.
a̬, ô.—a̬ll, a̬we, a̬ught, broa̬d, sta̬lk, na̬ught, ôught.
ă.—ădd, ănd, ăt, băde, plăid, cătch, măn, hănd.
â, ê.—âir, dâre, beâr, thêre, squâre, êre, hêir, ê'er.
a̍.—a̍nt, a̍sk, da̍nce, cha̍nce, gla̍ss, la̍st, sta̍ff, ga̍sp.
a̬, ŏ.—wa̬s, wa̬nd, wa̬sp, wha̬t, swa̬p, nŏt, blŏt, gŏd.
ē.—mē, wē, bee, bēan, fiērce, niēce, sēize, kēy, tēa.
ĕ.—ĕnd, drĕad, said, says, dĕaf, fĕoff, yĕs, ġĕt, yĕt.

TABLE OF VOCALS.—Continued.

ẽ, ĭ.—ẽrr, hẽr, ẽarth, wẽre, vẽrge, myrrh, thĭrst, work.
e̤, ā.—ve̤in, de̤ign, re̤in, the̤y, pre̤y, we̤ight, ne̤igh.
ê, â.—thêre, whêre, âir, êre, bâre, nê'er, câre, ê'er.
ī, ȳ.—īce, pīne, fīre, lȳre, līe, līar, aīsle, aȳes̩, eȳes̩.
ĭ.—ĭn, pĭn, been, hȳmn, mȳth, sĭeve, buĭld, sĭnce.
ĭ, ĕ.—thĭrst, fĭrst, gĭrl, ĕarn, lĕarn, bĭrd, thĭrd, worst.
ï, ē.—pïque, clïque, ob lïque', pol ïce', ma rïne'.
ō.—ōld, ōak, brōke, pōur, ōre, door, tōll, sew, tōw.
ŭ, a̤.—ŏdd, nŏt, dŏg, gŏd, lŏst, ŏff, cŏugh, mŏss, lŏss.
o̤, ōō, ṳ.—mo̤ve, mōōn, rṳle, do̤, ro̤ute, trṳe, grew, yo̤u.
ô, a̤.—ôr, nôr, hôrse, qua̤rt, wa̤rt, côrn, stôrm, bôrn.
ȯ, ŭ.—dȯne, sȯn, dȯes̩, dȯth, spȯnge, blood, flood, rŭn.
o̩, ōō, u̩.—wo̩lf, wo̩uld, wŏŏd, sho̩uld, bŏŏk, cŏŏk, pu̩t.
ū.—ūs̩e, mūs̩e, dūe, few, view, feūd, tūne, cūbe, tūbe.
ŭ, ȯ.—tŭb, bŭt, dŭst, trŭst, dȯne, dȯes̩, bȯmb, crŭmb.
u̩, ōō, o̩.—ru̩le, ru̩de, tru̩th, you̩th, spōōn, mo̩ve, pro̩ve.
û.—ûrġe, pûrġe, bûrn, tûrn, fûr, bûrr, cûr, cûrl, fûrl.
u̩, ŏŏ, o̩.—pu̩t, pu̩ll, pu̩sh, bu̩sh, pu̩ss, bŏŏk, tŏŏk.
oi, oy.—oil, boil, toil, boy, joy, cloy, roil, coil, foil.
ou, ow.—out, our, ounce, flour, power, sour, owl.

III. CONCERT DRILL.

In concert drill on the following table, observe the following directions.

1. Read the columns vertically.
2. Repeat with slow movement; moderate; fast.
3. Repeat in a forcible whisper.
4. Repeat with gentle force; moderate; loud.

ā–ā–ā	ẽ–ẽ–ẽ	ū–ū–ū
ä–ä–ä	ī–ī–ī	ŭ–ŭ–ŭ
a̤–a̤–a̤	ȳ–ȳ–ȳ	û–û–û
ă–ă–ă	ō–ō–ō	u̩–u̩–u̩
ē–ē–ē	ŏ–ŏ–ŏ	oi–oi–oy
ĕ–ĕ–ĕ	o̩–o̩–o̩	ou–ou–ow

IV. Vowel Sounds in Unaccented Syllables.

There are many delicate shades of sound in unaccented vowels which must be learned from the lips of the living teacher, or by noticing carefully the pronunciation of educated and critical people.

I. Final unaccented ar, er, ir, or, yr.

The vowels *a, e, i, o, u, y*, preceding *r* in final unaccented syllables, have the sound of *e* as in hĕr.

bĕg′gar	ạl′der	ür′mor	sŭl′phur
eŏl′lar	băn′ner	ür′dor	ạu′gur
dŏl′lar	lăd′der	eŏl′or	zĕph′yr
lī′ar	pā′per	ō′dor	mär′tyr
mō′lar	tā′pir	pär′lor	sā′tyr
pō′lar	nā′dir	fē′mur	hŏn′or
stĕl′lar	mī′nor	lē′mur	ī′ron(-urn)
çĕl′lar	mā′jor	mûr′mur	a′pron(-urn)

II. Final -ain like -ĕn.

eăp′tain	mŭr′rain	chiēf′tain
eûr′tain	vĭl′lain	chăp′lain
çêr′tain	bär′gain	plăn′tain

III. Words having a or o unaccented.

In words like the following, *a* or *o* in unaccented final syllables has a slightly obscured sound of short *u*.

fī′nal	vī′tal	phăn′tom	tĕn′ant
fĭs′eal	vō′eal	trăn′som	găl′lop
lē′gal	vē′nal	hănd′some	băl′lad
mĕn′tal	eŏm′mon	hăm′mock	săl′ad
môr′tal	eŭs′tom	hill′ock	sēa′man
nā′ṣal	blŏs′som	ôr′phan	fīre′man
nā′val	drăg′on	tru′ant	brāke′man
ō′val	sĕr′mon	sĕrv′ant	băl′ance

IV. Final unaccented a.

Unaccented *a*, at the end of a word, has the sound of intermediate *a*, verging towards short *u*, as cŏm'má or cŏm'mŭ.

cŏm'má	ăl'ġe brá	pï ăz'zá	va nĭl'lá
ē'rá	ā're á	co rō'ná	guer ĭl'lá
ĕx'trá	ā re'ná	vĕr'te brá	fa rï'ná
lā'vá	cū'po lá	man tĭl'lá	lăm'i ná
mī'cá	ŏp'e rá	scin tĭl'lá	mem o răn'dá
sō'fá	i dē'á	um brĕl'lá	a năth'e má

V. Sound of a in unaccented final syllables.

In words like the following, *a* has the sound of short *e*; as, -age = ĕj, and -ate = ĕt.

coŭr'aġe	măr'riaġe	săv'aġe	păl'ate
dăm'aġe	căr'riaġe	ūṣ'aġe	pī'rate
drāin'aġe	mīle'aġe	ăg'ate	frĭġ'ate
front'aġe	pōst'aġe	clī'mate	ad van'taġe
lēak'aġe	tĭll'aġe	prī'vate	per çent'aġe

VI. Unaccented a as an initial syllable.

In the first syllable of words like the following, the vowel *a*, when unaccented, has nearly the sound of short *a* a little obscured, or of *a* as in ask, verging towards short *u*; as ă bout', ă bove'; or á bout', á bove'. Avoid the common error of giving *a* the long sound; as ā bove', mā chīne'; also that of short *u*, as ŭ bout', ŭ bove'. In the dictionary this sound is unmarked.

a bóve'	a gain'	a līke'	ea dĕt'	ga zĕtte'
a bout'	a lärm'	a mông'	ea năl'	ma çhïne'
a būse'	a lás'	a pärt'	ea rĕss'	ma rïne'
a crŏss'	a līve'	a rīṣe'	ea närd'	ra vïne'
a dŭlt'	a lōne'	a sīde'	ea noe'	ca reen'

VII. Silent e and o.

In the following words and some others, e and o are silent before n or l, thus—heaven = hĕvn, evil = ēvl.

bācon	gōlden	lĭsten	ōpen	sēaṣon
bŭtton	gärden	lĕaven	ŏften	sŭdden
cŏtton	glădden	lĕaden	pẽrson	spōken
crĭmṣon	glĭsten	lĕngthen	pärson	slōven
dēacon	ḡĭven	lĭken	poison	shŏvel
dămṣon	glŭtton	lĕsson	rēaṣon	shrĭvel
dĕvil	grŏvel	lĕssen	rĕckon	snĭvel
drĭven	hēathen	māson	rāven	smĭtten
ēven	hĕaven	mŭtton	rāisin	sŭnken
ēvil	härden	māiden	rĭdden	tōken
ēaṣel	hāsten	moisten	rŏtten	tēaṣel
fallen	hăppen	mĭtten	răvel	wēaṣel
frōzen	hāzel	óven	sĕven	wēaken
frīghten	kĭtten	ouṣel	sĭlken	wĕapon

VIII. Short i in unaccented final syllables.

ăġ'ĭle	făç'ĭle	săn'guĭne	măs'cu lĭne
dŏç'ĭle	fẽr'tĭle	sŭb'tĭle	fĕm'ĭ nĭne
dĕs'tĭne	frăġ'ĭle	stẽr'ĭle	ġĕn'u ĭne
dŭc'tĭle	flĕx'ĭle	tĕx'tĭle	hẽr'o ĭne
ĕn'ġĭne	hŏs'tĭle	vĭ'rĭle	pū'er ĭle
ẽr'mĭne	mō'bĭle	vẽr'sa tĭle	jū've nĭle

IX. Short i in unaccented initial syllables.

dĭ vīde'	dĭ vĕst'	dĭ grĕss'	dĭ plō'ma
dĭ lāte'	dĭ vẽrt'	mĭ nūte'	dĭ ġĕs'tion
dĭ lūte'	dĭ vŭlġe'	ġĭ răffe'	dĭ vĭs'ion
dĭ rĕct'	dĭ vẽrġe'	çĭ gär'	dĭ lā'tion
dĭ ġĕst'	dĭ vôrce'	fĭ nănce'	dĭ rec'tion
dĭ văn'	dĭ vīne'	tĭ rāde'	bĭ tū'men

X. Sound of short i and y in unaccented syllables.

In words like the following, there is a tendency to give short e the sound of obscure e or a, and to prolong final -ty into -te.

ac tĭv′i ty	gul li bĭl′i ty	re spon si bĭl′i ty
a ġĭl′i ty	in tĕl′li ġi ble	tran quĭl′li ty
de bĭl′i ty	in cŭr′ri ġi ble	pos si bĭl′i ty
di vis i bĭl′i ty	in vĭn′ci ble	u tĭl′i ty
el i ġi bĭl′i ty	il lĕġ′i ble	u na nĭm′i ty
fu şi bĭl′i ty	in fĭn′i ty	in com pat i bĭl′i ty

XI. Sound of u in unaccented final syllables.

In the pronunciation of words of two syllables ending in -ture, -dure, or -sure, there is a slight difference in good usage. By some, the word creature, for example, is pronounced as if spelled thus—crēat′yẽr, verging towards crēa′cher; by others it is pronounced thus— crēat′yo͞or.

crēa′ture	frăc′ture	nā′ture	răp′ture
cŭl′ture	fū′ture	nûr′ture	scrĭp′ture
căp′ture	ġĕs′ture	păs′ture	strŭc′ture
fēa′ture	lec′ture	pĭc′ture	vĕn′ture
fĭx′ture	lēi′şure	pŏs′ture	vẽr′dure
vŭl′ture	sū′ture	vĕs′ture	rŭp′ture

XII. Sound of u in unaccented final syllables.

In words of more than two syllables, the sound of -ure is made somewhat longer than in words of two syllables; as furniture is pronounced fûr′nĭt yo͞or.

ăp′er ture	lĭt′er a ture	căr′i ea ture
ō′vẽr ture	tĕm′per a ture	jū′di ca ture
lĭġ′a ture	mĭn′i a ture	sĭġ′na ture
sĭġ′na ture	ăp′er ture	cûr′va ture

XIII. The syllable -tude.

ăp'ti tūde	lŏn'gi tūde	rĕc'ti tūde
ăl'ti tūde	lăs'si tūde	sŏl'i tūde
ăt'ti tūde	mŭl'ti tūde	sẽr'vi tūde

XIV. Long o unaccented.

mo rŏc'co	to băc'co	ăḡ'o ny
po tā'to	pro pōr'tion	ŏp'po site
o pĭn'ion	pi ä'no	ĕl'o quence

XV. Miscellaneous Hints.

1. The article *a* is sounded in connection with the word that follows it; as, "a book" is sounded as one word of two syllables, thus—a-book'. Here the article has the sound of long *a*, obscured and cut off suddenly. It is not good usage to give it the sound of short *u*, thus—ŭ-book', or of ûr-book'.

2. Before a word beginning with a consonant the article *the*, except when emphatic, is sounded as a syllable of the word which it precedes, as the-book', pronounced as a word of two syllables, accented on the last. In such cases the obscured *e* sound in *the* is really represented by short *i*, rather than by short *u;* as, thĭ-book', thĭ-horse', thĭ-school'. It is sometimes indicated thus— th'-book', th'-horse'.

3. Before words beginning with a vowel, as the-air', the-ice', *e* in *the* has the long sound, less obscured and shortened than when *the* precedes a word beginning with a consonant. The error in sounding the articles *a* and *the* frequently arises from attempts to give their phonic spelling independent of their connection with the words that follow them. In order to sound the articles correctly, notice how they are pronounced, by persons of good taste, in ordinary conversation.

SECTION III.
CONSONANT SOUNDS.

I. Articulation.

1. Distinct articulation is essential to good reading and speaking. "The first step towards becoming a good elocutionist," says Comstock, "is a correct articulation. A public speaker, possessed of only a moderate voice, if he articulates correctly, will be better understood, and heard with greater pleasure, than one who vociferates without judgment. The voice of the latter may indeed extend to a considerable distance, but the sound is dissipated in confusion. Of the former voice not the smallest vibration is wasted; every stroke is perceived at the utmost distance to which it reaches; and hence it has often the appearance of penetrating even farther than one which is loud, but badly articulated."

2. "In just articulation," says Austin, "the words are not hurried over, nor precipitated syllable over syllable; nor, as it were, melted together into a mass of confusion; they are neither abridged, nor prolonged; nor swallowed, nor forced, and, if I may so express myself, shot from the mouth; they are not trailed nor drawled, nor let slip out carelessly, so as to drop unfinished. They are delivered out from the lips, as beautiful coins newly issued from the mint, deeply and accurately impressed, perfectly finished, neatly struck by the proper organs, distinct, sharp, in due succession, and of due weight."

3. The best way of training the organs of speech to good articulation is by means of forcible phonic spelling and by drill-exercises on the elementary sounds, particularly on subvocals and aspirates.

4. "Articulate utterance," says Prof. Russell, "requires a constant exercise of discrimination of the mind, and of *precision or accuracy in the movements of the organs*

of speech. A correct articulation, however, is not belabored or artificial in its character. It results from the intuitive and habitual action of a disciplined attention. It is easy, fluent, and natural; but, like the skillful execution of an accomplished musician, it gives forth every sound, even in the most rapid passages, with truth and correctness.

5. "A good enunciation gives to every vowel and consonant its just proportion and character; none being omitted, no one blending with another in such a manner as to produce confusion, and none so carelessly executed as to cause mistake in the hearer, by its resemblance to another.

6. "A correct enunciation is the fundamental quality of a distinct and impressive elocution. It is an attainment of great value, for the ordinary purposes of communication; but it becomes doubly important, in the act of reading or speaking in public, whether we advert to the larger space which must be traversed by the voice, or the greater moment of the topics of discourse which are usual on such occasions.

7. "The appropriate style of modern eloquence is that of intellectual, more than of impassioned, expression; and enunciation being, of all the functions of the voice, that which is most important to the conveyance of thought and meaning, it justly requires, in the course of education, more attention and practice than any other branch of elocution."

II. CLASSIFICATION OF ELEMENTARY SOUNDS.

The elementary sounds are classified as follows:
1. Vocals, or tonics.
2. Subvocals, or subtonics.
3. Aspirates, or atonics.

Vocals, represented by vowels, are sounds consisting of pure tone only.

Subvocals, represented by consonants, are sounds that have *tone*, but are inferior to vocals in fullness. A consonant can not be *named* without the aid of a vowel, as *b* is *named* in the alphabet, *be*. Hence the term ,*consonant, sounded with*.

Aspirates, represented by consonants, are *sounds* without *tone*.

Letters are characters to represent articulate sounds.

III. DIACRITICAL MARKS OF CONSONANTS.
[*As given in Webster's Dictionary.*]

ç *soft*—çede, çent.
e *hard*—eall, lae.
ch *unmarked*—church.
çh *soft*—çhaise, çhute.
eh *hard*—ehyle, ehyme.
ḡ *hard*—ḡum, loḡ.
ġ *soft*—ġem, ġin.
ṣ *soft* = z—haṣ, hiṣ.
s *sharp* = ç—sin, gas.

th *sharp*—thing, bath.
ŧh *flat*—ŧhine, smooŧh.
ng *unmarked*— sing, ring.
ṇ—iṇk, liṇk.
x = ks—box, fox.
x̣ = gz—ex̣ist, ex̣alt.
ph = f—phlox, sylph.
qu = kw—queen, queer.
wh = hw—when, why.

IV. DRILL LESSONS ON CONSONANT SOUNDS.
1. SUBVOCALS.

In concert drill-exercises on the following table, observe the following directions:

1. Pronounce each word distinctly, and then give, *forcibly*, the phonic spelling.
2. Repeat, *forcibly*, each subvocal and aspirate three times, thus—*b, b, b; d, d, d*, etc.
3. After concert drill, require each pupil, in turn, to give the sounds.

b.—bĭb, bābe, bee, ĕbb, mŏb, rŏb, sŏb, eŏb.
d.—dĭd, dŏḡ, dĕad, ŏdd, drĕad, dīed, said, bĕd.
ḡ.—ḡăḡ, ḡĭḡ, ḡrŏḡ, ḡĕt, ḡīrl, ḡĭlls, ḡĭḡ'ḡle.

j.—joy, jŭst, jŏḡ, ġĭll, ġĕm, ġĭn, ġĭn'ġer.
l.—lŭll, lŏll, mĭll, bĕll, sāle, boil, toil, soil.
m.—măn, māim, mŭm, dĭm, rŭm, sóme.
n.—nŭn, nóne, noun, nāme, rŭn, ḡŭn.
r (*rough*).—rude, rule, rōōm, rōōd, rōll, rōar.
r (*smooth*).—ôr, ōre, mōre, ōar, yēar, deer.
v.—vălve, vāle, vīne, lĭve, ŏf, veer, vōte.
w.—wĭll, wōe, wē, wīne, wĕt, wĭnd, wŏŏd.
y.—yĕs, yĕt, you, yăm, yürn, yōke, yacht.
z.—zōne, ōōze, loṣe, nōṣe, blāze, crāze.
zh.—āzure, mĕaṣure, plĕaṣure, trĕaṣure.
th.—thy, thīne, thĭs, wĭth, blīthe, bāthe.
ng.—kĭng, rĭng, răng, rŭng, sĭng, săng, sŭng.
n̠.—ĭn̠k, lĭn̠k, thĭn̠k, wĭn̠k, blĭn̠k.
x̣ = gz.—ex̣ĭst, ex̣ămple, ex̣hôrt, ex̣haust.

II. ASPIRATES.

f.—fīfe, ĭf, fĭll, beef, bŭff, ŏff, läugh.
h.—how, hōme, hĭll, hăd, hēre, hâir, hāil.
k, c, ch.—kĭll, kĭck, cāke, cóme, chȳle, chȳme.
p.—pīpe, rīpe, pŭp, pŏp, pĭp, peep.
s.—ṣauçe, çēase, çīte, çĕll, sĕnse, çĕnts.
t.—tōō, dŏt, tĭlt, trŏt, trŭst, twĭt, wĭt.
sh, çh.—shăll, shăm, răsh, dăsh, çhāise, çhūte.
ch.—chĭn, chŏp, ĭch, dĭtch, chûrch, bīrch.
th.—thĭn, thĭck, pĭth, teeth, truth, youth.
x = ks.—bŏx, fŏx, lŏcks, vĕx, nĕcks, tăx, lăx, wăx.

V. MISCELLANEOUS HINTS.

1. Do not be over-particular about a heavy articulation of the *d* in *and*. The *d* should be sounded, but not so painfully emphasized as to become an elocutionary affectation.

2. *Th* is vocal, as in thine, in the following plurals: baths, laths, paths, moths, cloths, oaths, mouths, swaths, wreaths, booths; and in blithe, lithe, with, and beneath.

SECTION IV.

CLASSIFICATION OF ELEMENTARY SOUNDS.

I. Table of Elementary Sounds.

I. VOCALS.

ā	ā-ge,	n-ā-me	ĭ, y̆	ĭ-ll,	h-y̆-mn
ä	ä-lms,	ä-rt	ō	ō-ld,	n-ō
a̤	a̤-ll,	l-a̤w	ŏ	ŏ-n,	ŏ-dd
ă	ă-t,	ă-n	o̜, o͞o	m-o̜-ve,	m-o͞o-n
â	â-ir,	e-â-re	ū	ū-se,	d-ūe
ȧ	ȧ-sk,	el-ȧ-ss	ŭ	ŭ-p,	s-ŭ-n
ē	ē-ve,	m-ē	û	û-rge,	b-û-rn
ĕ	ĕ-nd,	ĕ-gg	u̜, o͝o	f-u̜-ll,	w-o͝o-l
ẽ	h-ẽ-r,	ẽ-rr	oi, oy	oi-l,	b-oy
ī, ȳ	ī-ce,	m-ȳ	ou, ow	ou-t,	ow-l

II. SUBVOCALS.

b	b-ĭ-b,	b-ā-be	r	r-ōa-r,	rē-a-r
d	d-ĭ-d,	dĕ-ad	th	th-īne,	wĭ-th
ḡ	ḡ-ŭ-ḡ,	ḡ-ĭ-ḡ	v	v-ăl-ve,	wā-ve
j	j-ăm,	ġ-ŏm	w	w-ĭll,	w-ĕll
l	l-ŭ-ll,	bĕ-ll	y	y-ĕs,	y-ĕt
m	m-āi-m,	mī-ne	z	z-ōne,	z-īne
n	n-ŭ-n,	nī-ne	zh, z	ă-z′ure,	seī′z-ure
ng, n̠	rī-ng,	ră-n̠-k			

III. ASPIRATES.

f	f-ī-fe,	ŏ-ff	t	t-ĕn-t,	t-är-t
h	h-ăt,	h-ĭll	ch	ch-ûr-ch,	ch-āin
k	k-ĭll,	bo͞o-k	sh	sh-ĭp,	wĭ-sh
p	p-ī-pe,	p-u̜t	th	thĭ-ck,	pä-th
s	s-ĕll,	s-ĕn-se	wh	wh-ĕn,	wh-êre

II. Vocals and Equivalents.

[Arranged according to the natural order of their formation by the organs of speech.]

I. LONG.			II. SHORT.		
ē	ē-ve,	m-ē	ĭ	ĭ-n,	ĭ-t
ā	ā-le,	ā-ge	ĕ	ĕ-nd,	m-ĕ-n
â	âi-r,	c-â-re	ă	ă-t,	ă-n
ä	ä-lms,	h-ä-lf	ȧ	ȧ-sk,	p-ȧ-ss
û	û-rge,	c-û-rl	ŭ	ŭ-p,	b-ŭ-d
a̤	a̤-ll,	l-a̤w	ŏ	ŏ-n,	d-ŏ-g
ō	ō-ld,	n-ō	ṳ	p-ṳ-ll,	p-ṳ-t
o̤	m-o̤-ve,	d-o̤			

COMPOUNDS AND DIPHTHONGS.—LONG.

ū = ĭ + ōō.—ū-se, m-ū-te.   ou = ä + ōō.—ou-t, th-ou.
ī = ä + ē.—ī-ce, m-ī-ne.   oi = a̤ + ĕ.—oi-l, b-oy.

III. Subvocals and Aspirates.

[Arranged according to the natural order of their formation by the organs of speech.]

I. COGNATES.

SUBVOCALS.			ASPIRATES.		
b	b-ĭ-b,	b-ā-be	p	p-ī-pe,	p-ŏ-p
w	w-ĭll,	w-ōō	wh	wh-ĕn,	wh-ȳ
v	v-ă-lve,	w-ā-ve	f	f-ī-fe,	f-ĕo-ff
th	th-īne,	wĭ-th	th	th-ick,	mŏ-th
z	z-ōne,	sī-ze	s	s-āy,	s-ee
d	d-ĭ-d,	d-rĕa-d	t	t-ĕn-t,	t-rŏ-t
j	j-oy,	j-āil	ch	ch-ûr-ch,	ch-īme
zh	a-z-ure		sh	sh-ăll,	sh-ow
y	y-ĕs,	y-ĕll	h	h-ow,	h-ōme
g	g-ăg,	ḡ-ĭ-g	k	e-ā-ke,	e-ō-ke

II. SUBTONICS WITHOUT COGNATES.

m.—m-āi-m, ă-m.
n.—n-ŭ-n, n-ī-ne.
l.—l-ŭ-ll, oi-l.

r (*rough*).—r-ule, r-ōōm.
r (*smooth*).—ō-re, mō-re.
ng.—sĭ-ng, rĭ-ng.

IV. TABLE OF CONSONANT SOUNDS.

[*Classified according to their formation by the organs of speech.*]

In order to secure correct and forcible articulation, it may be desirable to call the attention of pupils to the position of the organs of speech in making the consonant sounds. Teachers can do this without any detailed instructions in print.

Lip Sounds. [Labials.]	b m wh	p w	b-a-be, m-ai-m, wh-y,	p-i-pe w-ay wh-en
Lips and Teeth. [Labio-Dentals.]	f v		f-i-fe, v-ine,	f-eo-ff e-ve
Tongue and Teeth. [Linguo-Dentals.]	d th j s z	t th ch sh zh	d-i-d, th-is, j-oy, s-un, z-one,	t-en-t th-ink ch-ur-ch sh-un a-z'ure
Tongue and Palate. [Linguo-Palatals.]	ḡ l y	k r	g-ood, l-u-ll, y-et,	boo-k r-oa-r y-es
Nasal Passages.	n ng		n-o-ne, si-ng,	n-i-ne ri-ng
Glottis.	h		h-at,	h-ow

V. Phonic Drill.—Subvocals and Aspirates.

b.—bābe, brībe, rĭb, bĭd, rōbe, bĭrd, eûrb.
ç, s.—çĕnt, sĭnçe, onçe, Içe, fāce, rāce, sĕnse.
ch.—chûrch, bĭrch, lŭnch, cheeṣe, chīme.
d.—dĭd, dĕad, rīde, dīçe, dĕath, thrĕad, drīed.
f, gh.—fīne, ŏff, fīfe, fēar, dĕaf, fŏŏt, läugh.
ḡ.—ḡăḡ, ḡĭḡ, ḡāme, ḡĭlls, răḡ, ḡŏŏd, ḡāuġe.
h.—hōme, how, who, hâir, hāte, hĭll, hĭṣ.
j, ġ.—joy, jŭst, jĕt, āġe, pāġe, ġĕm, ġill.
k, e.—kĭll, kīte, lŏŏk, eāme, eould, eāke, erowd.
eh.—āehe, ehôrd, ehȳme, ehȳle, ehoir, ehōrus.
l.—lŏŏk, lŭll, ball, boil, lăd, wĕll, tall, pāle.
m.—māke, rōōm, māin, mōōn, nŭmb, māim.
n.—nōōn, nēat, tĕn, nīne, nŭn, pĭn, nóne.
ng.—sĭng, rĭng, thĭng, bănk, rănk, thănk.
p.—pīpe, eŭp, eāpe, hōpe, rīpe, drŏp, pāid.
r.—rōar, rēar, fīre, floor, door, stōre, mōre.
s, ç.—sauçe, sĭnçe, saw, Içe, ĭnçense, sōurçe.
sh, çh.—shīne, shăll, çhāiṣe, wĭsh, bush, çhute.
t.—tĕnt, dŏt, tĕll, wrīte, tīme, trŏt, thrĕat.
th.—thĭck, dĕath, thĭn, lĕngth, wĭdth, thrōat.
ₜh.—ₜhĭs, ₜhēṣe, ₜhōṣe, ₜhĕn, ₜhăt, wĭₜh, ₜhêir.
v.—vīne, ēve, vōte, move, veer, nêrve, vĕst.
w.—wĭnd, wĕt, wōe, wāit, weâr, wīṣe, wŏŏd.
wh.—whĕn, whêre, whȳ, what, whēat, wheel.
x = ks.—ŏx, bŏx, lŏcks, ăx, tăx, lăcks, vĕx, fŏx.
x̱ = gz.—ex̱ăct, ex̱ĭst, ex̱ămple, ex̱haust, ex̱ĕrt.
y.—yĕs, yĕt, yĕll, yēar, yóung, youth, truth.
z.—zōne, bŭzz, breeze, ōōze, loṣe, ĭṣ, zīne.
zh.—ăzure, plĕasure, mĕasure, trĕasure.

VI. Articulation Drill.

First, pronounce each word very distinctly and forcibly; then give the phonic spelling, and re-pronounce the word.

rb.—ôrb, hĕrb, vĕrb, cûrb, bärb, gärb.
rd.—bärd, lärd, bärd, eärd, bōard, hōard.
rk.—ärk, bärk, pärk, härk, märk, lärk.
spr.—sprĭng, sprăng, sprŭng, spray, sprite.
rt.—ärt, heärt, pärt, cärt, därt, stärt.
str.—strĭng, strŭng, strāight, strĕngth, strāy.
sts.—mȧsts, fȧsts, fists, nests, vests, pests.
sks.—ȧsks, tȧsks, bȧsks, cȧsks, mȧsks.
skt.—ȧsked, tȧsked, bȧsked, mȧsked, rȧsped.
sps.—gȧsps, clȧsps, rȧsps, hȧsps, grȧsps.
spt.—gȧsped, clȧsped, rȧsped, hȧsped, grȧsped.
th.—thĭs, thăt, thēṣe, those, with, bāthe.
th.—three, thrōat, thrĭll, thĭck, thĭn, bȧth.
wh.—whĕn, whêre, whȳ, whạt, whĭch, whēat.
dn.—laden, burden, harden, sadden, gladden.
kn.—heärken, līken, wēaken, spōken, brōken.
pn.—ōpen, wĕapon, hăppen, rīpen, deepen.
vn.—gĭven, sĕven, ȯven, hĕaven, lĕaven, ēven.
sn.—glĭsten, hāsten, fāsten, lĕsson, māson.

VII. Articulation Drill.

1. Round the rough rock the ragged rascal ran.
2. Shoes and socks shock Susan. (Repeat.)
3. The scene was truly rural. (Repeat.)
4. She uttered a sharp, shrill shriek. (Repeat.)
5. The difficulties were formidable, inexplicable, and irremediable.
6. Amidst the mists and coldest frosts,
   With stoutest wrists and loudest boasts,
   He thrusts his fists against the posts,
   And still insists he sees the ghosts.

7. Shrewd Simon Short sewed shoes. Seventeen summers' speeding storms, succeeding sunshine, successively saw Simon's small, shabby shop standing staunch, saw Simon's self-same sign still swinging, silently specifying: "Simon Short, Smithfield's sole surviving shoemaker. Shoes sewed, soled superfinely." Simon's spry, sedulous spouse, Sally Short, sewed shirts, stitched sheets, stuffed sofas. Simon's six stout, sturdy sons—Seth, Samuel, Stephen, Saul, Shadrach, Silas—sold sundries. Sober Seth sold sugar, starch, spices; simple Sam sold saddles, stirrups, screws; sagacious Stephen sold silks, satins, shawls; skeptical Saul sold silver salvers, silver spoons; selfish Shadrach sold shoe-strings, soaps, saws, skates; slack Silas sold Sally Short's stuffed sofas.

8. Theophilus Thistle, the successful thistle-sifter, in sifting a sieve full of unsifted thistles, thrust three thousand thistles through the thick of his thumb; now, if Theophilus Thistle, the successful thistle-sifter, in sifting a sieve full of unsifted thistles, thrust three thousand thistles through the thick of his thumb, see that thou, in sifting a sieve full of unsifted thistles, thrust not three thousand thistles through the thick of thy thumb. Success to the successful thistle-sifter.

9. Of all the saws I ever saw saw, I never saw a saw saw as this saw saws.

10. Peter Piper picked a peck of pickled peppers; a peck of pickled peppers Peter Piper picked. If Peter Piper picked a peck of pickled peppers, where's the peck of pickled peppers Peter Piper picked?

11. When a twister twisting, would twist him a twist,
    For twisting a twist three times he will twist;
    But if one of the twists untwist from the twist,
    The twist untwisting, untwists the twist.

SECTION V.

ORTHOEPY.

GOOD USAGE. The standard of correct pronunciation is *good usage*. Good usage implies the pronunciation of the educated and intellectual classes of society. The standard of good usage is found in the dictionaries of a language. In the United States, the standard dictionaries are Webster's and Worcester's.

The standard of pronunciation is never absolutely undeviating. Custom, from time to time, changes the pronunciation of words; but the number of these changes is not large. Whenever general good usage changes the pronunciation or the spelling of a word, this change soon finds its way into a new edition of the dictionary. The dictionary, then, remains the standard of good usage.

There are a few hundred words in our language that have two authorized pronunciations, either of which is allowable.

AFFECTATIONS. All affectations in pronunciation should be carefully avoided. The affectation of eī′ther and neī′ther, for ēither and nēither, is a case in point. Avoid in′quiry for in quir′y. There is no better test of culture, scholarship, and refinement, than a correct pronunciation.

On this point, Prof. William Russell says: "Individual opinion, when it is at variance with this important and useful principle of accommodation, gives rise to eccentricities, which neither the authority of profound learning, nor that of strict accuracy and system, can redeem from the charge of pedantry.

"It is a matter of great importance to recognize the rule of authorized custom, and neither yield to the influence of those errors which, through inadvertency, will creep into occasional or local use; nor, on the other hand, be induced to follow innovations or changes adopted without sufficient sanction. A cultivated taste is always perceptible in pronunciation, as in every other expression of mind; and errors in pronouncing are unavoidably associated with a deficiency in the rudiments of a good education."

PROVINCIALISMS. Provincialisms, or the peculiar pronunciation prevailing in certain localities or sections of our country, must be studiously corrected and avoided. It is to this class of errors that teachers must carefully direct their attention. The force of habit is so strong that pupils continue to mispronounce words long after they know the pronunciation to be incorrect.

Provincialisms most commonly consist of some variation or perversion of vowel sounds: as hălf for hälf, călf for cälf, laugh for läugh, etc.; of tew for tọ, trew for trụe, dew for dọ, yew for yọu; of grăss for grass, ăsk for ȧsk, lăst for lȧst, etc.; of dawg or dorg for dŏg; of gĭt for gĕt, gŭt for gŏt, etc.; of toon for tūne, noo for new, dōōty for dūty, etc.; of ŏp for ŭp, ŏnder for ŭnder; of skewl for schōōl, rewl for rụle.

Another class of these errors consists in misplacing the accent of words; as, ī′de a for i dē′a, ăd′ult for a dŭlt′, rē′cess for re cĕss′, con vĕx′ for con′vex, ex tănt′ for ĕx′tant, in ter ĕst′ing for ĭn′ter est ing, ĭl′lus trate for il lŭs′trate, rō′bust for ro bŭst′, tī′rade for tĭ rāde′, ve hē′ment for vē′he ment.

In this connection, the following lines from Oliver Wendell Holmes convey a valuable lesson:

1. A few brief stanzas may be well employed
   To speak of errors we can all avoid.
   Learning condemns beyond the reach of hope
   The careless churl that speaks of sŏap for sōap:
   Her edict exiles from her fair abode
   The clownish voice that utters rŏad for rōad,

Less stern to him who calls his cōat a cŏat,
And steers his bōat believing it a bŏat,
She pardoned one, our classic city's boast,
Who said, at Cambridge, mŏst instead of mōst;
But knit her brows, and stamped her angry foot,
To hear a teacher call a rōōt a rŏŏt.

2. Once more: speak clearly, if you speak at all;
Carve every word before you let it fall;
Do n't, like a lecturer or dramatic star,
Try over hard to roll the British *r;*
Do put your accents in the proper spot;
Do n't—let me beg you—do n't say "*How?*" for "*What?*"
And, when you stick on conversation's burrs,
Do n't strew the pathway with those dreadful *urs.*

I. Words Often Mispronounced.

[By misplacing the accent.]

The only variations from "Webster's Dictionary," in the following lists, include a few words in relation to which it may be said that good usage is in advance of the dictionary.

First, require pupils to pronounce the following words in concert; then require each pupil, singly, in turn, to pronounce five or more words.

ab dō'men	al lȳ'	ea nīne'
ac elī'māt ed	ā're a	ca băl'
är'mis tĭçe	au rē'o la	eāy ĕnne'
är'bĭ ter	an tĭp'o dēş	eon tour'
ăb'ject	al bū'men	eŏn'vex
ăd'verse	ba sạlt'	côr'net
ad drĕss'	bur lĕsque	eŏn'strūc
a dĕpt'	bĭ tū'men	eŏn'tents
a dŭlt'	bĕn'zĭne	eŏm'plex

con fi dănt'
com'bat ant
cŏm'pro mĭşe
cŏm'mun ist
cŏn'tro vert
cŏm'par a ble
con'ver sant
cŏn'tu me ly
com'plai şance
con trĭb'ūte
cog nō'men
cŏn fĭs'cate
cŏn dō'lence
chăs'tĭşe ment
çĭv il ĭ zā'tion
chĭv'al rĭc
com man dănt'
com pĕn'sate
con çĕn'trate
coy ō'te
dĕf'ĭ çit
dĕv'as tate
dŏl'or ous
dўn'am īte
de mŏn'strate
de cō'rous
dĕp rĭ vā'tion
dĕş'ul to ry
dĭ plō'ma çy
dis cōurse'
dis cärd'
ĕx'tant
dĭ'verse
ĕx'or çĭşe
ĕn'věl ōpe (n.)
ĕx'quĭ şĭte

ex'em pla ry
ex pō'nent
ex pûr'gate
ex ploit'
fĭ nănce'
frŏn'tier
fôr'mid a ble
frăg'ment a ry
grăn'ary
gŏn'do la
glăç'i er
guär'di an
grĭ māce'
gla dĭ'o lus
hăr'ass
ho rĭ'zon
hȳ'gĭ ēne
hȳ mĕ nē'al
ĭ dē'ȧ
il lŭs'trate
il lŭs'trat ed
in quīr'y
ĭn'grate
ĭn'ter stice
ĭn'ter est ing
ĭn'ter est ed
ĭm'pĭ ous
in cŏm'par a ble
in dĭs'pu ta ble
in ĕx'plĭ ca ble
ir rĕp'ar a ble
ir rĕf'ra ga ble
ir rĕv'o ca ble
lăm'en ta ble
lĕğ'is lā'tūre
lĕğ'is la tive

lĕğ'is lā tor
ly çē'um
leth är'gic
lith ŏğ'ra pher
mon sōōn'
mus tāche'
mag a zīne'
mis cŏn'strue
mū şē'um
mĕt'al lur ğy
mē'di o cre
ŏb'lĭ ga to ry
ôr'tho e py
ŏb'se quieş
ŏb'so lete
ŏn'er ous
ôr'nate
ō'vert
oc cŭlt'
op pō'nent
ō'a sis
pro lix'
pre tĕxt'
pre tĕnse'
pur loin'
plăc'ard
pre çēd'ence
prĕç'e dent (n.)
pre çēd'ent (adj.)
prom e nāde'
pў răm'i dal
quĭ'nīne
quan'da rў
re çĕss'
re flĕx'
re cōurse'

re sōurçe′	re trĭb′u tive	tĭ rāde′
re clūse′	strat′ĕġ ic	te lĕḡ′ra phy
re search′	sū i çī′dal	to pŏg′ra phy
ro bŭst′	sys tĕm′ic	vē′he ment
ro mance′	sub sīd′ence	va gā′ry
rọu tïne′	sȳs′to le	vā′ri o loid
rĕe′og nize	so nō′rous	vā′ri e gāt ed

II. Drill on Accent.

I shall absent′ myself to-day and shall be ab′sent to-morrow.
Accent′ the word with the proper ac′cent.
Affix′ an aff′ix properly.
I shall comment′ on your com′ment.
We confine′ the animal and erect his con′fines.
We conjure′ him not to con′jure.
He consorts′ with his con′sort.
I contest′ and so enter the con′test.
We contract′ and make a con′tract.
We contrast′ and produce the con′trast.
We convert′ and gain con′verts.
We convict′ and confine con′victs.
We desert′ into the des′ert without our dessert′.
We entrance′ him at the en′trance.
We escort′ with an es′cort.
I essay′ to produce an es′say.
We export′ our ex′ports.
We extract′ an ex′tract.
We frequent′ the hall and make fre′quent calls.
They misconduct′ and are punished for miscon′duct.
We object′ to your ob′ject.
Prefix′ the pre′fix.
We prelude′ with the proper prel′ude.
We premise′ and give the base of the prem′ise.
I present′ the letter and make a pres′ent.

The trans'ports will transport' the troops.
We progress' and make rapid prog'ress.
We protest' and file our pro'test.
We record' our names in the rec'ord.
We refuse' to accept such ref'use.
We reprint' and produce a re'print.
We subject' him and make him a sub'ject.
We survey' and make a sur'vey.

III. Monosyllables Often Mispronounced.

By giving a vowel sound incorrectly.

ȧnt	chȧff	găs	mōre	rṳle	tạlk
äunt	chȧnt	ḡĕt	mȯurn	ruṣe	true
ȧft	châir	häunt	nȯne	rĭnse	tọ
äre	eătch	häunch	nūde	rōot	tōast
ȧsk	däunt	hearth	ōre	sälve	tour
băde	drȧught	hȧlf	ōar	stäunch	tūbe
bälm	drȧft	hȧlves	pärse	sauce	tärt
bȧth	dȧnce	hȧsp	pȧth	sĭnce	tūne
bȧsk	dȯeṣ	hōme	pälm	sōurce	tōad
brȧss	dĕaf	jäunt	pȧss	scârce	twọ
bȧsque	ĕgg	jōwl	pȧst	shȧft	väunt
blȧst	êre	joist	pȧnt	stȧff	vȧst
bȯmb	ê'er	kĕg	prȧnce	slȧnt	wạnt
been	fȧst	läugh	pōrk	shọe	wạlk
bōne	flȧsk	läunch	pōrch	slōth	wau
bōrne	fläunt	lȧst	pōur	smōke	wȧft
bōurn	gäunt	lȧnce	prṳne	spōke	wand
cȧsk	găpe	lōre	psälm	stōne	wêre
cȧst	gȧsp	lạw	rȧft	sōon	wound
cȧlf	grȧsp	lieū	rȧsp	spōon	wō n't
clȧss	glȧnce	mȧss	rōof	täunt	wȯnt
chȧnce	grȧnt	mȧst	route	tȧsk	yĕt
crȧft	grȧss	maul	rude	trȧnce	yĕs
clȧsp	glȧss	mȧsk	rōod	truth	zouäves

IV. WORDS OFTEN MISPRONOUNCED
By giving a vowel sound incorrectly.

ăf'ter
ăr'id
ăn'swer
a läs
a mäss
a väst
ad vånce
a slänt
a gainst
ap pâr'ent
ap pa rā'tus
ad vän'tage
bås'ket
băr'rel
bŏn'net
bŏm'bast
baȳ'ou
eā'ret
eăr'rot
eăr'at
eåsk'et
eŭr'ry
eŏf'fee
eŏl'umn
châr'y
chāst'en
eāy ĕnne'
eom'mänd'
com mänd'ment
çȳn'o sure
däunt'less
drä'mȧ
dū'ty
dŏc'ĭle

dĭ vẽrge'
dĭ vĕst'
dĭ'verse
dĭ vōrce'
dĭ rĕct'
dĭ lāte'
dĭ ġĕst'
dĭ vŭlge'
dĭs'trict
dŭc'tĭle
dĭ rĕct'ion
dĭ ġĕst'ion
dĭ vẽr'sion
dŏm'ĭ çĭle
dȳn'a mite
ĕn'ġĭne
ĕp'oeh
ēi'ther
ē'dict
en grōss'
ex tŏl'
en chånt
ē'go tism
fạu'çet
fåst'en
fū'tĭle
fŭl'some
fĕt'id
fē'brĭle
fōrg'er
fĭ'brĭne
fōre'head
fŭr'row
for băde'

fŭl'mĭ nate
fĭ nä'le
ġĕn'u ĭne
glä'mọur
găn'der
gäunt'let
grăn'a ry
guä'va
guä'no
hŏs'tĭle
hŏv'er
hŭr'ry
hănd'some
häunt'ed
hein'ous
hĕr'o ĭne
ĭ'dyl
ĭ tăl'ics
ĭs'ŏ lāte
im plā'ca ble
ĭ so thẽr'mal
jäun'dice
jŏc'und
jo eōse'
jū'vĕn ĭle
jū'gu lar
kĕttle
llä'ma
läun'dry
lĭ'lac
lĭ'en
lēi'ṣure
lĕath'er
lăr'ynx

läugh′ter	pâr′ent	ru̇′by
lä′va	pal′frey	ru̇′mor
lē′ver	prāi′rie	rĕp′tĭle
lĭ′chen	pȧs′tor	ru̇′in
līve′long	pȧs′ture	rȧ′tion al
mā′tron	pȧs′tīme	rāil′le ry
măr′ry	plä′zȧ	rā′ti o
māy′or	plăt′ter	rĕt′ro spect
mŏn′ad	plȧs′ter	rā′dix
mĕt′ric	pū′pil	răth′er
mĕaṣ′ure	pōr′ter	ru̇′ral
mȧs′ter	pōr′tion	răp′ĭne
mȧs′tiff	pōr′trait	säun′ter
măt′ter	prŏç′ess	sau′cer
mō′bĭle	prŏd′uct	stal′wart
măr′i tīme	prŏd′uce (n.)	sŭp′ple
măs′cu lĭne	phŏn′ic	sū′et
mū ṣē′um	prĕl′ate	suăv′i ty
mau so lē′um	prĕf′ace	squĭr′rel
mêr′can tĭle	pru̇′dent	slăn′der
nā′ked	pā′tri ot	sўn′od
nēi′ther	pā tri ŏt′ic	sўr′up
năr′row	pā′tri ot ism	sē′nĭle
nŏth′ing	prĕṣ′en ta tion	stĭr′rup
ō′ral	pi ä′no	squal′or
ōn′ly	pi ä′nist	tru̇′ant
ŭn′er ous	pū′is sance	tĕn′et
o bĕs′i ty	pȧth′wāy	tī′ny
ō′ro tund	pā′tri arch	tū′tor
ob lïque′	păt′ron īze	trī′o
pā′tron	pĕd′a gō ġy	to mā′to
păt′rŏn age	plăt′i num	tū′ber ōse
pȧss′a ble	plĕaṣ′ure	tăp′est ry
păs′sage	plĕth′o ric	trĭb′une
pȧss′pōrt	por trāy′	tăs′sel
păs′sive	rā′tion	waṣ′sail

V. Pronunciation and Spelling.

Some of the following words from the French are fully Anglicized; others, partly so; while some retain the French pronunciation.

cou′pon	grĭ māce′	cogn′ac (cōn′yac)
frā′cas	gui pūre′	dē′pot (dē′po)
prĕṣ′tĭġe	mo räle′	mĕm′oir (mĕm′wôr)
pûr′lieu	ou tre′	côr′tege (côr′tāzh)
truf′fle	pe lisse′	bou quet′ (boo kā′)
bla ṣe′	phy̆ sïque′	me lee′ (mā lā′)
deṣ ṣĕrt′	rou tïne′	me lauge′ (mā lŏngz′)
de tour′	rou lĕtte′	quad rille′ (ea drĭl′)
e meūte	souve nir′	re gime′ (ra zheem′)
fa çāde	rou e′	vign ette′ (vin yĕt′)
fĭ nesse′	ta bleau′	băd′i naġe (băd′ĭ näzh)
fū′ṣi lier	trous seau′	am a teur′ (am a tōō:′)

VI. Proper Names Often Mispronounced.

Agassiz (ag′a se)
Arab (ăr′ab)
Aryan (ä′ry an)
Asia (ā′shē a)
Avon (ā′von)
Beatrice (bē′a trĭce)
Berlin (bĕr′lin)
Bingen (bĭng′en)
Calliope (cal lī′o pe)
Caucasian (eaw eā′shun)
Charon (chā′ron)
Cheops (chē′ops)
Concord (cŏng′curd)
Daniel (dăn′yel)
El Dorado (el do rä′do)
European (eu ro pē′an)
Faneuil Hall (făn′el)
Froude (frōōd)
Goethe (gŭr′tĕ)
Gratiano (grä she ä′no)
Guyot (ḡe′ō)
Guise (gwēz)
Heine (hī′nĕ)
Hemans (hĕm′ans)
Iowa (ī′o wa)
Ixion (ix ī′on)
Khedive (kā dēve′)
Lewes (lew′is)
Milan (mĭl′an)
Oberon (ŏb′e ron)
Orion (o rī′on)
Orpheus (ôr′fūs)
Portia (pōr′shĭ a)
Persia (pĕr′shĭ a)

VII. Words of Difficult Enunciation.

Divide into syllables, and mark the accented syllables.

abominably	inviolably	peculiarly
assassination	insuperable	peculiarity
anthropophagi	indissolubly	perpendicularly
differentiation	infinitesimal	ratiocination
dicotyledonous	indefatigable	tergiversation
hypochondriacal	irremediable	unintelligible
inexplicable	lugubrious	unconformability
intolerable	meteorological	uninhabitable
impracticable	monocotyledonous	unhospitable
indisputable	numismatics	valetudinarian
incorrigible	particularly	viviparous

VIII. Miscellaneous Words.

ex cur'sion (ex eûr'shun)
hŏm'age (*h* sounded)
hŭm'ble (*h* sounded)
hŏn'or (*h* silent)
hŏn'est (*h* silent)
hū'mor (*h* silent)
al'mond (*l* silent)
ŏf'ten (ŏf'n)
sŏf'ten (sŏf'n)
thĭs'tle (thĭs'sle)
whĭs'tle (whĭs'sle)
çẽr'tain (çer'tŏn)
chās'ten (chās'n)
lithe (*th* vocal)
blīthe (*th* vocal)

baths (*th* vocal)
oaths (*th* vocal)
par quet' (par kā')
pret'ty (prĭt'ty)
quay (kē)
span'iel (spăn'yel)
sub'tile (sŭb'tĭle)
sub'tle (sŭt'tle)
tor'toise (tôr'tis)
truths (*th* aspirate)
vase (vāçe)
youths (*th* aspirate)
kept (*t* sounded)
slept (*t* sounded)
crept (*t* sounded)

PART II.

PART II.

PRINCIPLES IN ELOCUTION.

CHAPTER I.

EMPHASIS, PAUSES, AND INFLECTIONS.

SECTION I.

EMPHASIS.

I. INTRODUCTORY.

1. Emphasis, as the term is used in its restricted signification, is the special force or energy of voice applied to words in order to give prominence to leading ideas.

2. In its widest signification, however, *emphasis* is used to include *any* means of distinguishing words, phrases, or clauses, whether by means of force, or inflection, or stress, or quantity, or pauses.

3. A word may be made emphatic by an intense whisper; by a strong rising, falling, or circumflex slide; by prolonging vowel or liquid sounds; or by rhetorical pauses.

4. As commonly used, however, *emphasis* relates to the degree or intensity of *force*. But the stronger the *emphatic force*, the longer are the *slides*, and the more

prolonged the *vowel* and the *liquid sounds*. It may here be remarked that the *liquid* sounds capable of being prolonged in emphasis are *l, m, n*, and *r*. The short vowel sounds and the consonant sounds, with the exception of *l, m, n, r*, cannot be prolonged in emphasis.

5. "Every sentence," says Prof. William Russell, "contains one or more words which are prominent, and peculiarly important, in the expression of meaning. These words are marked with a distinctive inflection; those, in particular, which illustrate the reading of strong emotion, or of antithesis.

6. "The words which are pronounced with peculiar inflection, are uttered with more force than the other words in the same sentences. This *special force* is what is called *emphasis*. Its use is to impress more strikingly on the mind of the hearer the thought, or portion of thought, embodied in the particular word or phrase on which it is laid.

7. "It gives additional energy to important points in expression, by causing sounds which are peculiarly significant, to strike the ear with an appropriate and distinguishing force. It possesses, in regard to the sense of hearing, a similar advantage to that of 'relief,' or prominence to the eye, in a well-executed picture, in which the figures seem to stand out from the canvas.

8. "Emphasis, then, being the manner of pronouncing the most significant words, its office is of the utmost importance to an intelligible and impressive utterance. It is the manner of uttering emphatic words which decides the meaning of every sentence that is read or spoken.

9. "A true emphasis conveys a sentiment clearly and forcibly to the mind, and keeps the attention of an audience in active sympathy with the thoughts of the speaker; it gives full value and effect to all that he utters, and secures a lasting impression on the memory."

II. Faults in Emphasis.

In animated conversation, most persons emphasize correctly because they know clearly what they wish to express; but, in reading the long and involved sentences of literary composition, the faults of untrained readers are numerous.

1. Sometimes the emphasis is misplaced because the reader does not clearly comprehend the sense of what is read.

2. Sometimes the emphasis is applied at random, without reference to prominent ideas.

3. Sometimes the untrained reader reads in a dull, monotonous tone, without any emphasis whatever.

4. Not unfrequently the pupil overdoes the emphasis, and reads in a jerky, dogmatic manner.

5. There is often a tendency to a regular recurrence of emphasis, combined with the falling inflection, on random words, particularly at the end of every line of poetry, or of every alternate line, or at the end of every phrase or clause.

III. General Principles of Emphasis.

1. Words or groups of words that express leading ideas are *emphatic;* those that express what is comparatively unimportant, or that merely repeat what has been previously stated, are *unemphatic*.

2. Words expressing contrast of ideas are *emphatic*.

3. The subject and predicate of a sentence are, in general, *emphatic*.

4. Articles, pronouns, and connectives are, in general, *unemphatic*, though any part of speech may sometimes become emphatic.

5. The emphatic words of a sentence are generally the words most strongly marked by the rising, falling, or circumflex inflection.

IV. Distinction of Emphasis.

Emphasis may be divided into two kinds, *antithetic* or relative emphasis, and *absolute* emphasis.

Antithetic emphasis is applied to words that indicate contrast of ideas: *Absolute* emphasis is used to show the importance of a single word or to express feeling, emotion, or passion.

The *degree* of emphasis to be applied to words may be considered as *slight*, *moderate*, or *strong*.

V. Examples of Antithetic Emphasis.

1. He is not a *friénd* but an *ènemy*.
2. *Hĕ* raised a *mórtal* to the skíes.
   Shĕ drew an *àngel dòwn*.
3. To *bé* or *nòt* to be—that is the question.
4. I come to *bŭry* Cæsar, not to *prăise* him.
5. As for *mé*, give me *líberty* or give me *dèath*.
6. You cannot *dó* wrong without *sùffering* wrong.
7. He that cannot *béar* a jest should not *màke* one.
8. I said my *fàther*, not my *móther*.
9. *Tálent* is *pówer* ; *tàct* is *skĭll*.
10. After the *snów*, the emerald *lèaves*,
    After the *hárvest*, golden *shèaves*.
11. He spoke *fór* education, not *agàinst* it.
12. The clerk, in letting Scrooge's nephew *óut*, had let two other people *ìn*.
13. Put not your trust in *mŏney*, but put your *mŏney* in *trŭst*.
14. The *nóblest* mind the best *còntentment* has.
15. Be thou *famíliar*, but by no means *vùlgar*.
16. Give every man thine *éar*, but few thy *vòice*.
17. Take each man's *cénsure*, but reserve thy *jùdgment*.

18. COMPENSATION.

Polárity, or *áction* and *reáction*, we meet in every part of *nàture*—in *dárkness* and *light*; in *héat* and *còld*; in the *ébb* and *flòw* of waters; in *mále* and *fèmale*; in the *ínspiration* and *èxpiration* of *plánts* and *ànimals*; in the equation of *quántity* and *quàlity* in the fluids of the animal *bòdy*; in the *sýstole* and *diàstole* of the *hèart*; in the undulations of *flúids* and of *sòund*; in the *centrífugal* and *centrìpetal* gravity; in *electrícity*, *gálvanism*, and chemical *affìnity*. Superinduce magnetism at *óne* end of a needle, the opposite magnetism takes place at the *òther* end. If the south *attrácts*, the north *repèls*. To empty *hére*, you must condense *thère*. An inevitable *dùalism* bisects *nàture*, so that each thing is a *hùlf* and suggests *anóther* thing to make it *whòle*; as, *spírit*, *màtter*; *mán*, *wòman*; *ódd*, *èven*; *súbjective*, *òbjective*; *ín*, *òut*; *úpper*, *ùnder*; *mótion*, *rèst*; *yéa*, *nùy*.

All things are *dòuble*, *óne* against *ànother*—*tít* for *tàt*; an *eýe* for an *eỳe*; a *tóoth* for a *tòoth*; *blóod* for *blòod*; *méasure* for *mèasure*; *lóve* for *lòve*. *Gíve* and it shall be *gìven* you. He that *wátereth* shall be watered *hìmself*. What will you *háve?* quoth Gód; *páy* for it and *tàke* it. Nothing *vénture*, nothing *hàve*. Thou shalt be paid exactly for what thou hast *dòne*, no *móre*, no *lèss*. Who doth not *wórk* shall not *èat*. EMERSON.

VI. EXAMPLES OF ABSOLUTE EMPHASIS.

Absolute emphasis is applied to words according to their importance in the sentence, or according to the degree of emotion or passion to be expressed. When words are repeated for the purpose of intensifying emotion, each successive repetition is more forcibly emphasized.

1. It *was* a turkey! He never could have stood upon his *légs*, *thăt* bird. He would have snapped 'em *short òff* in a minute, like sticks of *sèaling*-wax.

2. What is it that gentlemen *wìsh?* What would they hàve?

3. "*Revènge! revènge!*" the Saxons cried.

4. Then rose the terrible cry of *fìre! fíre! fìre!*

5. We must *fìght;* I repeat it, sir, we must *fíght!*

6. "To *àrms!* to *àrms!* to *àrms!*" they cry.

7. Háppy, háppy, háppy páir!
   None but the brấve,
   None but the brấve,
   None but the brấve deserves the fàir!

8. CHRISTMAS CAROL.

"Why, bless my soul!" cried Fred, "who's *thàt?*"

"It's *I.* Your uncle *Scròoge.* I have come to *dìnner.* Will you let me *ín,* Fred?"

Let him ín! It is a mercy he didn't shake his *àrm* óff. He was at home in five mìnutes. Nothing could be heàrtier. His niece looked just the sáme. So did Topper, when *hĕ* cáme. So did the plump sister, when *shĕ* cáme. So did every one when *thĕy* cáme. Wŏnderful párty, wŏnderful gámes, wŏnderful unanímity, wŏnderful hàppiness!

DICKENS.

9. GRANDMOTHER'S STORY OF BUNKER-HILL BATTLE.

Then we cried, "The troops are *routed!* they are *beat*—it can't be doubted!

God be thanked, the fight is over!"—Ah! the grim old soldier's smile!

Tell us, TELL us why you *loŏk* so? (we could hardly speak we *shoŏk* so.)

"Are they *béaten? àre* they béaten? *àre* they beaten?"—"Wait awhile."

* * * * * *

And we shout, "At last they're *dòne* for; it's the *barges* they have *rùn* for:

They are bèaten! *bèaten!* BEATEN! and the battle's over now."

HOLMES.

10. INDEPENDENCE.

But whatever may be *oúr* fate, be assúred—*be assúred* that this *declarátion* will *stánd*. It may cost *tréasure*, and it may cost *blóod;* but it will *stánd*, and it will richly compensate for *bòth*. Through the thick gloom of the *présent*, I see the brightness of the *fúture*, as the *sùn* in *hèaven*. We shall make this a *glòrious*, an *immòrtal* day. When *wé* are in our gràves, our *chíldren* will *hònor* it. They will celebrate it with *thanksgìving*, with *festívity*, with *bònfires*, and *illuminàtions*. On its annual *retúrn*, they will shed *tèars*, *còpious*, *gùshing* tèars; not of *subjéction* and *slávery*, not of *ágony* and *distréss*, but of *exultàtion*, of *gràtitude*, and of *jòy*.

My judgment *appróves* this measure, and my whole *heàrt* is in it. All that I *háve*, and all that I *àm*, and all that I *hòpe* in this life, I am now ready here to *stáke* upon it; and I leave off as I began, that, *líve* or *dìe*, *survíve* or *pèrish*, *I* am for the declaration.
WEBSTER.

11. UNCLE TOBY.

"In a fortnight or three weeks," said my uncle Toby, smiling, "he might *màrch*." "He will *néver* march, an' please your honor, in *thís* wórld," said the córporal. "He *wíll* march," said my uncle Tóby, rising up with one shoe óff. "An' please your honor," said the corporal, "he will *néver* march but to his *gráve*." "He *shàll* march," cried my uncle Toby; "he shall march to his *régiment*." "He can not *stánd* it," said the corporal. "He shall be *suppórted*," said my uncle Toby. "Ah, well-a-day, do what we can for him," said Trim, maintaining his point, "the poor soul will *díe*." "He shall *nót*," shouted my uncle Toby, with an oath. The Accusing Spirit which flew up to heaven's chancery, blushed as he gave it in, and the Recording Angel, as he wrote it down, dropped a tear upon the word and blotted it out forever.
STERNE.

SECTION II.

PAUSES.

1. The pauses made in reading or speaking may be classed as grammatical, rhetorical, and emphatic or emotional.

2. *Grammatical* pauses are those indicated by punctuation; *rhetorical* pauses are those required by the structure of the sentence, or by emphasis; and *emphatic* pauses, those expressive of deep feeling or passion.

3. These pauses may be relatively long, moderate, or short, according to the general style of expression appropriate to what is read; but without due attention to them, it is impossible properly to emphasize prose, or to express the melody of verse.

4. Concerning pauses, Prof. Russell says: "The cessation of the voice at proper intervals has the same effect, nearly, on clauses and sentences with that of articulation on syllables, or of pronunciation on words: it serves to gather up the sounds of the voice into relative portions, and aids in preserving clearness and distinction among them. But what those elementary and organic efforts do for syllables and words—the minor portions of speech—pausing does for clauses, sentences, and entire discourses.

5. "The great use of pauses is to divide thought into its constituent portions, and to leave the mind opportunity of contemplating each distinctly, so as fully to comprehend and appreciate it, and, at the same time, to perceive its relation to the whole. Appropriate pauses are of vast importance, therefore, to a correct and impressive style of delivery; and without them, indeed, speech cannot be intelligible.

6. "Pausing has, further, a distinct office to perform in regard to the effect of feeling as conveyed by utterance. Awe and solemnity are expressed by long cessa-

tions of the voice; and grief, when it is deep, and at the same time suppressed, requires frequent and long pauses.

7. "The general effect, however, of correct and well-timed pauses, is what most requires attention. The manner of a good reader or speaker is distinguished, in this particular, by clearness, impressiveness, and dignity arising from the full conception of meaning, and the deliberate and distinct expression of it; while nothing is so indicative of want of attention and of self-command, and nothing is so unhappy in its effect, as haste and confusion."

I. GRAMMATICAL PAUSES.

Grammatical pauses, or the pauses indicated by punctuation, have no fixed length. They depend, to some extent, on the character of the piece to be read. When the general movement or rate is slow, the pauses are relatively *long;* when the movement is fast, the pauses are relatively *short*. The general principles that govern grammatical pauses may be stated as follows:

1. *In general, a slight pause at a comma; a longer pause at a semicolon; and a still longer pause at a period.*

2. *A full pause, longer than at a period, is required at the end of a paragraph of prose, or of a stanza of poetry.*

This pause is made to enable the hearer to note the subdivisions of a piece, and to afford the reader time for a slight rest.

II. RHETORICAL PAUSES.

1. *Rhetorical* pauses are pauses not indicated by punctuation, but which are made in reading, generally for the purpose of emphasis or expression. Attention to these pauses is absolutely essential to good reading.

2. The general tendency of pupils to read too fast is

owing, in no small degree, to a neglect of the pauses necessary to effective utterance. Both the *hearer* and the *reader* must have *time to think.* These pauses, too, afford the reader time to renew the breath, and thus keep the lungs well supplied with air.

3. A continuous stream of rapid utterance soon wearies the hearer, because the speaker neither takes time to think, nor allows his hearers time to do so. The trained extemporaneous speaker talks with deliberation, and the trained reader reads in the same manner.

4. We read words by groups, not by disconnected units. The beginner laboriously calls out each word of a sentence independently, with a pause after each word, thus:

"The | black | cat | caught | a | big | rat | in | the | barn."

A good reader will read this sentence in groups, as indicated by the hyphenized words, thus:

"The-black-cat | caught-a-big-rat | in-the-barn."

5. Pupils, whose attention is directed to the manner in which they run words together in speaking and reading, with pauses between the groups, will notice that adjectives are grouped with the nouns which they modify; adverbs, with verbs or adjectives or other adverbs; prepositions, with their objects; pronouns, with the words they modify; and auxiliaries, with their principal verbs —in other words, that we speak in phrases and clauses.

6. They will notice, further, that when the subject of a verb is a noun, or when it is modified by a phrase or a clause, there is a rhetorical pause between the subject and the predicate.

A COMMON FAULT.

7. "The common fault in regard to pauses," says Prof. Russell, "is that they are made too short for clear and distinct expression.

8. "Feeble utterance and defective emphasis, along with rapid articulation, usually combine to produce this fault in young readers and speakers. For, whatever force of utterance or energy of emphasis, or whatever rate of articulation we accustom ourselves to use, our pauses are always in proportion to it.

9. "Undue brevity in pausing has a like bad effect with too rapid articulation: it produces obscurity and confusion in speech, or imparts sentiment in a manner which is deficient and unimpressive, and prevents the proper effect both of thought and language.

10. "To be fully convinced how much of the clearness, force, and dignity of style depends on due pauses, we have only to revert for a moment to the effect of rapid reading on a passage of Milton, and observe what an utter subversion of the characteristic sublimity of the author seems to take place. This instance is, no doubt, a strong and peculiar one. But a similar result, though less striking, may be traced in the hurried reading of any piece of composition characterized by force of thought or dignity of expression.

11. "When habitual rapidity of voice, and omission of pauses, are difficult to correct, the learner may be required *to accompany the teacher's voice* in the practice of sentences. This simultaneous reading, if sufficiently long continued, will probably prove effectual for the cure of habitual faults. A second stage of progress may be entered on, when the learner's improvement will warrant it; and he may be permitted to read *after* the teacher.

12. "Pupils who possess an ear for music, may be taught to observe that there is in reading and speaking a 'time,' as distinct and perceptible, and as important, as in singing, or in performing on any instrument; and that pauses are uniformly measured with reference to this time."

DRILL EXERCISES.

13. The careful study of a few selections for the purpose of marking pauses, emphasis, and inflection, is also an excellent exercise in parsing and analysis. This method is a slow one, but it will lead to thoughtful, careful, and expressive reading.

14. For the purpose of aiding pupils to gain a clear comprehension of this subject, general principles are applied under a number of definite rules, which are illustrated by copious examples. The value of thorough drill on these examples cannot be overestimated.

15. If any teachers object to formal rules, the following remarks of Prof. Russell are commended to their attention:

16. "Persons, even, who admit the use of rules on other subjects, contend, that, in reading and speaking, no rules are necessary; that a correct ear is a sufficient guide, and the only safe one. If, by a 'correct ear,' be meant a vague exercise of feeling or of taste, unfounded on a principle, the guidance will prove to be that of conjecture, fancy, or whim. But if, by a 'correct ear,' be meant an intuitive exercise of judgment or of taste, consciously or unconsciously recognizing a principle, then is there virtually implied a latent rule; and the instructor's express office, is, to aid his pupil in detecting, applying, and retaining that rule.

17. "Systematic rules are not arbitrary; they are founded on observation and experience. No one who is not ignorant of their meaning and application, will object to them, merely because they are systematic, well defined, and easily understood: every reflective student of any art, prefers systematic knowledge to conjectural judgment, and seizes with avidity on a principle, because he knows that it involves those rules which are the guides of practice."

III. Rules for Rhetorical Pauses.

Rule I. A rhetorical pause should be made between the subject and the predicate of a sentence when the subject is emphatic, or when it consists of a phrase or a clause, or of a noun modified by a phrase or a clause.

EXAMPLES.

1. *Art* | is long, and *time* | is fleeting,
    And the *grave* | is *not* its goal.
2. To *err* | is human, to *forgive,* divine.
3. To reach the Indies | was the object of Columbus.
4. How he found his way out | is not known.
5. Whom the gods love | die young | was said of you.
6. Who steals my purse | steals trash.
7. No wind that blew | was bitterer than he.
8. Not to know *me* | argues *yourself* | unknown.
9. It was for *hím* | that the *sùn* had been darkened, that the *ròcks* | had been rent, that the *dèad* | had risen, that *all nàture* | had shuddered at the sufferings of her expiring God. *Déath* | had lost its *térrors* | and *pléasure* its *chárms.*

Turn to any unmarked selection in Part III. and require pupils to point out further illustrations of this rule.

Rule II. Make a rhetorical pause before a clause used as a predicate nominative, or as the object of a verb.

EXAMPLES.

1. The truth is | he knows nothing about the subject.
2. It was in midwinter | that the Pilgrims landed at Plymouth.
3. I do not know | where he went.
4. He did not say | when he should go.
5. I wish | that friends were always true,
    And motives always pure ;
   I wish | the good were not so few,
    I wish | the bad were fewer.

Rule III. Make a rhetorical pause after introductory or transposed adverbial words, phrases, or clauses.

EXAMPLES.

1. Slowly and sadly | we laid him down.
2. Forth in the pleasing spring | thy beauty walks.
3. In their ragged regimentals | stood the old continentals.
4. If he did that | he ought to be punished.
5. During that terrible storm | the ship foundered.
6. Who she was | nobody knows.
7. In all its history | the Constitution has been beneficent.
8. And up the steep | barbarian monarchs ride.
9. *Down* | came the blow! but in the heath
   The erring blade found bloodless sheath.

Rule IV. Unless the phrases or clauses are short or very closely connected, make a rhetorical pause before adjective or adverbial phrases or clauses.

EXAMPLES.

1. There is a reaper | whose name is Death.
2. He is the same man | that you spoke of.
3. I will go | when you are ready.
4. Let me have men about me | that are fat.
5. The swallows | that build their nests in the old barn | migrate | when winter comes.
6. Our fathers raised their flag against a power | to which, for purposes of foreign conquest and subjugation, Rome, in the height of her glory, is not to be compared—a power | which has dotted the surface of the whole globe | with her possessions | and military posts; whose morning drum-beat, following the sun in his course, and keeping pace with the hours, daily circles the earth | with one continuous and unbroken strain | of the martial airs of England. WEBSTER.

Rule V. Make a pause before and after adverbs or adverbial phrases transposed so as to break the regular order of arrangement.

EXAMPLES.

1. The plowman | homeward | plods his weary way.
2. And some | to happy homes | repair.
3. As we | to higher levels | rise.
4. Who | of this crowd | to-night | shall tread
     The dance | till daylight | gleam again?
5. If Memory | o'er their tomb | no trophies raise.
6. Await | alike | the inevitable hour.
7. Their furrow | oft | the stubborn glebe has broke.

Rule VI. In sentences introduced by idiomatic it or there, make a rhetorical pause before the subject-phrase or clause that is placed after the predicate.

EXAMPLES.

1. There came to the beach | a poor exile of Erin.
2. It is not known | how the prisoner made his escape.
3. It is not true | that the poet paints a life that does not exist.
4. There lies | on the table before me | all that he had written of his latest and last story.

Rule VII. Make a rhetorical pause after predicate adjectives used to introduce a sentence, and after nouns or pronouns in the objective case when they are transposed so as to come before the verbs which govern them.

EXAMPLES.

1. Sweet | are the uses of adversity.
2. Few and short | were the prayers we said.
3. How sweet and solemn | is this midnight scene.
4. Thee | I revisit now | with bolder wing.
5. And all the air | a solemn stillness | holds.

Rule VIII. When an ellipsis of the verb occurs in a sentence, make a rhetorical pause.

EXAMPLES.

1. Homer was the greater genius; Virgil | [was] the better artist. In the one | we most admire the man; in the other—[we most admire] the work.

2. Death had lost its terrors, and pleasure | [had lost] its charms.

3. Their palaces were houses | not made with hands; their diadems | [were] crowns of glory which should never fade away.

4. Lands | he could measure, terms and tides | [he could] presage.

5. Thy waters wasted them while they were free, and many a tyrant [has wasted them] since.

Require the class to find five additional examples.

Rule IX. Unless the grammatical connection is very close, a short pause should be made at the end of every line of poetry, to mark the poetic rhythm.

EXAMPLES.

1. PARADISE LOST.

Anon | out of the earth | a fabric huge |
Rose like an exhalation, with the sound |
Of dulcet symphonies, and voices sweet,
Built like a temple, where pilasters | round
Were set, and Doric pillars, overlaid |
With golden architrave. MILTON.

2. POWER OF MUSIC.

'T was at the royal feast, for Persia won |
   By Philip's warlike son—
 Aloft in awful state |
 The godlike hero sate |
   On his imperial throne. DRYDEN.

3. THE SHIPWRECK.

'T was twilight, for the sunless day went down |
  Over the waste of waters, like a veil |
Which, if withdrawn, would but disclose the frown |
  Of one | whose hate | is masked but to assail.
Thus to their hopeless eyes | the night was shown,
  And grimly darkled o'er their faces pale,
And the dim, desolate deep; twelve days | had Fear |
Been their familiar, and now *Death* | was here.
BYRON.

4. THE LADDER OF ST. AUGUSTINE.

All these | must first be trampled down |
  Beneath our feet | if we would gain |
In the bright fields of fair renown |
  The right | of eminent domain.
LONGFELLOW.

IV. EMPHATIC PAUSES.

Rule I. Emphatic pauses occur when the reader desires to call marked attention to some word or group of words.

EXAMPLES.

1. The penalty was | | | *death.*
2. My answer would be | | *a blow.*
3. You call me *dŏg ;* and for these *coŭrtesies*
  I'll lend you | *thus* | *much* | *moneys.*
4. Hath a *dŏg* | *mŏney ?* Is it possible |
  A cŭr | | can lend | | | *three* | | *thousand* | | *ducats !*
5. Rider and horse, friend, foe, in *one* | *red* | *burial* | blent.
6. They did not see *óne* | *màn,* not | *óne* | *wòman,* | | not | *óne* | *chìld,* not *óne* | *four-footed bèast* | | *of àny description* | | *whatèver.* One | *dead* | *uniform* | *silence* | | *reigned* | over the whole region`.
BURKE.

7. The love that loves a *scarlet* coat
Should be | | more *uniform*.

8. BUNKER HILL.

Just a glimpse (the air is clearer), they are nearer | |
nearer | | nearer,
When a flash—a curling smoke-wreath—then a crash—
the steeple shakes;
The deadly truce is ended; | | the tempest's shroud is
rended; | |
Like a morning mist it gathered, | | like a thunder cloud
| | it breaks.

All through those hours of trial, I had watched a calm
clock-dial,
As the hands kept *creeping*, | | *creeping*, | | | they were
creeping | | round to four. HOLMES.

V. RECAPITULATION OF PAUSES.

1. *In general, a rhetorical pause should be made between the subject and the predicate, when the subject is emphatic, or when it consists of a phrase, a clause, or a noun modified by a phrase or a clause.*

2. *A rhetorical pause should be made whenever the regular order of a sentence is broken by the inversion of words, phrases, or clauses.*

3. *An emphatic pause occurs before any word that is very strongly emphatic, or to which the reader or speaker desires to call marked attention.*

SECTION III.
INFLECTION.

I. Introductory Remarks.

1. In all good speaking or reading, there must be ever-varying upward and downward slides of the voice. Inflection is a means, not only of expressing emotion, passion, and emphasis, but, also, of conveying the finer distinctions and contrasts of ideas, and the more delicate shades of feeling and sentiment.

2. Inflection forms an important element of emphasis: for emphasis consists, not only in *force*, but also in the *slides* and in *quantity*.

3. Reading, when it lacks the melody of varied emphasis and inflection, becomes like the monotonous droning of children who laboriously pronounce the successive words of their reading lesson in the conventional school tone.

4. In animated conversation, and in the reading of simple stories, the inflections take care of themselves without thought by the speaker or reader; but in the long and often inverted sentences of finished prose or poetry, involving a higher and more complicated order of thought, the proper application of emphasis and inflection requires some knowledge of the principles of elocution.

5. While it is true that a clear conception of the spirit and meaning by the reader is essential to good reading, it is equally true that, having the right conception, the reader may fail to convey it to the hearer, from ignorance of the principles that govern the correct expression of thought and feeling.

6. Good reading, like fine singing, is the result of systematic training—is the product of culture and art. There are good *natural* voices both for singing and

reading, but a fine singer, without training in the science and art of music, is as rare as is a good reader of general English literature, who is ignorant of the principles of elocution, and untrained in the management of the voice.

7. The real object of school elocution is, not to enable pupils to read by imitation a few selected pieces in the style of an actor, but to make thoughtful and intelligent readers independent of the assistance of teachers.

8. One reason for the full treatment of inflection in this book is the great importance of the subject as a means of *expressive* and *impressive* reading.

9. Another reason is the cursory manner in which the few introductory rules and illustrations are taken up in the grammar school. Teachers of high schools and normal schools are aware of the fact that many of their pupils come into school not only ignorant of the principles of inflection, but also so untrained in the management of the voice that they cannot give the correct inflections even when indicated, and sometimes cannot even imitate them when given by the teacher.

10. It is not unreasonable to expect that, in high and normal schools, there should be training enough to enable students themselves to apply the general principles of elocution; and that there should be practice enough to secure some flexibility in the management of the voice.

11. *Expression* in reading depends largely on the variety produced by the proper and effective application of the slides. There is no excuse for the neglect that leads to the monotonous and lifeless style of reading characteristic of many high schools and colleges.

"This school-tone," says Prof. Russell, "can be tolerated only in a law paper, a state document, a bill of lading, or an invoice, in the reading of which the mere distinct enunciation of the words is deemed sufficient.

In other circumstances, it kills, with inevitable certainty, everything like feeling or expression."

12. The careful study of an extract from some standard author, for the purpose of marking it for inflection, emphasis, and pauses, is an intellectual discipline of no mean order. It combines, in one lesson, rhetoric, grammar, and elocution.

13. It matters little whether aspiring elocutionists *can* or can *not* render effectively such pieces as "The Raven," "The Bells," or "Catiline's Defiance"; but it is a matter of solid importance for them to be able to read intelligently and effectively such extracts as Macaulay's "Puritans," Bryant's "Winds," Byron's "Apostrophe to the Ocean," one of Webster's "Speeches," or an extract from Milton or Shakespeare. The trained reader is able not only to read well, but also to give good *reasons* for reading with good taste, discrimination, and judgment.

14. As an aid both to teachers and pupils in applying principles and rules, a considerable number of extracts and examples are marked for inflection, emphasis, and pauses. When these have been carefully studied and read, pupils ought to be able to apply, to some extent at least, principles and rules to unmarked extracts, thus becoming independent of imitation and of teachers.

II. Distinctions of Inflection.

1. *Inflection* may be defined as an upward or downward slide of the voice, generally on the emphatic word or words of a sentence. In words of more than one syllable, the inflection falls chiefly on the vowel of the accented syllable; hence the mark of inflection is placed over the vowel in the accented syllable.

2. The rising inflection, indicated by the acute accent

(´), is used in direct questions, and, in general, whenever the sense is incomplete.

3. The falling inflection, indicated by the grave accent (`), is used in complete declarative, exclamatory, or very emphatic statements, and, in general, wherever the sense is *complete*, or does not depend on something to follow.

4. The *circumflex*, a combination of the rising and falling inflections on the same sound or word, indicated thus (ˇ or ˆ), is used in surprise, sarcasm, irony, wit, humor, and in expressing a pun, or a double meaning. The rising circumflex is used in place of the direct rising inflection to add force to the emphasis, and the falling circumflex in place of the direct falling inflection.

5. The monotone (.– –), that is, one uniform tone, is merely the absence of any marked rising or falling slide above or below the general level of the sentence.

III. Length of Slides.

1. The length of the rising or the falling inflection, in ascending or descending the scale, depends on the force of emphasis applied to words marked by inflection.

2. The *degrees* of inflection may be roughly distinguished as corresponding to the *second, third, fifth,* and *eighth* notes in the musical scale, including the semitones, or chromatic notes, of the minor second, third, fifth, and eighth notes.

3. The "second" and "third" are classed as the *unemotional* slides, as contrasted with the "fifth" and "eighth," which are the *emotional* inflections.

IV. The Slide of the Second.

1. The inflection of the second is a very slight upward or downward slide of the voice, expressing what

may be termed the current melody of the sentence, in quiet conversation and in unemotional reading. It is the distance in tone between *C* and *D*, or *Do* and *Re* on the scale in music.

2. "The simple rise and fall of the second, and perhaps its wave," says Dr. Rush, "when used for plain narration, or for the mere statement of an unexcited idea, is the only intonated voice of man that does not spring from a passionate, or, in some degree, an earnest condition of his mind. If we listen to his ignorance, doubt, selfishness, arrogance, and injustice, we hear the vivid forms of vocal expression, proceeding from these and related passions.

3. "Thus we have the rising intervals of the fifth and octave, for interrogatives, not of wisdom but of envious curiosity; the downward third, fifth, and octave, for dogmatic or tyrannical command; waves for the surprise of ignorance, the snarling of ill-humor, and the curling voice, along with the curling lip of contempt; the piercing height of pitch for the scream of terror; the semitone, for the peevish whine of discontent, and for the puling cant of the hypocrite and the knave, who cover beneath the voice of kindness, the designs of their craft.

4. "Then listen to him on those rare occasions, when he forgets himself and his passions, and has to utter a simple idea, or plainly to narrate; and you will hear the second, the least obtrusive interval of the scale, in the admirable harmony of Nature, made the simple sign of the unexcited sentiment of her wisdom and truth."

V. INFLECTION DRILL ON THE SECOND.

1. Count, in a gentle tone, from one to twenty, with the slight rising inflection, thus—óne, twó, thrée, fóur, etc.

2. Count from one to twenty with the slight falling inflection, thus—òne, twò, etc.

3. Count with alternate rising and falling, thus—óne, twò, thrée, fòur, etc., to thirty.

4. Sound the long vocals, ā, ē, ī, ō, ū: (1) With the rising second. (2) With the falling second. (3) Alternate rising and falling.

VI. THE SLIDE OF THE THIRD.

1. The slide of the third corresponds to the interval, on the scale, between *C* and *E*, or *Do* and *Mi*.

2. When the voice *rises* on a word through an interval of two tones, or a major third, it expresses moderate emphasis, interrogation, contrast, or slight surprise; when the voice *falls* through the same interval, it expresses moderate emphasis, assertion, command, contrast, or the conclusion of a proposition.

3. The inflection of the third is the prevailing slide of animated and earnest conversation, and of the slightly emphatic words of narrative, didactic, or descriptive composition. It is the slide of antithesis in contrasted words.

VII. UNEMOTIONAL SLIDES.

The slides of the second and third are the sentential or *unemotional* inflections as contrasted with the fifth and the eighth, which are the slides of emotion and passion.

VIII. INFLECTION DRILL ON THE THIRD.

1. Count, with moderate force and emphasis, from one to twenty with the rising third, thus: óne, twó, thrée, etc.

2. Count from one to twenty with the falling third, thus: òne, twò, thrèe, etc.

3. Count with alternate rising and falling third, thus: óne, twò, threé, fòur, etc.

4. Will you gó or stày?

IX. THE SLIDES OF THE FIFTH AND THE EIGHTH.

1. The slide of the fifth corresponds to the interval between *C* and *G*, or *Do* and *Sol*, and the slide of the eighth, or the octave, to the interval between *C* and *C*, or *Do* and *Do*.

2. When the voice *rises* through the interval of the fifth, it expresses impassioned interrogation, extreme surprise, or strong negation; when it *falls* through the same interval, it expresses deep conviction, strong determination, emphatic declaration, stern command, or strong emotion.

3. Under the influence of intense excitement or passion, the voice sometimes rises or falls through the whole octave. The rising octave expresses amazement, astonishment, excited interrogation, intense irony, and the falling octave expresses fierce determination, impassioned scorn, imprecation, and defiance.

4. Thus, when Douglas cries out under the influence of intense anger—

"And dar'st thou then
To beard the *líon* in his *dén*,
The *Dóuglas* in his *háll?*"

The voice on "hall" rises through the whole octave. And when Coriolanus cries out: "*Meásureless* liar," the voice on "measureless" falls through the octave.

5. The words "*ăh! indĕed!*" uttered so as to express the greatest possible degree of astonishment, illustrate the rising octave.

X. INFLECTION DRILL.

1. Sound the long vocals, ā, ē, ī, ō, ū, with the rising fifth; the falling fifth.

2. Sound the long vocals, ā, ē, ī, ō, ū, with the rising eighth; with the falling octave.

3. Count from one to twenty with the rising fifth; the falling fifth.

I. THE RISING INFLECTION.

1. *The rising inflection calls attention to what is to follow. It is the inflection of incomplete statement, of appeal, of inquiry, and of negative antithesis.*

2. *It is the prevailing inflection of sentiment, of tenderness, and of pathos.*

3. *It is the characteristic inflection used in stating what is comparatively unimportant, trite, questionable, doubtful, or parenthetical.*

Rules for the Rising Inflection.

Rule I. Questions requiring YES *or* NO *for an answer have the rising inflection, except when very emphatic.*

EXAMPLES.
[*Rising Third.*—Light Emphasis.]

1. Have you recited your *léssons?*
2. Is it, O mán, with such discordant *nóises,*
   With such accurséd instruments as *thése,*
   Thou drownest Nature's sweet and kindly *vóices,*
   And jarrest the celestial *hármonies?*
3. Breathes there the man with soul so *déad,*
   Who never to himself hath said,
   This is my *ówn,* my *native lánd?*
   Whose heart hath ne'er within him *búrned,*
   As *hóme* his footsteps he hath *túrned,*
   From wandering on a *foreign stránd?*

[*Fifth and Eighth.*—Strong Emphasis.]

4. Hates ăny man the thing he would not kĭll?
5. Whăt! wouldst thou have a serpent sting thee twĭce?
6. And dar'st thou then
   To beard the *líon* in his *dĕn,*
   The Douglas in his *hăll?*

7. Art thou a *friend* to Roderick?—Nò.
Thou dar'st not call thyself his *fŏe?*

8. Is it come to *thĭs?* Shall an inferior *mágistrate,* a góvernor, who holds his whole power of the *Roman péople,* in a Roman *próvince,* within sight of *Italy, bínd, scoúrge, tórture,* and put to an infamous *déath,* a Roman *cítizen?* Shall neither the cries of *innócence* expiring in *ágony,* the tears of pitying *spectátors,* the majesty of the *Roman Cómmonwealth,* nor fear of the justice of his *coúntry,* restrain the merciless monster, who, in the confidence of his riches, strikes at the very root of *líberty,* and sets mankind at *defíance?* And shall *thĭs* man *escápe?* Fathers, it must not *bè! It must not bè,* unless you would undermine the very foundations of social *sáfety,* strangle *jùstice,* and call down *ànarchy, mássacre,* and *rùin* on the Commonwealth! CICERO.

9. Canst thou bind the *únicorn* with his band in the *fúrrow?* or will he harrow the *válleys* after thee? Wilt thou *trúst* him because his *stréngth* is greát? or wilt thou leave thy *lábor* to him?

Gavest thou the goodly wings unto the *péacocks?* or wings and feathers unto the *óstrich?* Canst thou draw out *levíathan* with a *hóok?* or his *tóngue* with a *córd* which thou lettest dówn? Canst thou put a *hóok* into his *nóse?* or bore his *jáw* through with a *thórn?* Wilt thou *pláy* with him as with a *bírd?* or wilt thou *bínd* him for thy *máidens?* Canst thou fill his *skín* with barbed *írons?* or his *héad* with *fĭsh* spears? Book of Job.

Rule II. Words repeated in surprise take the rising inflection, and are emphatic.

EXAMPLES.

1. Must I endure all *thĭs? All thĭs?* Ay, mòre.

2. CATILINE'S REPLY.

"*Banished from Róme!*" What's banished but set free
From daily contact with the things I lòathe?
"*Tríed and convícted tráitor!*" Whò says thìs? CROLY.

3. SQUEERS.

"Who cried *stòp?*" said Squeers, turning savagely round.

"*I`*," said Nicholas, stepping forward. "*This must not go òn.*"

"*Must not go ón!*" cried Squeers, almost in a shriek.
"*Nò!*" thundered Nicholas. DICKENS.

Call on the class to find five additional illustrations.

Rule III. Words and phrases of address, unless very emphatic, take the slight rising inflection.

EXAMPLES.

1. Sír, I believe the hour has còme.
2. Mr. Président, I desire to offer a resolùtion.
3. Friénds, Rómans, cóuntrymen, lend me your eàrs.
4. Fellow-cítizens, the time for action has còme.
5. *Góod* friends, *swéet* friends, let me not stir you up
   To such a sudden flood of mutiny.

Call on each pupil to find one additional illustration.

EXCEPTION.

6. O còmrades! wàrriors! Thràcians! if we mŭst fight, let us fight for oursélves.
7. Prínces! pòtentates! wàrriors!

Rule IV. The language of entreaty, coaxing, or flattery, takes the rising inflection.

EXAMPLES.
1. ARTHUR IN KING JOHN.

Alás, what need you be so boisterous-*roúgh?*
I will not *strúggle;* I will stand *stóne-still.*

For heaven's sake, Hubert, let me not be *boúnd;*
Náy, *héar* me, Húbert; drive but these *mèn awáy,*
And I will sit as quiet as a *làmb;*
I will not *stír,* nor *wínce,* nor speak a wòrd,
Nor *lóok* upon the iron *ángerly:*
Thrust but these *mén awáy,* and I'll forgive you,
Whatever torment you do *pùt* me to. SHAKESPEARE.

2. MRS. CAUDLE'S CURTAIN LECTURES.

I.

Now, Caudle, déar, do let us talk comfortably. After all, lóve, there's a good many folks who, I dare sáy, don't get on half so well as we've dóne. We've both our little témpers, perháps; but you *are* ággravating; you must own *thăt,* Caúdle. Wéll, never mínd; we won't tálk of it; I won't scold you *nŏw.*

II.

I'm sure I don't object to your being a *Măson;* not at *ăll,* Cáudle. I dare say it's a very good *thĭng;* I dare say it *ĭs:* it's only your making a *sĕcret* of it that *vĕxes* mé. But you'll *tĕll* me—you'll tell your own *Măgaret? You wŏn't?* You're a *wrétch,* Mr. Caudle. HARROLD.

Rule V. Negative expressions, whether of words, phrases, clauses, or sentences, take the rising inflection when they carry the attention forward to a contrasted affirmation, or backward to an affirmative statement.

EXAMPLES.

1. I come not here to *tálk.*
    Ye know *too wéll* the story of our *thràlldom.*
2. The battle, sir, is not to the *stróng* alóne.
    It is to the *vígilant,* the *àctive,* the *bràve.*
3. Tell me *nòt,* in mournful númbers,
    Life is but an empty *dréam;*
    For the soul is *deàd* that slúmbers,
    And things *àre* not what they sèem.

4. I come not, friends, to steal away your *heárts;*
I am no orator, as *Brŭtus* is :
But, as you know me all, a plain, blunt *màn.*

5. Cleon hath a million *ácres*—ne'er a *one* have I':
Cleon dwelleth in a *pàlace*—in a *cottage,* I';
Cleon hath a *dozen fòrtunes*—not a *penny,* I';
But the *poorer* of the twain is *Clèon,* and *nót* I'.

6. FREEDOM.

O *Fréedom!* thou art not, as *pŏets* dream,
A fair young *gĭrl,* with light and delicate *lĭmbs,*
And wavy tresses gushing from the cap
With which the Roman master crowned his *sláve,*
When he took off the *gýves.* A *bearded màn,*
Armed to the *tèeth,* art thòu.

BRYANT.

7. THE OCEAN.

The armaments | which thunderstrike the walls |
Of rock-built cities, bidding nations quake,
And monarchs | tremble in their cápitals,
The oak leviathans, whose huge ribs make
Their clay creator | the vain title | take |
Of lord of thee, and arbiter of wár;—
Thése, are thy *tòys,* and as the snowy *flàke* |
They melt into thy yeast of waves, which mar |
Alike | the Armada's príde | or spoils of Trafalgàr.

BYRON.

8. LIBERTY.

Tell me not of the honor of belonging to a *frce coúntry.* I ask, does our liberty bear *gcnerous frùits!* Does it exalt us in manly *spĭrit,* in *publĭc vìrtue,* above countries trodden under foot by *dèspotism ?*—Tell me not of the *extént* of our *coúntry.* I care not how *lárge* it is, *if it multĭply degencrate mén.* Speak not of our *prospérity.* Better be one of a *poor pèople,* plain in *mánners,* reverencing Gód, and respecting themselves, than belong to a *rich* country, which knows no higher good than *riches*. CHANNING.

9. WHAT CONSTITUTES A STATE?

What constitutes a Stàte?
 Not high-raised *báttlement* or labored *móund*,
Thick *wáll* or moated *gáte;*
 Not *cíties* proud with *spíres* and *turrets* crowned.
Not *báys* and broad-armed *pórts*,
 Where, laughing at the storm, rich *návies* ride:
Not starred and spangled *cóurts*
 Where low-bred baseness wafts perfume to *príde:*
Nò; mèn, high-minded *mén;* men, who their *dúties* know;
 But know their *ríghts;* and knowing, dare *maintàin;*
Prevent the long-aimed blow,
 And crush the *týrant* while they rend the *chàin.*
Thèse constitute a State. JONES.

Call on pupils to find additional examples.

Rule VI. Incomplete expressions, whether of phrases or clauses, when they carry the mind forward to something to be stated, require the rising inflection.

EXAMPLES.

1. Born to inherit the most illustrious monarchy in the *wórld*, and early united to the object of her *chóice*, the amiable *princess*, happy in hersélf, and joyful in her future *próspects*, little anticipated the fate that was so soon to *overtàke* her.

2. THE PILGRIM FATHERS.

And yet, do you not *thínk*, that who so *cóuld*, by adequate *description*, bring before you that *wínter* of the *Pílgrims*, its brief *súnshine*, the nights of *stórm*, slow *wáning;* the damp and icy *bréath*, felt to the pillow of the *dýing;* its *destitútions*, its *cóntrasts* with all their former *expérience* in life; its utter *insulátion* and *lóneliness;* its *déath-beds* and *búrials;* its *mémories;* its ap-

prehénsions; its *hópes;* the *consultátions* of the *prúdent;* the *práyers* of the *píous;* the occasional cheerful *hýmn,* in which the strong heart threw off its *búrthen,* and, asserting its unvanquished *náture, went úp,* like a bird of *dáwn,* to the *skíes;*—do ye not *thínk* that whoso could *descríbe* them calmly waiting in that *defíle,* lonelier and darker than *Thermópylæ,* for a *mórning* that might never *dáwn,* or might *shów* them, when it *díd,* a *míghtier* arm than the Pérsian, raised as in act to *stríke,* would he not sketch a scene of more difficult and rarer *héroism?* A scéne, as Wordsworth has sáid, "*mélancholy,* yea, *dísmal,* yet consolatory and full of *jóy;*" a *scéne,* even better fitted, to *súccor,* to *exált,* to *léad,* the forlorn hopes of all *great cáuses,* till *tíme* shall be *nò mòre.*

Choate.

3. THE STRIFE.

Notice that the last four stanzas constitute one sentence.

> The wish that of the living whole
>   No life may *fáil* beyond the *gráve*—
>   Derives it not from what we have
> The likest *Gód* within the *sóul?*
>
> Are *Gód* and *náture* then at *strífe,*
>   That *náture* lends such evil dréams?
>   So *cáreful* of the type she séems,
> So *cáreless* of the single lífe,
>
> That *Í,* considering everywhere
>   Her secret meaning in her déeds,
>   And finding that of *fífty* seeds
> She often brings but *óne* to *béar*—
>
> I *fálter* where I *firmly tród;*
>   And, falling with my weight of *cáres*
>   Upon the great world's *áltar*-stairs,
> That slope through darkness up to *Gód,*

I stretch lame hands of *fáith*, and grópe,
    And gather dust and *cháff*, and call
    To what I feel is Lord of áll,
And faintly trust the *larger hòpe.*
TENNYSON's *In Memoriam.*

4. THE LADDER OF ST. AUGUSTINE.

The low desíre, the base desígn,
    That makes another's virtues léss;
The revel of the treacherous wíne,
    And all occasions of excéss;

The longing for ignoble thíngs,
    The strife for triumph more than trúth;
The hardening of the heart that brings
    Irreverence for the dreams of yoúth;

All thoughts of ill; all evil deeds
    That have their *root* in thoughts of ill;
Whatever hinders or impedes
    The action of the noble wíll,—

All these must first be trampled dówn
    Beneath our feet, if we would gáin
In the bright fields of fair renówn,
    The right of eminent domàin.
LONGFELLOW.

Rule VII. Conditional phrases and clauses, when introductory, take the rising inflection, because the sense is carried forward to the principal statements on which they depend.

EXAMPLES.

1. FROM "THE ARMORY."

Were half the power that fills the world with *térror;*
    Were half the wealth, bestowed on camps and *cóurts,*
Given to redeem the human mind from *érror,*
    There were no *nèed* of arsenals or fòrts.
LONGFELLOW.

2. FROM "JULIUS CÆSAR."

As Cæsar *lóved* me, I *wèep* for him; as he was *fórtunate*, I *rejòice* at it; as he was *váliant*, I *hònor him;* but, as he was *ambítious*, I *slèw* him. There is tears for his lóve; joy for his fórtune; honor for his válor; and death for his ambìtion.

3. WATER.

Of all *inorganic súbstances*, acting in their own proper *náture*, and without assistance or *combinátion*, *wàter* is the most *wònderful*. If we think of it as the source of all the changefulness and beauty which we have seen in *cloúds;* then as the instrument by which the earth we have contemplated was modeled into *sýmmetry*, and its crags chiseled into *grácc;* then, as in the form of *snów*, it robes the mountains it has *máde* with that *transcendent líght* which we could not have *concéived* if we had not *séen;* then as it exists in the foam of the *tórrent*—in the *íris* which *spáns* it, in the morning *mìst* which *ríses* from it, in the deep crystalline *pòols* which mirror its hanging *shóre*, in the broad *làke* and glancing *ríver;* finally, in that which is to all human minds the best emblem of unwéaried, uncónquerable *pówer*, the wíld, várious, fantástic, támeless *unity* of the *sèa;* what shall we *compàre* to this *mìghty*, this *univèrsal* element, for *glóry* and for *beaùty?* or how shall we follow its *etérnal chángefulness* of *fèeling?* It is like trying to paint a *sòul*.

RUSKIN.

4. FROM WEBSTER'S SPEECHES.

I.

If disastrous *wár* sweep our *cómmerce* from the *ócean*, *anóther* generation may *renèw* it; if it exhaust our *trèasury*, future industry may *replènish* it; if it desolate and lay waste our *fiélds*, still, under a *néw* cultivation, they will grow *gréen* again, and ripen to *future hárvests*.

II.

If discord and disunion shall *woúnd* it; if party strife

and blind ambition shall *háwk at* and *téar* it; if folly and *mádness,* if uneasiness under salutary *restráint,* shall succeed to separate it from that Union, by which alone its existence is made *súre,* it will stand, in the ènd, by the side of that cradle in which its infancy *was ròcked;* it will stretch forth its *árm* with whatever of vigor it may *still retáin,* over the friends who gather roùnd it; and it will *fàll,* if *fall* it *múst,* amid the *proudest mònuments* of its glóry and on the very *spòt* of its òrigin.

<small>Require each pupil, at the next lesson, to read one additional illustration, selected from some extract in this book.</small>

Rule VIII. In poetic description, whether of prose or verse, the prevailing inflection is the slight rising inflection of the "third."

EXAMPLES.

1. FROM WHITTIER'S "RANGER."

Nowhere fáirer, swéeter, rárer,
Does the golden-locked frúit-beárer,
   Through his painted woodlands stráy,
Than where hillside oaks and béeches
Overlook the long, blue réaches,
Silver cóves and pebbled béaches,
   And green isles of Casco Bày:
Nowhere dáy, for deláy,
With a tenderer look beséeches,
   "Let me with my charmed earth stày."

2. WATER.

Gleaming in the déw-drop, singing in the summer ráin, shining in the íce-gem till the trees seem turned to living jéwels, spreading a golden véil over the setting sún, or a white gáuze around the midnight móon; sporting in the cátaract, sleeping in the glácier, dancing in the háil-shower, folding bright snów-curtains softly above the wintry wórld, and weaving the many-colored íris, that seraph's zone of the sky, whose warp is the ráin of éarth, whose wóof is the sunbeam of héaven, all checkered over with celestial flowers by the mystic hand of rarefáction—still always it is beaùtiful, that blessed cold wàter! No poison bubbles on its brínk—its foam brings not mádness and múrder—no blóod stains its liquid gláss—pale wídows and starving órphans weep not burning tears in its clear dépths—no drunkard's shrieking ghost from the gráve curses it in words of despàir! *Speak òut,* my frìends; would yoú exchange it for the demon's drínk—*álcohol?*

A shout like the roar of the tempest answered "*Nò! No*'!"

DENTON.

3. THE VOICE OF SPRING.

The fisher is out on the sunny séa;
And the reindeer bounds o'er thè pasture frée;
And the pine has a fringe of softer gréen,
And the moss looks bright, where my fòot hath been.
From the streams and founts I have loosed the cháin.
They are sweeping on to the silvery máin,
They are flashing down from the móuntain brows,
They are flinging spray o'er the fórest boughs,
They are bursting fresh from their sparry cáves;
And the earth resounds with the joy of wàves.

HEMANS.

Rule IX. Pathos and tender feeling incline the voice to the slight rising inflection.

EXAMPLES.

1. BABIE BELL.

And what did dainty Babie Bèll?
She only crossed her little hánds!
She only looked more meek and fáir!
We parted back her silken háir;
We laid some buds upon her brów—
Déath's bride arrayed in *flòwers!*

ALDRICH.

2. THE RANGER.

When the shadows vail the méadows,
And the sunset's golden ládders
   Sink from twilight's walls of gráy—
From the window of my dréaming,
I can see his sickle gléaming,
Cheery-voiced can hear him téaming
   Down the locust-shaded wáy;
   But awáy, swift awáy,
Fades the fónd, delusive seéming,
   And I kneel again to pràs.   WHITTIER.

Rule X. In a series of words or phrases, if the particulars enumerated are unimportant, or if they are to be taken as constituting a whole, each particular, except the last in a closing series, takes the rising inflection.

EXAMPLES.

1. The sún, the plánets, their sátellites, the cómets, and the méteors, compose the solar system.
2. The solar system consists of the sún, the plánets, their sátellites, the cómets, and the mèteors.
3. The minerals of California are góld, sílver, cópper, íron, tín, and quìcksilver.
4. Whéat, flóur, pórk, béef, cótton, tobácco, and petróleum are exported from the United States.
5. The Góth, the Chrístian, Tíme, Wár, Flóod, and Fíre,
   Have dealt upon the seven-hilled city's prìde.

6. CHRISTMAS MARKETS.

Heaped upon the flóor, to form a kind of thróne, were túrkeys, géese, gáme, bráwn, great joints of méat, súcking-pígs, long wreaths of sáusages, mince-píes, plumpúddings, barrels of óysters, red-hot chéstnuts, cherry-cheeked ápples, juicy óranges, luscious péars, immense twélfth-cákes, and great bowls of pùnch.   DICKENS.

7. BOARDING-SCHOOL CURRICULUM.

And thus their studies they pursùed:—On Súnday,
  Béef, cóllects, bátter, téxts from Dr. Príce;
Mútton, Frénch, páncakes, grámmar—of a Mónday;
  Túesday—hard dúmplings, glóbes, Chapone's Advíce.
Wédnesday—fáncy-wórk, ríce-mílk (no spíce);
Thúrsday—pórk, dáncing, currant-bólsters, réading;
  Fríday, béef, Mr. Bútler, and plain ríce;
Sáturday—scráps, short léssons and short féeding,
Stócks, báck-boards, hásh, steel-cóllars, and good bréeding.

HOOD.

8. FROM DICKENS'S "CHRISTMAS CAROL."

It was a game called Yes and No, where Scrooge's nephew had to think of something, and the rest must find out what; he only answering to their questions yes or no, as the case was. The fire of questioning to which he was exposed elicited from him that he was thinking of an *ánimal*, a *líve* animal, rather a *disagrée-able* animal, a *sávage* animal, an animal that *grówled* and *grúnted* sometimes, and *tálked* sometimes, and lived in *Lóndon*, and walked about the *stréets*, and was n't made a *shów* of, and was n't *léd* by anybody, and did n't live in a *menágerie*, and was never killed in a *márket*, and was not a *hórse*, or an *áss*, or a *ców*, or a *búll*, or a *tíger*, or a *dóg*, or a *píg*, or a *cát*, or a *beàr*.

9. FROM DICKENS'S "CHRISTMAS CAROL."

Sitting-room, bedroom, lumber-room, all as they *should* be. Nobody under the táble; nobody under the sófa; a small fire in the gráte; spoon and basin réady; and the little saucepan of gruel (Scrooge had a cold in his head) upon the hob. Nobody under the béd; nobody in the clóset; nobody in his dressing-gown, which was hanging up in a suspicious attitude against the wáll. Lumber-room as úsual. Old fíre-guard, old shóes, two fish-baskets, washing-stand on three légs, and a pòker.

II. THE FALLING INFLECTION.

1. *The falling inflection is the slide of the complete statement.*

2. *It is the characteristic inflection of assertion, of confidence, of command, of emotion, and of passion.*

3. *It denotes what is important, interesting, or decisive. It is the prevailing inflection of impressive oratory.*

RULES FOR THE FALLING INFLECTION.

Rule I. The close of a declarative, imperative, or exclamatory sentence is generally marked by the falling inflection.

EXAMPLES.

1. The liberty of the press is the highest safeguard to all free gòvernment. It is like a greát, exúlting, and abóunding rìver.

    2. Maud Muller, on a summer's dáy,
       Raked the meadow sweet with hày.

3. Ye crágs and péaks, I'm *with* you once *agàin!*
   I hold to you the hands you first beheld,
   To show they still are *frèc.* Methinks I hear
   A spirit in your echoes *ànswer* me,
   And bid your tenant welcome to his *hòme*
   Again! O sacred fórms, how *proùd* ye look!
   How *hìgh* you lift your heads into the skỳ!
   How *hùge* you are! how *mìghty* and how *frèe!*

Rule II. The answer to a direct question generally takes the falling inflection.

EXAMPLES.

1. Are you going to schóol? Yès, I àm.

    2. Shall traitors lay that greatness lów?
       Nò! land of hope and blessing, nò.

EXCEPTIONS.

Answers given in a careless or an indifferent manner sometimes take the rising inflection, as,

1. What do you wànt? Nóthing.
2. Which will you hàve? I do n't cáre.
3. What did you sáy? Not múch.
4. May I stáy here? Yés, you may if you líke.
5. Out spoke the ancient fisherman: "O what was that, my dàughter?"
   "'T was nothing but a pébble, sir, I threw upon the wáter."
   "And what is that, pray tell me, love, that paddles off so fàst?"
   "It's nóthing but a pórpoise, sìr, that's been a swimming pást."

Rule III. Impassioned exclamation or very emphatic assertion is characterized by the falling inflection—usually the fifth or eighth.

EXAMPLES.
[Falling Fifth.]

1. *Rìse*, fellow-mèn, our *coùntry* yet remains.
2. Clèarness, fòrce, and èarnestness are the qualities which produce convìction.
3. Eloquence is *àction, nòble, sublìme, gòdlike* action.
4. *Strìke*—till the last armed foe *expìres;*
   Strìke—for your *àltars* and your *fìres;*
   Strìke—for the *green gráves* of your *sìres,*
   Gòd—and your *native lànd!*

[Falling Eighth.—Emotional.]

5. O hòrrible! O hòrrible! most hòrrible!
6. O my prophetic sòul! my ùncle!

7. We heard the piercing shriek of *mùrder! mùrder! mùrder!*

8. I have done my *dùty:*—I stand acquitted to my *cónscience* and my *còuntry:*—I have opposed this measure *throughòut;* and I now *protèst* against it as *hàrsh,* oppressive, *uncàlled* for, *unjùst,*—as establishing an *ínfamous prècedent* by retaliating *crìme* against *crìme,*—as *tỳrannous—crùelly* and *vindìctively* tyrannous. O'CONNELL.

    9. The mustering place is Lanrick mead,
       Speed forth the sìgnal, Norman, *spèed;*
       Her summons dread brooks no *delày,*
       Stretch to the ràce—awày, awày!

    10. Thy threats, thy mercy, I *defỳ,*
       Let recreant yield who fears to *dìe.*

    11. "Can naught but *blóod* our feud *atóne?*
       Are there *nó* means?" *Nò,* stranger, *nòne.*

Rule IV. Indirect questions and very emphatic direct questions generally take the falling inflection.

Interrogative sentences beginning with *who, which, when, where, why,* and *how,* generally take the falling inflection. A *direct* question if repeated a second or third time, frequently takes the *falling* inflection for emphasis.

EXAMPLES.

1. What constitutes a *Stàte?*
2. What is it that gentlemen *wìsh?*
3. When was he *gràduated?*
4. Why do you not study your *lèsson?*
5. "Speak louder; I did not hear your *quèstion.*" "Are you going to *Bòston?*"
6. O why should the spirit of mortal be *pròud?*

7

7. "Do you hear the ràin, Mr. Càudle ? I sày, *do you hear the ràin ?* Do you héar it against the wìndows? Do you héar it, I sày ? Ôh ! you dó héar it !"

Rule V. Completeness of thought or expression, whether in the clauses of a complex sentence, or in the propositions of a compound sentence, generally requires the falling inflection.

EXAMPLES.

1. DEAD HEROES.

They fell | devóted, but undýing ;
The very gàle | their names seemed sìghing ;
The wáters | murmured of their nàme ;
The wóods | were peopled with their fáme ;
The silent píllar, lone and gráy,
Claimed kíndred | with *their* sacred clày :
Their spírits | wrapped the dusky mòuntain,
Their mémory | sparkled o'er the fòuntain ;
The meanest ríll, the mightiest rìver,
Rolled mingling | with their fáme forèver.

BYRON.

2. FROM GOLDSMITH'S "DESERTED VILLAGE."

Imagination fondly stoops to trace
The parlor splèndor of that festive plàce :
The whitewashed wàll, the nicely sanded flòor,
The varnished clòck that clicked behind the door ;
The chèst, contrived a double debt to pay,
A bed by níght, a chest of drawers by dày ;
The píctures placed for órnament and ùse,
The twelve good rùles, the royal game of gòose ;
The heàrth, except when winter chilled the dáy,
With aspen bòughs and flòwers and fènnel gay ;
While broken tèacups, wisely kept for shów,
Ranged o'er the chimney, glistened in a ròw.

3. BACON'S PHILOSOPHY.

It has lengthened *lífe ;* it has mitigated *páin ;* it has extinguished disèases ; it has increased the fertility of the *sòil ;* it has given new securities to the *máriner ;* it has furnished new arms to the *wárrior ;* it has spanned great rivers and estuaries with *brìdges* of form unknown to our fathers ; it has guided the *thùnderbolt* innocuously from héaven to eàrth ; it has lighted up the *níght* with the splendor of the *dày ;* it has extended the range of the human *vìsion ;* it has multiplied the power of the human *mùscles ;* it has accelerated *mòtion ;* it has annihilated *dìstance ;* it has facilitated *ìntercourse, correspòndence,* all friendly *óffices,* all despatch of *bùsiness ;* it has enabled men to descend to the depths of the *séa,* to soar into the *àir ;* to penetrate securely into the noxious recesses of the *eárth,* to traverse the land in *cárs* which whirl along without *hòrses,* and the ócean in ships which run ten knots an hòur against the wind. MACAULAY.

4. FREEDOM.

I love *Fréedom* better than *Slàvery.* I will speak *her wòrds ;* I will listen to *her mùsic ;* I will acknowledge *her ìmpulses ;* I will stand beneath *her flàg ;* I will fight in *her rànks ;* and, when I *dó* so, I shall find myself surrounded by the *grèat,* the *wìse,* the *gòod,* the *bràve,* the *nóble* of every *lánd.* BAKER.

5. CHOATE'S EULOGY ON WEBSTER.

We seem to see *his fórm* and hear *his déep, gráve spéech èverywhere.* By some felicity of his *personal lífe ;* by some wise, deep, or *beautiful wòrd* spóken or wrìtten ; by some service of his *ówn,* or some commemoration of the services of *óthers,* it has come to páss that " our *gránite hìlls,* our *ìnland sèas, práiries,* and fresh, unbounded, *magnìficent wìlderness ;"* our *encìrcling òcean ;* the *résting-place* of the *Pìlgrims ;* our new-born *sìster* of the *Pacífic;* our *pópular assèmblies;* our *frée schòols;* all our cherished doctrines of *educàtion,* and of the influence of *relìgion,* and national *pólicy* and *làw,* and the *Constitùtion,* give us back *his nàme.* What American *làndscape* will you *lòok* on; what subject of American interest will you *stùdy;* what source of *hópe* or of *ànxiety,* as an Américan, will you *acknówledge,* that it does not *recàll* him?

Rule VI. In commencing a series of emphatic particulars, each particular except the last takes the slight falling inflection of the "third," and in a concluding series, each particular except the last but one takes the falling inflection.

EXAMPLES.

1. The *àir,* the *èarth,* the *wáter* teem with delighted existence.

2. Vàlor, humànity, coùrtesy, jùstice, and hónor, were the characteristics of chivalry.

3. The ministers of *relìgion,* the priests of *lìterature,* the historians of the *pàst,* the illustrators of the *prèsent, càpital, scìence, àrt, invèntion, discòveries,* the works of *génius—àll thèse* will attend us in our march, and we shall *cònquer.*
BAKER.

4. The characteristics of chivalry were vàlor, humànity, coùrtesy, jùstice, and hònor.

  5. A TROPICAL SCENE.

 The *mòuntain* wooded to the pèak, the *làwns*
 And winding *glàdes* high up like ways to *hèaven,*
 The slender *còco's* drooping crown of *plùmes,*
 The lightning flash of insect and of *bìrd,*
 The luster of the long *convòlvuluses*
 That coiled around the stately stems, and ran
 Even to the limit of the *lànd,* the glows
 And glories of the broad belt of the *wòrld,*

All *thèse* he *sàw;* but what he *fain* had seen
He *còuld* not sèe, the kindly human *fàce,*
Nor ever hear a *kindly vòice,* but heard
The myriad shriek of wheeling *òcean*-fowl,
The league-long *ròller* thundering on the *rèef,*
The moving whisper of *huge trèes* that branched
And blossomed in the *zènith,* or the sweep
Of some precipitous *rìvulet* to the wàve,
As down the *shòre* he ranged, or all day long
Sat often in the seaward-gazing *górge,*
A shipwrecked *sáilor,* waiting for a *sàil;*
No *sàil* from *dáy* to *dày,* but *èvery dáy*
The *sùnrise* broken into scarlet shafts
Among the palms and ferns and prècipices;
The blaze upon the waters to the *èast;*
The blaze upon his *ìsland* overhead;
The blaze upon the *wàters* to the west;
Then the great *stárs* that globed themselves in hèaven,
The hollower-bellowing *òcean,* and again
The scarlet shafts of *sùnrise,—but no sàil.*

Tennyson's *Enoch Arden.*

ILLUSTRATION.

The contrast in the rendering of a series with the rising inflection and the unemphatic tone of indifference, or with the falling inflection and the emphasis of feeling, is illustrated by the following:

> The one with yawning made reply:
> "What have we seen? Not *múch* have I!
> Trées, méadows, móuntains, gróves, and stréams,
> Blue sky̌, and clóuds, and sunny gléams."
>
> The other, smiling, said the same;
> But, with face transfigured and eye of flame:
> "*Trèes, mèadows, moùntains, gròves, and strèams,*
> *Blue sky̌ and clouds and sunny glèams!*"

Rule VII. The cadence, or falling inflection at the end of a sentence, must not be made too abruptly.

The closing descent in tone at the end of a sentence falls lower than the falling inflection at the end of the propositions that make up a compound sentence, and lower than the slide on emphatic words or clauses. The longer the sentence, the more marked is the cadence. The common errors in cadence are: (1) Dropping the tone suddenly on the last word of the sentence. (2) Falling too soon in the sentence. (3) A gradual diminishing in force towards the end of a sentence, so that the last few words are feebly uttered. (4) A monotonous sameness of inflection.

The difference between the partial falling inflection in the body of a sentence and the cadence at the close, must be illustrated by the living voice of the teacher. Take the following sentence from Addison for illustration:

"Our sight is the most perfect and most delightful of all our sènses. It fills the mind with the largest variety of *idèas*, converses with its objects at the greatest *dìstance*, and continues the longest in áction without being tired or satiated with its proper *enjòyments.*"

Here the slide on "ideas" and "distance" is the partial falling, say the falling third, while the cadence on "enjoyment" runs to the falling fifth. It will be noticed, also, that the voice slides upward on "action," to prepare for the cadence at the close of the sentence.

EXAMPLES.

1. I have done my *dùty;* I stand acquitted to my conscience and my *còuntry;* I have opposed this measure *throughòut;* and I now protest against it, as *hàrsh, oppressive, uncàlled* for, *unjùst;* as establishing an infamous precedent, by retaliating crime against *crìme;* as *tỳrannous—crùelly* and *vindìctively* tyrannous.

2. Ill fares the land, to hastening ills a prey,
Where wealth accumulates and men decày:
Princes and lords may flourish, or may fàde —
A breath can make them, as a breath *hàs* made;
But a bold peasantry, their country's prĭde,
When once destróyed, can *nèver* be *supplĭed.*

3. God of the earth's extended plàins!
The dark green fields contented lìe:
The mountains rise like holy towers,
Where man might commune with the sky;
The tall cliff challenges the storm
That lowers upon the vale belòw,
Where shaded fountains send their strĕams,
With joyous *mùsic* in their flòw.

Rules for Contrasted Inflections.

Rule I. When negation is opposed to affirmation, negation has the rising, and affirmation the falling inflection. Contrasted words are emphatic.

EXAMPLES.

1. He did not call *yóu*, but *mè.*
2. He called *yòu*, not *mé.*
3. He called neither *yóu* nor *mè.*
4. Man never *ís*, but always *to bè* blest.

5. JOHN HOWARD.

He visited *all Eùrope—nót* to survey the sumptuousness of *pálaces*, or the stateliness of *témples; nót* to make accurate measurements of the remains of ancient *grándeur*, nor to form a scale of the curiosities of modern *árt*, nor to collect *médals*, or collate *mánuscripts;* but to dive into the depths of *dùngeons*, to plunge into the infection of *hòspitals*, to survey the mansions of *sorrow* and *pàin;* to take the gauge and dimensions of *mìsery*, *depréssion*, and *contèmpt;* to remember the *forgòtten*, to attend to the *neglècted,* to visit the *forsáken,* and compare and collate the distresses of all men in all coùntries. His plan is *orìginal;* it is as full of *génius* as of *humànity.* It was a voyage of *discòvery*—a circumnavigation of *chàrity.*

BURKE.

Rule II. When the conjunction OR *connects contrasted words or phrases, it is preceded by the rising, and followed by the falling inflection. Contrasted words are emphatic.*

EXAMPLES.

1. Did he call *Jáne* or *Màry?*
2. Is this book *yóurs* or *mìne?*
3. *Sínk* or *swìm, líve* or *dìe, survíve* or *pèrish,* I give my *hánd* and my *heàrt* to this vote.
4. Do we mean to *carry ŏn* or to *give ŭp* the war?

<small>*Require an additional example from each pupil.*</small>

Rule III. Contrast or antithesis is denoted by opposite inflections on the contrasted words of a sentence, and the contrasted words are emphatic.

Pupils should be cautioned against the common fault of substituting, in examples of contrast, the circumflex inflections for the direct rising and falling inflections. The following example is often incorrectly read thus:

1. In the *ŏne* we most admire the *măn;* in the *ŏther,* the *wôrk.*

It should be read as follows:

2. In the *óne* we most admire the *mán;* in the *óther,* the *wòrk.*
3. *Incorrect:* As is the *begínning,* so is the *ènd.*
4. *Correct:* As is the *begínning,* so is the *ènd.*
5. *Incorrect:* What we gain in *pŏwer* is lost in *tĭme.*
6. *Correct:* What we gain in *pówer* is lost in *tìme.*

The circumflex inflections are properly applied in cases of very emphatic contrast, or in the expression of irony, sarcasm, wit, and humor.

Selection 3, at the end of this chapter, affords good illustrations of contrasted circumflex, while selections 1, 2, and 5 are examples of the use of the direct rising and falling inflections.

"A fault of local usage, prevailing throughout New England," says Prof. Russell, "is that of giving all emphasis with the tone of the circumflex. It is a tone incompatible with simplicity and dignity of expression, and belongs properly to irony or ridicule, to the peculiar significance of words and phrases embodying logical or grammatical niceties of distinction, or to the studied and peculiar emphasis which belongs to the utterance of a word intended to convey a pun. This fault would be avoided by giving emphasis with the direct inflection, instead of the circumflex."

EXAMPLES OF CONTRAST.

1. I said *gòod*, not *bád;* *vìrtuous*, not *vícious;* *èducated*, not *illíterate*.

2. He spoke *fòr* education, not *agáinst* it.

3. After the *shówer*, the tranquil *sùn;*
Silver *stárs* when the *dày* is done.
After the *snów*, the emerald *lèaves;*
After the *hárvest*, golden *shèaves;*
After the *cloúds*, the violet *skỳ;*
Quiet *wóods* when the *wìnds* go by.
After the *témpest*, the lull of *wàves;*
After the *báttle*, peaceful *gràves*.
After the *knéll*, the *wèdding*-bells;
Joyful *gréetings* from sad *farewèlls*.
After the *búd*, the radiant *ròse;*
After our *wéeping*, sweet *repòse*.

After the *búrden*, the blissful *mèed;*
After the *fúrrow*, the waking *sèed.*

After the *flíght*, the downy *nèst;*
Beyond the shadowy *rìver—rèst.*

4. Thus the Puritan was made up of *twò* different *mèn:* the *óne*, all self-abásement, pénitence, grátitude, *pássion;* the *óther*, pròud, càlm, inflèxible, sagàcious. He prostrated himself in the dust before his *Máker;* but he set his *fòot* on the neck of his *kìng.*

5. ROME AND CARTHAGE.

The catastrophe of this stupendous drama is at hànd. What àctors are mèt! *Twó ràces*—that of *mérchants* and *màriners,* that of *làborers* and *sòldiers; twó nàtions*—the one dominant by *góld*, the other by *stèel; twó repùblics*—the one *théocratic*, the other *àristocratic. Ròme* and *Càrthage! Róme* with her *àrmy, Cárthage* with her *flèet; Cárthage, óld, rích,* and *cráfty—Róme, yoùng, pòor,* and *robùst;* the *pást,* and the *fùture;* the spirit of *discóvery,* and the spirit of *cònquest;* the genius of *cómmerce,* the demon of *wàr;* the East and the South on *óne* side, the West and the North on the *òther;* in short, *twó wòrlds*—the civilization of *África,* and the civilization of *Eùrope.*

VICTOR HUGO.

6. I have always preferred *chéerfulness* to *mìrth.* The *látter* I consider as an *áct,* the *fórmer* as a *hàbit* of the mind. *Mĭrth* is *shórt* and *tránsient, chéerfulness fĭxed* and *pèrmanent. Mĭrth* is like a flash of *líghtning,* that breaks through a gloom of *cloúds,* and glitters for a *móment; chéerfulness* keeps up a kind of *dàylight* in the mind, and fills it with a *stèady* and *perpétual serènity.*

7. THE ONE-HOSS SHAY.

For the *whéels* were just as strong as the *thĭlls,*
And the *flóor* was just as strong as the *sĭlls,*

And the *pánels* just as strong as the *flòor,*
And the *whípple*-tree neither less nor *mòre,*
And the *báck* crossbar as strong as the *fòre,*
And spring, and áxle, and húb *èncore,*
And yet, as a whole, it is past a doubt
In another hour it will be worn out! _{HOLMES.}

8. DUST TO DUST.

"Eárth to *éarth,* and *dúst* to *dùst!*"
Here the *évil* and the *jùst,*
Here the *yóuthful* and the *òld,*
Here the *féarful* and the *bòld,*
Here the *mátron* and the *màid,*
In ōne sīlent bēd āre lāid;
Here the *vással* and the *kìng*
Side by side lie withering;
Here the *swórd* and *scèpter* rùst—
"Eārth tō ēarth, ānd dūst tō dūst!" _{CROLY.}

9. HUDIBRAS.

He was in logic a great *crític,*
Profoundly skilled in *analŷtic,*
He could distinguish and divide
A hair 'twixt *sŏuth* and *sŏuth-west* side;
On either which he would dispute,
Confute, change hands and *stĭll* confute.
He'd undertake to prove by force
Of argument a *măn's* no *hŏrse;*
He'd prove a *bŭzzard* is no *fŏwl,*
And that a *lŏrd* may be an *ŏwl;*
A *călf* an *ălderman,* a *gŏose* a *jŭstice,*
And *rŏoks commĭttee*-men and *trŭstees.*
He'd run in debt by *disputătion,*
And pay with *ratiocinătion.* _{BUTLER.}

10. TACT AND TALENT.

Take them into the church. Talent has always something worth *hĕaring,* tact is sure of abundance of *hĕarers;*

talent may *obtăin* a living, tact will *măke* one; talent gets a *gŏod* name, tact a *greăt* one; talent *convĭnces*, tact *convêrts;* talent is an *honor* to the *profĕssion*, tact *găins* honor from the profession. Take them to court. Talent feels its *wĕight*, tact finds its *wăy;* talent *commănds*, tact is *obĕyed;* talent is honored with *approbătion*, and tact is blessed by *prefêrment*.

Rule IV. Direct questions generally require the rising inflection, and their answers, the falling inflection.

EXAMPLES.

1. Have you studied your lésson? Yès.
2. Are you going to New Yórk? Nò.

3. OUR COUNTRY.

Oh, country, marvel of the éarth!
   Oh, realm to sudden gréatness grown!
The age that gloried in thy bírth,
   Shall it behold thee *overthrówn?*
Shall *trăitors* lay that greatness lów?
Nò! Land of Hópe and Bléssing, *Nò!*
BRYANT.

4. THE INQUIRY.

Tèll me, my secret sóul,
   Oh, tèll me, Hópe and Fáith,
Is there no resting-place
   From sórrow, sín, and déath?
Is there no happy spót
   Where mortals may be bléssed,
Where grief may find a bálm,
   And weariness a rést?
Fáith, Hópe, and Lóve—best boons to mortals gíven—
Waved their bright wíngs, and whíspered "Yès, in hèaven!"
MACKAY.

5. FROM "HAMLET."

Hamlet. Hold you the *wátch* to-níght?
Mar. and *Ber.* We dò, my lórd.
Hamlet. Ármed, say yóu?
Mar. and *Ber.* Ármed, my lòrd.
Hamlet. From top to *tóc?*
Mar. and *Ber.* My lord, from *héad* to *fòot.*
Hamlet. Then you saw not his *fáce?*
Hor. Oh, yés, my lórd; he wore his beaver *ùp.*
Hamlet. Whát, looked he *frówningly?*
Hor. A countenance more in *sòrrow* than in *ănger.*
Hamlet. *Pále* or *rèd?*
Hor. Nay, *very pàle.*
Hamlet. And fixed his *eýes* upon you?
Hor. Most cònstantly.
Hamlet. I would *Ĭ* had been thére.
Hor. It would have much *amàzed* you. SHAKESPEARE.

III. INFLECTIONS OF THE PARENTHESIS.

Rule I. The words included in a parenthesis, or between two dashes used as a parenthesis, and any phrase corresponding in effect to a parenthesis, are read with the same inflection as the clause immediately preceding them.

"A lower and less forcible tone, and a more rapid utterance, than in the other parts of a sentence, together with a degree of monotony, are required in the reading of a parenthesis. The form of parenthesis implies something thrown in as an interruption of the main thought in a sentence. Hence its suppressed and hurried tone; the voice seeming to hasten over it slightly, as if impatient to resume the principal object. The same remark applies, with more or less force, to all intervening phrases, whether in the exact form of parenthesis or not." RUSSELL.

EXAMPLES.

1. Uprightness is a habit, and, like all other habits, gains strength by time and exercise. If then we éxercise upright prínciples (and we cannot have them, unless we éxercise thém), they must be perpetually on the increase.

2. "And thís," said hé—putting the remains of a crust into his wállet—"and this should have been *thỳ* portion," said hè, "hadst thou been alive to have shared it with me."

3. To my mínd—though I am native here,
   And to the manner bórn—it is a custom
   More honored in the breach than the observance.
                                                SHAKESPEARE.

SUMMARY OF INFLECTION.

1. *The stronger the emphasis, the longer the slides.*

2. *In unimpassioned reading, the emphasis is slight and the slides are short: in bold and dignified composition, the emphasis is stronger and the slides are longer: and in highly impassioned or dramatic reading, the emphasis is strongest and the slides are longest.*

3. *The general principle that underlies all the rules of inflection is as follows: The rising inflection in general denotes incompleteness of statement, comparatively unimportant statement, interrogation, or negation; the falling inflection denotes completed or emphatic statement.*

GENERAL INFLECTION DRILL.

1. Sing the scale, upward and downward.

2. Substitute in place of the note names the long vocals, thus : ā, ē, ī, ō, ū, ā, ē, ō.

3. Sound the third, fifth, and eighth notes of the

scale; then substitute for the note names the following: ē, ü, ōō.

4. Give the long vowel sounds, ā, ē, ī, ō, ū, (1) with the rising "second;" (2) with the rising "third;" (3) with the rising "fifth;" (4) with the rising "eighth."

5. Give the long vowel sounds, ā, ē, ī, ō, ū, with the *falling* "second," "third," "fifth," and "eighth."

6. Give the long vowel sounds, ā, ē, ī, ō, ū, with the rising wave of the "third;" of the "fifth;" of the "octave;" the falling wave with the same degrees.

IV. THE CIRCUMFLEX INFLECTION.

The circumflex, or wave, is a combination of the rising and falling inflections on the same word or sound.

The *rising* circumflex ends with the rising inflection, and is denoted thus (ˇ); the *falling* circumflex ends with the downward slide, and is marked thus (ˆ).

The circumflex is more emphatic than the direct rising and falling inflections. The circumflex may be divided into the *distinctive* and the *emotional*.

I. THE DISTINCTIVE CIRCUMFLEX OF THE THIRD.

The *distinctive*, or unimpassioned, circumflex occurs when the voice rises or falls through the interval of the third. It is the characteristic inflection of good-natured raillery, of humor, and of wit. It is used in expressing a pun, or a play upon words. It expresses a double meaning, or a double relation. It carries the mind back to something that *has been* said, or forward to something *to be* said. This form of circumflex is a delicate wave of the voice, and is very expressive; but great care should be taken not to overdo it. Carried to excess, it becomes ridiculous.

II. Inflection Drill.

1. Sound the long vocals, ā, ē, ī, ō, ū, with the slight rising circumflex of the third; with the slight falling circumflex.

2. Count from one to twenty, with the slight rising circumflex; with the falling wave of the third.

3. It is n't the *sĕcret* I care about, Mr. Caudle. It's the *slîght*.

4. Do you hear the *răin*, Mr. Caudle?

5. When lawyers *tăke* what they would *gîve*,
And doctors *gîve* what they would *tăke*.

6. I should do Brutus wrong, and Cassius wrong,
Who, you all know, are *hŏnorable mĕn*.

7. Men, *indêed!* call themselves *lŏrds* of *creătion!* Prĕtty *lŏrds*, when they can't even take care of an *umbrĕlla!*

8. Let any man resolve to do right *nŏw*, leaving *thĕn* to do as it can; and if he were to live to the age of *Methûselah*, he would never do wrong. But the common error is to resolve to act right *ăfter brĕakfast*, or *ăfter dînner*, or *to-mŏrrow môrning*, or *nĕxt tîme*. But *nŏw*, just *nŏw*, this *ŏnce*, we must go on the *sáme* as *èver*.

III. Emotional Circumflex.

The *emotional* circumflex occurs when the voice rises or falls through an interval of the fifth or the eighth.

It is the wave of irony, sarcasm, scorn, contempt, hatred, revenge, astonishment, or amazement. It is the inflection of very strong emphasis.

The rising circumflex occurs where, otherwise, the direct rising inflection would be used; and the falling wave where, otherwise, the falling slide would be applied.

IV. Inflection Drill.

1. Sound the long vocals, ā, ē, ī, ō, ū, with the rising circumflex of the fifth; with the falling circumflex.

2. Repeat, five times, with surprise, the words, "ăh! indĕed!" with the rising circumflex of the fifth.

3. Gone to be mărried! gone to swear a pĕace!

4. Hath not a Jew hănds, ŏrgans, dimĕnsions, sĕnses, affĕctions, păssions?

5. Repeat, with irony and the falling wave of the fifth, the expression, "I tóld you sô."

6. Sound the long vocals, ā, ē, ī, ō, ū, with the rising wave of the eighth; the falling wave of the eighth.

7. Repeat, five times, with the greatest possible astonishment, the following: ăh! indĕed! is it trŭe!

8. O nôble judge! O ĕxcellent young man!

9. Nô! by St. Bride of Bothwell, nô!

10. Soars thy presumption then so hígh,
 Because a wretched kĕrn ye slew,
 Homage to name to Roderick Dhŭ?

V. Examples of the Distinctive Circumflex.

The distinctive circumflex is the delicate wave of the voice, generally of the rising or falling *third*, indicative of mirth, fun, wit, humor, and good-natured raillery. In the following examples, be careful not to overdo the inflection or the emphasis.

EXAMPLES.

1. THE DEBTOR.

A dĕbtor is a man of mârk. Many êyes are fixed upon him; many have ínterest in his well-being; his mŏvements are of concêrn; he can not disappear unhêeded;

his name is in many *mŏuths;* his name is upon many *bŏoks;* he is a man of *nôte*—of *prŏmissory* note; he fills the *speculâtion* of many minds; men *conjĕcture* about him, *wŏnder* about him—*wŏnder* and *conjĕcture* whether he will *pây*. He is a man of *cônsequence,* for many are *rŭnning* after him. His door is thronged with *dŭns*. He is *inquîred* after every hour of the day. *Jûdges* hear of him and knòw him. Every *mĕal* he *swâllows*, every *côat* he puts upon his *bâck*, every *dŏllar* he *bôrrows*, appears before the country in some *formal dôcument*. Compare *hĭs* notoriety with the obscure lot of the *crédĭtor*—of the man who has nothing but *clâims* on the world; a *lândlord*, or *fûnd*-holder, or some *sŭch* disagreeable, hard chàracter.

2. FALSTAFF'S INSTINCT.

Why, I *knéw* ye as well as he that *mâde* ye. Why, hear me, my masters: was it for *mĕ* to kill the *hĕirappărent?* Should *I* turn upon the *trŭe prĭnce?* Why, thou knowest I am as valiant as *Hércules;* but beware înstinct; the lion will not touch the true prince; *ĭnstinct* is a great matter; I was a *côward* on *ĭnstinct*. I shall think the better of myself and thee during my life; *I* for a valiant *lĭon*, and thou for a *trŭe prĭnce*.

3. FALSTAFF'S HONOR.

How *thĕn?* Can *hŏnor* set a *lĕg?* Nô. Or au *ărm?* Nô. Or take away the *grĭef* of a wóund? Nô. Honor hath no skill in *sŭrgery, thĕn?* Nô. What *ĭs* honor? A wôrd. What is that word? *Air*. A trim reckoning! Who *hâth* it? He that *díed* o' Wednesday. Doth he *fĕel* it? Nô. Doth he *hĕar* it? Nô. Is it insensible, then? Yea, to the *dĕăd*. But will it not live with the *lĭving?* Nô. Why? *Detrăction* will not suffer it; therefore I'll *nŏne* of it.—Hónor is a mere 'scŭtcheon—and so ends my catechism.

4. PORTIA, IN THE MERCHANT OF VENICE.

If to *dŏ* were as easy as to know what were *gŏod* to do, *chăpels* had been *chúrches*, and poor men's *cŏttages* princes' *pálaces*. It is a good divine that follows his own *instrúctions*. I can easier teach *twénty* what were *gŏod* to be done than be *ŏne* of the twenty to follow mine own *teáching*. The brain may devise laws for the blôod; but a hot temper leaps over a cold *decrèc;* such a hare is madness, the youth, to skip o'er the meshes of good counsel, the cripple. But this reasoning is not in the fashion to choose me a *húsband*. O me! the word *chôose!* I may neither choose whom I *woŭld*, nor refuse whom I *dislíke;* so is the will of a *living dăughter* curbed by the will of a *dead fáther*. Is it not *hárd*, Nerissa, that I can not choose *ŏne*, nor refuse *nóne?*

5. ROMEO AND JULIET.

Jul. Oh! swear not by the *mŏon*, the inconstant *mŏon*
That monthly changes in her circled *ŏrb;*
Lest that thy love prove *líkewise* variable.
  Rom. What *sháll* I swear by?
  Jul. Do not swear at *áll;*
Or, if thou *wĭlt*, swear by thy gracious *sélf*,
Which is the god of my idolatry,
And I'll believe thee.

6. NELLY GRAY.

O, Nelly Gray! O, Nelly Gray!
  Is *thĭs* your love so *wárm?*
The love that loves a *scărlet coat*
  Should be more *úniform!*   Hood.

7. THE WITCH'S DAUGHTER.

Her *mŏther* only killed a *ców*,
  Or witched a churn or dairy-pan;
But *shĕ*, forsooth, must charm a *mán*.   Whittier.

8. Contentment.

Lĭttle I *ăsk;* my wants are *fĕw:*
  I only wish a hut of *stône*
(A *very plain brôwn* stone will *dŏ*),
  That I may call my *ôwn;*
And close at hand is such a one,
In yonder street that fronts the sun.

I always thought *cŏld* victual *nĭce.*
My *chôice* would be *vanilla-îce.*

I only ask that fortune send
A *lĭttle* more than I can *spĕnd.*   Holmes.

9. Aunt Tabitha.

Whatever I do, and whatever I say,
Aunt Tabitha tells me *thăt* is n't the *wăy.*
When *shĕ* was a girl (forty summers ago),
Aunt Tabitha tells me they never did *sŏ.*
                                    Holmes.

VI. Examples of Emotional Circumflex.

The emotional circumflex runs into the fifth and eighth, and requires strong emphasis. This form of the circumflex is expressive of sarcasm, irony, astonishment, revenge, and hatred.

EXAMPLES.

1. From Dickens's "Christmas Carol."

"Let me hear another sound from *yŏu,*" said Scrooge, "and you 'll keep *yôur* Christmas by losing your situation. You 're quite a powerful *spĕaker,* sir," he added, turning to his nephew. "I wonder you do n't go into *Pârliament.*"

2. King John.

Thŏu wear a *lîon's hîde?* Doff it for *shâme,*
And hang a *câlf*-skin on those recreant limbs.

3. CORIOLANUS.

Mĕasurelĕss liar! thou hast made my heart
Too great for what contains it.
Bôy! Cut me to *pìeces*, Vòlscians; men and *làds*,
Stain *áll* your edges on me. *Bôy!*—
If you have writ your annals true, 't is *thêre*
That, like an eagle in a dovecot, *I*
Fluttered your Volscians in Corioli:
Alône I did it. *Bôy!*

4. SHYLOCK.

If it will feed nothing *ĕlse*, it will feed my *revênge*. He hath disgrâced me, and hindered me of *hălf a mìllion;* *lăughed* at my *lósses*, *môcked* at my *gâins*, *scôrned* my *nâtion*, thwărted my *bârgains*, *côoled* my *friênds*, heated my *ênemies*. And what's his *rêason?* *I* am a *Jĕw!* Hath not a Jew *eyes?* Hath not a Jew *hănds*, *ŏrgans*, *dimĕnsions*, *sĕnses*, *affĕctions*, *păssions?* Is he not fed with the same *fôod*, hurt with the same *wĕapons*, subject to the same *disĕases*, healed by the same *mĕans*, warmed and cooled by the same *sŭmmer* and *wĭnter*, as a *Chrĭstian* is? If you *stăb* us, do we not *blĕed?* If you *tĭckle* us, do we not *lăugh?* If you *pŏison* us, do we not *dĭe?* And if you *wrŏng* us, shall we not *revĕnge?*

5. SCHOOL FOR SCANDAL.

Sir Peter. Very *wĕll*, ma'am, very *wĕll;* so a husband is to have no *ĭnfluence*, no *áuthority?*

Lady Teazle. Authôrity! *Nô*, to be *sŭre;* if you wanted *authŏrity* over me, you should have *adôpted* me, and not *mărried* me; I'm sure you were *ŏld* enoúgh.

Sir Peter. Old enôugh! ay, there it *ĭs*. *Wĕll, wĕll*, Lady Teazle, though my life may be made unhappy by your *tĕmper*, I'll not be ruined by your *extrăvagance*.

Lady Teazle. *Mŷ* extravagance! Sir Peter, am *I* to blame because flowers are *dĕar* in cold *wĕather?* You should find fault with the *clĭmate,* and not with mĕ. For my part, I'm sure, I wish it was *sprĭng* all the year round, and that rôses grew under our fêet.

Sir Peter. Zounds! Madam, you had no *tăste* when you married mĕ.

Lady Teazle. That's very *trŭe,* indeed, Sir Péter; and after having married *yŏu,* I should *never pretend* to taste *agăin,* I allôw.

6. OTHELLO.

Iago. My noble lord———

Othello. What dost thou say, Iago?

Iago. Did Michael Cassio, when you wooed my lady, knŏw of your love?

Othello. He did, from first to last. Why dost thou ásk?

Iago. But for a satisfaction of my thought;
No *fŭrther* hárm.

Othello. Why of thy *thôught,* Iago?

Iago. I did not think, he had been acquainted with her.

Othello. O yés; and went between us very oft.

Iago. Indĕed?

Othello. Indéed! ày, indêed:—Discern'st thou aught in *thăt?* Is he not *hŏnest?*

Iago. Hŏnest, my lórd?

Othello. Ay, hônest.

Iago. My lord, for aught Ĭ know.

Othello. What dost thou *thĭnk?*

Iago. Thĭnk, my lórd?

Othello. Thĭnk, my lórd? By heavens! he echoes me, As if there were some monster in his thought Too hideous to be shown. Thou dost *méan* something.

7. FROM THE "HONEYMOON."

Julia. I will go *hôme!*

Duke. You *âre* at home *alréady.*

Julia. I'll not *endŭre* it!—But remember this—
Duke or *nó* duke, I'll be a *dŭchess*, sir!
  Duke. A *dŭchess!* You shall be a *quéen*—to all
Who, by the courtesy, will *cáll* you so.
  Julia. And I will have *attĕndance!*
  Duke. So you *shăll,*
When you have learned to wait upon *yoursélf.*
  Julia. To wait upon *mysĕlf!* Must I bear *thĭs?*

. . . . . .

  Duke. Ĕxcellent!
How *wĕll* you sum the duties of a *wĭfe!*
Why, what a *blĕssing* I shall *háve* in you!
  Julia. A *blĕssing?*
  Duke. When they talk of *yŏu* and *mĕ,*
Darby and Joan shall no more be remembered:—
We shall be *háppy!*
  Julia. Shăll we?
  Duke. Wóndrous happy!
Oh, you will make an *ádmirable* wife!
  Julia. I will make a *vĭxen.*
  Duke. Whăt?
  Julia. A *vĕry vĭxen.*
  Duke. Oh, *nó!* We'll have *nŏ vĭxens.*
  Julia. I'll not *béar* it!
I'll to my *fáther's!*— TOBIN.

V. THE MONOTONE.

The *monotone* is one uniform tone, which neither rises nor falls in pitch above or below the general level of the sentence. It is a continuous flow of sound, corresponding, in some degree, to the chanting tone in vocal music. It is generally associated with *low* pitch and slow movement. When the voice is under the influence of awe or horror, the monotone strikes upon the ear like the recurring pulsations of a deep-toned bell.

The monotone is the natural expression of voice when the feelings are under the influence of awe, adoration, reverence, sublimity, grandeur, or horror.

"Grandeur of thought and sublimity of feeling," says Tower, "are always expressed by this movement. The effect produced by it is deep and impressive. When its use is known, and the rule for its application is clearly understood, the reading will be characterized by a solemnity of manner, a grandeur of refinement, and a beauty of execution, which all will acknowledge to be in exact accordance with the dictates of Nature, and strictly within the pale of her laws."

The monotone, one of the most effective tones in elocution, must not be confounded with *monotony*, one of the worst faults in school reading.

There is one form of monotone, prevailing in the poetry of sentiment, that is not combined with low pitch. This may be called *poetic* monotone, as contrasted with the monotone on a low pitch, which may be termed *grave* monotone.

In poetic monotone, the key is not necessarily lower than the middle pitch, though there is always something of the suppressed force of pathos and sentiment. In examples of the poetic monotone, the slight or suspensive rising inflection takes the place of monotone.

I. Inflection Drill on the Monotone.

1. Repeat, five times, the long vowel sounds, ā, ē, ī, ō, ū.

2. Count, in low pitch combined with monotone, from one to twenty, thus: ōne, twō, thrēe, etc.

3. Rōll ōn, thōu dēep and dārk blūe ōcean, rōll!
   Ten thōusand flēets swēep ōver thēe in vàin.

4. An ancient time-piece says to all—
   Fōrēvēr—nēvēr!
   Nēvēr—fōrēvēr!

II. EXAMPLES OF POETIC MONOTONE.

1. FROM POE'S "RAVEN."

Then, methought, the air grew denser, perfumed from
    an unseen censer
Swung by Seraphim, whose footfalls tinkled on the
    tufted floor.
This I sat engaged in guessing, but no syllable expressing
To the fowl, whose fiery eyes now burned into my bosom's
    core ;
This and more I sat divining, with my head at ease
    reclining
On the cushion's velvet lining that the lamp-light
    gloated o'er,
But whose velvet violet lining with the lamp-light
    gloating o'er
        She shall press, ah, nevermore!

2. FROM "THE CLOSING SCENE."

Long, but not loud, the droning wheel went on,
  Like the low murmur of a hive at noon;
Long, but not loud, the memory of the gone
  Breathed through her lips a sad and tremulous tune.
At last the thread was snapped: her head was bowed;
  Life dropped the distaff through his hands serene,—
And loving neighbors smoothed her careful shroud,
  While Death and Winter closed the autumn scene.
                              READ.

3. PASSING AWAY.

While yet I looked, what a change there came!
  Her eye was quenched, and her cheek was wan;
Stooping and staffed was her withered frame,
  Yet just as busily swung she on.
The garland beneath her had fallen to dust:
The wheels above her were eaten with rust.

The hands, that over the dial swept,
Grew crooked and tarnished, but on they kept;
And still there came that silver tone
From the shriveled lips of the toothless crone—
    Let me never forget, to my dying day,
    The tone or the burden of that lay—
    "*Passing away! Passing away!*"
PIERPONT.

III. Low, or Grave, Monotone.

The low, or grave, monotone is pitched on the lower notes of the voice. It is indicated by the macrons placed over the vowels:

1. ALEXANDER'S FEAST.

He chose a mōurnful mūse,
Soft pity to infūse:
He sung Darius grēat and gōōd,
  By tōō sēvēre a fāte,
Fāllen, fāllen, fāllen, fāllen,
  Fāllen from his hīgh estāte,
And wēltering in hīs blood.   DRYDEN.

2. THE SEA.

Breāk, breāk, breāk,
  On thy cōld grāy stōnes, O Sēa!
And I wōuld that my tōngue cōuld ūtter
  The thōughts thāt arīse in mē.

O wēll for the fishērman's bōy,
  That he shōuts with his sīster at plāy!
O wēll for the sāilor lād,
  That he sīngs in his bōat on the bāy!

And the stātely shīps gō ōn
  To their hāven ūnder the hīll;

But O for the touch of a vanished hand,
  And the sound of a voice that is still!

Break, break, break,
  At the foot of thy crags, O Sea!
But the tender grace of a day that is dead
  Will never come back to me.   TENNYSON.

3. DEATH.

Leaves have their time to fall,
And flowers to wither at the north-wind's breath,
  And stars to set—but all,
Thou hast all seasons for thine own, O Death!
                                         HEMANS.

4. DRIFTING.

From the strong Will, and the Endeavor
    That forever
Wrestles with the tides of Fate;
From the wreck of Hopes far scattered,
    Tempest-shattered,
Floating waste and desolate;—

Ever drifting, drifting, drifting
    On the shifting
Currents of the restless heart;
Till at length in books recorded,
    They, like hoarded
Household words, no more depart.   LONGFELLOW.

5. THE BATTLE.

Heavy and solemn,
A cloudy column,
Through the green plain they marching came—
  Measureless spread, like a table dread,
For the wild, grim dice of the iron game.

Looks are bent on the shaking ground,
Hearts beat low with a knelling sound;
Swift by the breast that must bear the brunt,
Gallops the major along the front.
  "*Halt!*"
And fettered they stand at the stark command,
And the warriors, silent, halt. SCHILLER.

6. THE PRISONER OF CHILLON.

For all was blank, and bleak, and gray;
It was not night—it was not day;
It was not even the dungeon light,
So hateful to my heavy sight—
But vacancy absorbing space,
And fixedness—without a place;
There were no stars—no earth—no time—
No check—no change—no good—no crime—
But silence, and a stirless breath
Which neither was of life nor death:
A sea of stagnant idleness—
Blind, boundless, mute, and motionless. BYRON.

7. What this grim, ungainly, ghastly,
  Gaunt, and ominous bird of yore
  Meant in croaking "Nevermore."

8. To-morrow, and to-morrow, and to-morrow,
Creeps in this petty pace from day to day,
To the last syllable of recorded time;
And all our yesterdays have lighted fools
The way to dusty death. Out, out, brief candle!
Life's but a walking shadow; a poor player,
That struts and frets his hour upon the stage,
And then is heard no more: it is a tale
Told by an idiot, full of sound and fury,
Signifying nothing.

9. THE OCEAN.

Thou glorious mirror, where the Almighty's form
Glasses itself in tempests; in all time,
Calm or convulsed, in breeze, or gale, or storm,
Icing the pole, or in the torrid clime
Dark-heaving—boundless, endless, and sublime;
The image of Eternity—the throne
Of the Invisible; even from out thy slime
The monsters of the deep are made; each zone
Obeys thee; thou goest forth, dread, fathomless alone.
BYRON.

10. SONG OF THE SHIRT.

  Work—work—work!
Till the brain begins to swim;
  Work—work—work!
Till the eyes are heavy and dim!
  Seam, and gusset, and band,
   Band, and gusset, and seam,
Till over the buttons I fall asleep,
  And sew them on in a dream!   HOOD.

11. THE GHOST IN HAMLET.

Ghost. I am thy father's spirit;
Doomed for a certain term to walk the night;
And, for the day, confined to fast in fires,
Till the foul crimes, done in my days of nature,
Are burnt and purged away. But that I am forbid
To tell the secrets of my prison-house,
I could a tale unfold, whose lightest word
Would harrow up thy soul; freeze thy young blood;
Make thy two eyes, like stars, start from their spheres;
Thy knotted and combined locks to part,
And each particular hair to stand on end,
Like quills upon the fretful porcupine.   SHAKESPEARE.

Recapitulation of Inflections.

1. *The rising inflection is the slide of appeal, of inquiry, of incompleteness, and of negation contrasted with affirmation.*

2. *The falling inflection is the slide of assertion, of command, and of complete statement.*

3. *The circumflex is the wave of wit, humor, raillery, irony, sarcasm, satire, and revenge.*

4. *The monotone is the tone expressive of grandeur, sublimity, reverence, awe, amazement, and horror.*

Inflection Drill Review.

1. Repeat, three times, the long vowel sounds, ā, ē, ī, ō, ū. (1) With the rising second. (2) With the rising third. (3) With the rising fifth. (4) With the rising octave.

2. Repeat, three times, ā, ē, ī, ō, ū. (1) With the falling second. (2) With the falling third. (3) With the falling fifth. (4) With the falling eighth.

3. Repeat, three times, with the same degrees of inflection as above, ē, ā, ä, ō, ọ.

4. Repeat, three times, ā, ē, ī, ō, ū. (1) With the rising circumflex of the third. (2) Fifth. (3) Octave. (4) Falling circumflex of the third. (5) Falling fifth. (6) Falling octave.

5. The same degrees of the circumflex as above, on ē, ā, ä, ō, ọ.

6. Repeat, three times, ā, ē, ī, ō, ū, with the low monotone.

7. Repeat, three times, ē, ā, ä, ạ, ō, ọ, with the low monotone.

School Elocution.

Inflection Drill on Vocals.

Read, in concert, the words of the following Table:

1. *With the rising inflection.*
2. *With the falling inflection.*
3. *With the rising circumflex.*
4. *With the falling circumflex.*

ā, ẹ.—āle, māde, brāid, ḡāuġe, veil, plāy, wẹight.
ä.—älms, chärt, heärt, läugh, häunt, äunt, päth.
ạ, ô.—ạll, ạwe, lạw, fạll, hạul, bạwl, crạwl, ôught.
ă.—ădd, thăt, brăt, hănd, lănd, plăid, băde.
â.—âir, bâre, dâre, prâyer, thêre, hâir, scârçe.
à.—àsk, eàsk, tàsk, pàss, gràss, dànce, glànce.
a, ŏ.—whạt, spŏt, wạd, wạnd, wạs, wạtch, wạn.
ē.—ēat, bēat, beet, thēṣe, sēize, freeze, lēaveṣ.
ĕ.—ĕnd, lĕt, thrĕat, ḡĕt, ġĕm, brĕad, yĕt, said.
ẽ, ĭ.—ẽarth, hẽard, lẽarn, ẽarn, ẽrr, thĭrd, gĭrd.
ẹ, ā.—thẹy, wẹigh, nāy, nẹigh, slẹigh, prẹy, prāy.
ī.—īçe, īsle, āisle, wīne, heīght, whīle, rhȳme.
ĭ.—ĭll, ĭt, wĭn, thĭn, been, ġin, sĭnce, zĭnc.
ĭ, ẽ.—mĭrth, gĭrl, dĭrt, vẽrse, tẽrse, worse, world.
ï, ē.—pïque, elïque, creek, oblïque, ravïne.
ō.—ōld, thōṣe, grōan, fōrce, pōur, rōar, mōre.
ŏ.—ŏdd, ŏn, blŏt, spŏt, ḡŏt, ḡŏd, rŏd, phlŏx.
ọ, o͞o, ụ.—mọve, pro͞of, loṣe, lo͞oṣe, ro͞of, cho͞oṣe.
ô, ạ.—ôr, nôr, wạr, fôr, lôrd, côrd, fought, cạught.
ȯ, ŭ.—dȯne, dȯth, dȯst, dŭst, blȯod, flȯod, cȯme.
o, o͝o, ụ.—wolf, would, wo͝od, could, shọuld, go͝od.
ū.—ūṣe, mūte, mūṣe, feūd, lieū, view, new, tūbe.
ŭ, ȯ.—ŭp, bŭt, hŭt, sȯn, blȯod, ḡŭn, dŭck, sȯme.
û.—ûrge, pûrge, sûrge, cûrd, ûrn, bûrn, chûrn.
u, o͞o, ọ.—rule, school, brute, route, wọund, rude.
u, o͝o, ọ.—put, pull, push, bull, wo͝ol, wolf, wo͝od.
oi, oy.—oil, toy, boil, coil, roil, joy, boy, cloy.
ou, ow.—out, noun, proud, now, how, gout, pout.

Examples of Emphasis, Pauses, and Inflection.

1. John Bunyan.

Bunyan | is almost the only writer | that ever gave to the *abstráct* | the interest of the *concrètc.* In the works of many celebrated authors | *mén* are mere *personificátions.* We have not an *Othéllo,* but *jèalousy;* not an *Iágo,* but *pèrfidy;* not a *Brútus,* but *pàtriotism.* The mind of *Búnyan,* on the cóntrary, was so imáginative | that *personificátions,* when *hĕ* dealt with them, became *mèn.* A dialogue between two *quàlities,* in *his drĕam,* has more dramatic efféct | than a dialogue between *two human bèings* | in most *pláys.*

The *stỳlc* of Búnyan | is delightful· to every reader, and invaluable | as a stúdy | to every pérson | who wishes to obtain a wide commánd over the *English làngnage.* The *vocábulary* | is the vocabulary of the *cómmon pèople.* There is not an *exprèssion,* if we except a few technical terms of theólogy, which would puzzle the *rúdest pèasant.* We have observed several *páges* | which do not contain a *single wòrd* | of more than *twó sỳllables.* Yet *nò* writer | has said more *exáctly* | what he *mèant* to say. For magnífícence, for páthos, for vehement exhortátion, for subtile disquisítion, for every purpose of the póet, the órator, and the divíne, this homely *díalect,* the dialect of plain *wórkingmen,* was *pérfectly sufficient.* There is no book in our *líterature* | on which we would so readily stake the *fáme* | of the old unpolluted *English làngnage;* no *bóok* | which shows so well | how rich that language *ìs,* in its own proper wéalth, and how little it has been *impróved* | by all that it has *bòrrowcd.*

Cowper sáid, fifty or sixty years agó, that he dared not name John Búnyan in his verse, for fear of moving a *snèer.* *Wĕ* | live in *bétter tìmes;* and we are not *afràid* | *to sày,* that though there were many clever men in England | during the latter half of the seventeenth cén-

tury, there were only *twò | gréat | creátive | mìnds*. *One* of these produced the "Paradise Lóst," the *óther* | the "Pilgrim's Prògress."
MACAULAY.

2. HYDER ALI.

[*This extract must be read with strongly marked rising and falling inflections.*]

Whilst the authors of all these evils | were idly and stupidly gazing on this *menacing métcor*, which blackened all the *horízon*, it suddenly *bùrst*, and poured down the whole of its contents | upon the plains of the Carnàtic. Then ensued a scene of *wóe*, the like of which | *no cýe* | had *sèen*, *no heárt* | *concèived*, and which *no tóngue* | can adequately *tèll*. The miserable inhábitants, flying from their flaming víllages, in part | were *slàughtered;* óthers, without regard to *séx*, to *áge*, to *ránk*, or sacredness of *fúnction—fáthers* | torn from *chíldren*, *húsbands* | from *wíves*—enveloped in a whirlwind of *cávalry*, and amidst the goading *spears* of *drívers*, and the trampling of pursuing *hórses*, were swept into *cáptivity*, in an unknówn and *hóstile lànd*. Those who were able to *evàde* this tempest, fled to the walled *cìties*. But, escaping from *fíre*, *swórd*, and *éxile*, they fell into the jaws of *fàmine*.

For *eighteen mònths*, without *intermìssion*, this destruction | raged | from the gates of *Madrás* | to the gates of *Tanjòre;* and so completely did these masters in their árt, Hyder Ali, and his more ferocious són, absolve themselves | of their *ímpious vów*, that when the *British ármies* | traversed, as they díd, the Carnátic | for hundreds of miles in all *diréctions, through the whòle lìne of their màrch* they did not see *óne* | *màn*, not *óne* | *wòman*, not *óne* | *chìld*, not *òne* | *four-fóoted bèast* | of *àny descríption* | *whatèver*. One dēad | ūniform | sīlence | rēigned | ōver the whōle rēgion.
BURKE.

3. CONTRAST OF TACT AND TALENT.

[*This extract affords a good illustration of distinctive or unimpassioned circumflex.*]

Tălent | is *sŏmething*, but tăct | is *ĕvery* thing. Talent | is sèrious, sòber, gráve, and respèctable: tact | is all *thăt*, and *more tŏo*. It is not a *sixth sĕnse*, but it is the *lĭfe* of all the *fĭve*. It is the open *eўe*, the quick *ĕar*, the judging *tȧste*, the keen *smĕll*, and the lively *tŏuch;* it is the *intĕrpreter* of all *rĭddles*, the *surmŏunter* of all *dĭfficulties*, the *remŏver* of all *ŏbstacles*. It is useful in all *plȧces*, and at all *tĭmes;* it is useful in *sŏlitude*, for it shows a man *ĭnto* the wòrld; it is useful in *sŏciety*, for it shows him his way | *thrŏugh* the wòrld.

Tálent | is *pŏwer*, *táct* | is *skĭll;* *tálent* | is *weĭght*, táct | is *momĕntum;* *tálent* | knows *what to dŏ*, táct | knows *how to dŏ it;* *tálent* | makes a man *respĕctable*, *tăct* | will make him *respĕcted;* *tálent* is *wĕalth*, *táct* | is *ready mŏney*. For all the *prăctical* purposes, *táct* | carries it against *tálent* | *tĕn* to *ŏne*.

Take them to the *thèater*, and put them against each other on the stáge, and *tálent* | shall produce you a trágedy that shall scarcely live long enough to be *condèmned*, while *tăct* | keeps the house in a *ròar*, night after night, with its successful fàrces. There is no want of dramatic *tálent*, there is no want of dramatic *táct;* but they are seldom *togèther:* so we have successful pĭeces |, which are not *respĕctable*, and *respĕctable* pĭeces | which are not *succĕssful*.

Take them to the *bàr*, and let them shake their learned curls at each other in *lègal* rivalry; *tálent* | sees its way *clĕarly*, but *tăct* | is first at its joúrney's *ènd*. Tálent | has many a *cŏmpliment* from the bénch, but *tăct* | touches *fèes*. *Tálent* makes the world wonder that it gets on no *făster*, *tăct* | arouses astónishment | that it gets on so *făst*. And the *sécret* is, that it has no *weĭght* to carry; it makes no fálse *stĕps;* it hits the right *nȧil* on the head; it loses no *tĭme;* it takes all *hĭnts;* and by keeping its eye on the *wéather-*cock, is ready to take advantage of every wínd that blóws.

Take them into the chùrch: *tálent* | has always something worth *hĕaring, táct* | is sure of abundance of *héarers; tálent* | may *obtăin* a living, *tăct* will *măke* one; *tálent* | gets a *gŏod* name, *táct* | a *grĕat* one; tálent | con*vĭnces,* táct | *convérts; tálent* | is an honor to the *profĕssion,* táct | gains honor | *frŏm* the profession.

Take them to còurt: *tálent* | feels its *wĕight,* táct | finds its *wáy; tálent* | *commănds, táct* | is *obéyed; tálent* | is honored with *approbătion,* and táct | is blessed by *preférment.* Place them in the *sènate: tálent* | has the *ĕar* of the house, but táct | wins its *héart,* and has its *vótes; tálent* | is *fĭt* for employment, but *táct* | is *fitted* for it. It has a knack | of slipping into place with a *swéet sĭlence* and glibness of *mòvement,* as a *bĭlliard*-ball *insĭnuates* itself into the *pòcket.*

It seems to know *ĕvery* thing, without learning *ăny* thing. It has served an extemporary *apprénticeship;* it wants no *drĭlling;* it never ranks in the *ăwkward* squad; it has no *lĕft hănd,* no *dĕaf ĕar,* no *blĭnd sĭde.* It puts on no look of *wŏndrous wĭsdom,* it has no air of *profŭndity,* but plays with the details of place | as dexterously as a well-taught *hănd* | flourishes over the keys of the *piáno-forte.* It has all the air of *cŏmmonplace,* and all the force and power of *génius.* London Atlas.

4. THE PURITANS.

[Marked for emphasis, inflection, and rhetorical pauses. Require the class to give the reasons for the marking. To be read with strongly marked emphasis and inflections.]

We would speak first of the *Pùritans,* the most remarkable body of men, perhaps, which the world has ever produced. The *ódious* and *ridículous* parts of their character | lie on the *sùrface.* He that *rùns* | may *rèad* them; nor have there been wanting | attentive and malicious *obsèrvers* | to point them out. For many years after the Restorátion, they were the theme | of unmeasured *invéctive* and *derìsion*. They were exposed | to the utmost licentiousness of the *préss* | and of the *stáge*, at the time when the press and the stáge | were *mòst licèntious*. They were *nòt men of létters;* they *wére* | as a body | *unpòpular;* they could not *defènd* themselves; and the *públic* | would not take them | under its *protèction*. They were therefore abandoned | without *rescrve* | to the tender *mércies* | of the *sátirists* and *drámatists*. The ostentatious simplicity of their *dréss*, their *sour áspect*, their *nasal twáng*, their *stiff pósture*, their *long gráces*, their *Hebrew námes*, the scriptural *phráses* which they introduced on *every occásion*, their contempt of *human léarning*, their detestation of *polite amúsements*, were indeed fair *gáme* for the láughers. But it is not from the *làughers* alóne | that the *philósophy of hìstory* | is to be learned. And he who approaches this súbject | should carefully guard against the influence | of that *potent rídicule* | which has already misled so many excellent wrìters.

Those who roused the people to *resístance*, who directed their measures through a long series of *evcntful yéars*, who fórmed, out of the most unpromising *matérials*, the finest *ármy* | that Europe had ever *sécn*, who trampled down *kíng, Chúrch,* and *aristócracy,* who, in the short intervals of domestic *sedítion* and *rebéllion*, made the name of England | terrible to every nation on the face of the *éarth,* were no *vúlgar fanàtics*. *Most* of their absurdities | were mere *èxternal bádges,* like the signs of *freemásonry,* or the dresses of frìars. We *regrèt* | that these badges | were not more attractive. We *regrèt* | that a *bódy* | to whose courage and talents | mankind has owed *inestimable obligátions* | had not the *lofty élegance* | which distinguished some of the adherents of

Charles Í., or the easy *good bréeding* | for which the court of Charles ÍI. was celebrated. But, if we must *make our chóice*, we shall, like Bassanio in the plày, turn from the *spĕcious* caskets, which contain only the *déath's* head and the *fóol's* head, and fix our choice | on the plain leaden *chést* | which conceals the *trèasure*.

The *Púritans* | were men | whose minds | had derived a *pecúliar chàracter* | from the daily contemplation | of *supèrior béings* | and *etérnal ìnterests*. Not *contènt* | with acknowledging, in general terms, an *overruling Próvidence*, they habitually ascribed *évery evènt* | to the will of the *Great Béing*, for whose *pówer* | nothing was *too vást*, for whose *inspéction* | nothing was *tóo minùte*. To *knòw* him, to *sèrve* him, to *enjóy* him, was with them | the *great énd* of *exìstence*. They rejected with *contèmpt* | the ceremonious homage | which *óther* sects | substituted for the *pure wórship* of the *sòul*. Instead of catching occasional *glímpses* of the Deity | through an *obscuring vĕil*, they aspired to gaze *fùll* | on the *intólerable brìghtness*, and to commune with him | *fáce* to *fàce*. Hence originated | their *contèmpt* | for *terréstrial distìnctions*.

The difference between the *gréatest* and the *mèanest* of mankínd | seemed to *vànish*, when compared with the *boundlesś ìnterval* | which separated the *whole ràce* | from him | on whom their *ówn* eyes | were constantly fixed. They recognized *no títle* to superiority | but *hís fàvor;* and, *cónfident* of that favor, they despised all the *accómplishments* | and all the *dígnities* of the *wòrld*. If they were unacquainted with the works of *philósophers* and *póets*, they were *dèeply réad* | in the oracles of *Gòd*. If their names were not found in the registers of *héralds*, they felt assured that they were recorded in the *Book of Lìfe*. If their steps were not accompanied by a splendid train of *ménials*, legions of ministering *àngels* | had charge over them. Their *pálaces* | were houses |

not made with *hánds*, their *díadems* | crowns of *glóry* | which should never *fáde* awày.

On the *rích* and the *éloquent*, on *nóbles* and *príests*, they looked down with *contèmpt;* for they esteemed themselves | *rích* in a *more prècious* treasure, and *éloquent* in a *more sublìme language, nòbles* | by the right of an *éarlier creàtion*, and priests | by the imposition | of a *míghtier hànd*. The very *mèanest* of them | was a *béing* | to whose fate | a *mystérious* and *terríble impòrtance* | belònged—on whose *slíghtest àctions* | the spirits of *líght* and *dàrkness* | looked with *ánxious ìnterest*—who had been déstined, before heaven and earth were *creàted*, to enjoy a *felícity* | which should continue | when heaven and éarth | should have passed awày. *Evénts* | which short-sighted politicians | ascribed to *eàrthly* causes | had been ordained on *hís* account. For *hís* sake | empires had rísen, and flourished, and decàyed. For *hís* sake | the *Almìghty* | had proclaimed his wíll | by the pen of the evángelist | and the hárp of the pròphet. He had been rescued by no *cŏmmon* delíverer | from the grasp | of no *cómmon fòe*. He had been ransomed | by the sweat of no *vŭlgar* ágony, by the blood of no *éarthly sàcrifice*. It was for *hím* | that the *sùn* | had been darkened, that the *ròcks* | had been rent, and the *dèad* had arisen, that *áll nàture* | had shuddered at the sufferings | of her expiring *Gôd!*

Thus the *Púritan* | was made up | of *twò dífferent mèn*, the *óne* | all self-*abásement, pénitence, grátitude, pássion;* the *óther* | pròud, càlm, inflèxible, sagàcious. He prostrated himself in the *dúst* before his *Măker;* but he set his *fŏot* | on the neck of his *kíng*. In his *devòtional* retírement, he prayed with *convùlsions*, and *gróans*, and *tèars*. He was *half-màddened* by *glórious* | or *tèrrible illùsions*. He heard the lyres of *ángels* | or the tempting whispers of *fìends*. He caught a gleam of the *Beatífic Vísion*, or woke *scrèaming* | from dreams of *everlàsting fĭre.* Like Váne, he thought himself intrusted with the scepter | of the *millénnial yèar.* Like Flĕetwood, he cried in the bitterness of his soul | that *Gòd* | had hid his *fàce* from him. But when he took his seat in the *còuncil,* or girt on his sword for *wár,* these tempestuous workings of the soul | had left *nò percéptible tràce* behind them. People who saw nothing of the *gódly* | but their uncouth *vísages,* and *héard* nothing from them | but their groans | and their *whining hýmns,* might *làugh* at them. But those had little *réason* to láugh | who encountered them | in the hall of debáte | or in the field of bàttle.

These *fanátics* | brought to civil and military affáirs | a coolness of *júdgment* | and an immutability of *púrpose* | which some writers have thought | *inconsìstent* with their *relígious zèal,* but which were, in fact, the necessary *èffects* of it. The intensity of their feelings on *óne* subject | made them *trànquil* | on *every òther.* One *overpówering sèntiment* | had subjected to itself | píty and hàtred, ámbition and fèar. *Déath* | had lost its *tèrrors,* and *pléasure* | its *chàrms.*

They had their *smíles* | and their *tèars,* their *ráptures* | and their *sòrrows,* but *nòt* | for the things of *thîs* world. Enthusiasm | had made them *stòics,* had cleared their minds from every *vúlgar* passion and prèjudice, and raised them above the influence of dánger and of corrùption. It sometimes might lead them to pur̄sue unwise *ĕnds,* but never to choose unwise *méans.*

They went through the world | like Sir Artegale's iron man Tàlus with his flàil, crushing and trampling down oppréssors, mingling with human béings, but having neither párt nor lòt | in *húman infĭrmities;* insensible to *fatígue,* to *pléasure,* and to *pàin;* not to be pierced by any *wéapon,* not to be withstood by any *bàrrier.*

MACAULAY.

5. THE RIGHT TO TAX AMERICA.

"But, Mr. Speaker, we have a *right* to tax Amèrica." Oh, *inéstimable* right! Oh, *wónderful, transcéndent* right! the assertion of which has cost this country *thírteen pròvinces*, six *ìslands, one húndred thóusand lìves,* and *séventy míllions* of *mòney!* Oh, *inváluable* right! for the sake of which we have sacrificed our rank among *nàtions,* our importance abròad, and our happiness at hòme.

Oh, ríght, more dear to us than our *existence*, which has already cost us so *múch,* and which seems likely to cost us our *àll!* Infatuated *màn!* miserable and undone *coùntry!* not to knòw that the *cláim* of ríght, without the power of *enfórcing* it, is *núgatory* and *ìdle.* We have a *ríght* to tax America, the noble lord téls us, therefore we *óught* to tax America. This is the profound logic which comprises the whole *cháin* of his *rèasoning.*

Not inferior to this was the wisdom of him who resolved to shear the *wólf. Whát—shéar a wólf!* Have you considered the *resístance,* the *dífficulty,* the *dánger,* of the attémpt?

Nô, says the madman, I have considered nothing but the *ríght.* Man has a *right of domínion* over the beasts of the fórest; and, therefore, I will shear the *wólf.* How *wónderful* that a nation could be thus *delùded!* But the noble lord *dèals* in cheats and *delùsions.* They are the daily *tràffic* of his *invèntion;* and he will *contìnue* to play off his cheats on this hóuse, so long as he thinks them necessary to his púrpose, and so long as he has money enough at command to bribe gentlemen to pretend that they *belièvc* him.

But a black and bitter day of *rèckoning* will surely còme; and *whenéver* that day *cómes,* I trust I shall be able, by a parliamentary *impéachment,* to bring upon the heads of the *áuthors* of our *calámities* the punishment they *desèrve.*

BURKE.

6. FLOWERS.

Spake full well, in language quaint and olden,
    Óne who dwelleth by the castled *Rhíne*,
When he called the *flówers*, so blue and gólden,
    Stàrs, that in earth's *fìrmament* do shine.

Stars they àre, wherein we read our history,
    As astrologers and seers of èld;
Yet not so wrapped about with awful mystery,
    Like the burning stars which *théy* beheld.

Wondrous *trùths*, and *mánifold* as *wòndrous*,
    God hath written in those stars *abòve ;*
But not less | in the bright flowerets *únder* us |
    Stands the revelation of His love.

Bright and glorious | is that revelation
    Writ all over this great *wòrld* of ours;
Making evident our own creation |
    In these *stars of èarth*—these *gólden flòwers.*

And the Póet, faithful and far-séeing,
    Sees, alike in *stárs* and *flówers*, a part |
Of the self-same, universal being,
    Which is throbbing | in his *bráin* and *hèart.*

Gorgeous *flòwerets* in the *sùnlight* shining;
    Blòssoms | flaunting in the eye of dày;
Tremulous *lèaves*, with soft and silver lining;
    Bùds | that ópen | only to decày!

Brilliant *hòpes*, all woven in gorgeous tissues,
    Flaunting gayly in the golden light;
Large *desìres*, with most uncertain ìssues ;
    Tender *wìshes* | blossoming at night!

These in flowers and men | are *mòre* than séeming;
    Wòrkings | are they | of the self-same pówers,

Which the Poet, in no idle dreaming,
  Seeth in *himself,* and in the *flòwers.*

Everywhere about us | are they glòwing—
  Some like *stárs,* to tell us *Sprìng* is born;
Óthers, their blue eyes | with *tèars* o'erflówing,
  Stand like *Rùth* | amid the golden còrn;

Not *alóne* | in Spring's armorial bearing,
  And in Summer's | green emblazoned *fiéld,*
But in arms | of brave old *Aùtumn's* wearing,
  In the center | of his brazen shièld;

Not *alóne* in meadows | and green álleys,
  On the moúntain-top, and by the brink |
Of sequestered pools | in woodland válleys,
  Where the slaves of nature | stoop to drínk;

Not *alóne* in her vast dome of glóry,
  Not on graves of bird and *béast* alone,
But on old *cathèdrals* | high and hòary,
  On the tomb of *hèroes,* carved in *stòne;*

In the cottage of the rudest *pèasant,*
  In ancestral homes, whose crumbling tówers,
Speaking of the *Past* | unto the *Prèsent,*
  Tell us of the ancient Games of Flòwers;

In all *plàces,* then, and in all *sèasons,*
  Flowers expand their light and soul-like wíngs,
Teaching us, by most persuasive réasons,
  How akin they are | to *hùman* things.

And with child-like, credulous affection,
  We behold their tender buds expànd;
Emblems of our own *great resurréction,*
  Emblems | of the bright | and *better lànd.*

LONGFELLOW.

7. THE SEVEN AGES OF MAN.

All the *wórld's* a *stàge,*
And all the *mén* and *wómen* merely *pláyers:*
They have their *éxits* and their *èntrances;*
And *one mán* in his time plays *many pàrts,*
His *ácts* being *séven àges.* At first, the *Ìnfant,*
Mewling and puking in the nurse's àrms.
And then, the whining *Schòol-boy,* with his sàtchel,
And shining morning fáce, creeping like *snàil*
Unwillingly to *schòol.* And then, the *Lòver,*
Sighing like *fùrnace,* with a woful bállad
Made to his mistress' *eyebrow.* Then a *Sòldier,*
Full of strange *òaths,* and bearded like the *pàrd,*
Jealous in *hònor,* sudden and quick in *quàrrel,*
Seeking the bubble *reputátion*
Even in the *cànnon's* mouth. And then, the *Jùstice,*
With eyes *sevère,* and beard of formal *cùt,*
Full of wise *sàws* and modern *ìnstances;*
And so he plays *hís* part. The sixth age shifts
Into the lean and slippered *Pantalòon,*
With spectacles on *nóse,* and pouch on *sìde;*
His youthful *hóse,* well sáved, a world too wíde
For his *shrúnk shànk;* and his big manly *vóice,*
Turning again toward childish *tréble, pípes*
And *whístles* in his *sòund.* Last scene of *áll,*
That ends this *strange eventful hístory,*
Is second *chìldishness* and mere *oblìvion,*
Sans *téeth,* sans *eýes,* sans *táste,* sans *èverything.*

SHAKESPEARE.

8. BURIAL OF SIR JOHN MOORE.

Not a *drùm* | was heard, not a funeral *nòte,*
  As his corse | to the *ràmpart* | we hurried;
Not a *sòldier* | discharged his farewell *shòt*
  O'er the grave | where our hero | we buried.

We buried him darkly, at dead of *nìght*,
  The sods with our *bàyonets* turning;
By the struggling *mòonbeam's* misty light,
  And the *làntern* | dimly burning.

No useless *cóffin* | inclosed his breast,
  Not in *shéet* | nor in *shroùd* | we wóund him;
But he lay | like a warrior taking his *rèst* |
  With his martial *clòak* | around him.

Féw and shòrt | were the *pràyers* we sáid,
  And we spoke not a word of sórrow,
But we steadfastly gazed on the face of the dead,
  And we *bítterly* thought of the *mòrrow*.

We thought, as we hollowed his narrow béd,
  And smoothed down his lonely píllow,
That the foe and the stranger | would *trcad* o'er his héad,
  And *wé* | far *awáy* on the billow!

Lightly they'll talk of the spirit that's gone,
  And o'er his cold ashes | *upbráid* him,—
But nothing he'll reck, if they let him sleep on |
  In the grave | where a *Brìton* | has laid him.

But *hàlf* | of our heavy task | was done |
  When the clock | struck the hour for retìring;
And we heard the distant and random *gún* |
  That the fóe | was sullenly firing.

Slowly and sadly | we laid him down,
  From the field of his fame | fresh and góry;
We carved not a line, and we raised not a stone,
  But left him | alone with his glòry.

CHAPTER II.

FORCE AND STRESS.

SECTION I.
FORCE OF VOICE.

1. *Force* of utterance relates to the degree of loudness or intensity of voice.

2. The three main divisions of force are soft, moderate, and loud. These, for convenience, may be subdivided as follows: (1) Very soft (corresponding to *pianissimo* in music). (2) Soft (*piano*). (3) Moderate (*mezzo-forte*). (4) Loud (*forte*). (5) Very loud (*fortissimo*).

3. The general rule of force is, to read with an intensity appropriate to the thoughts or emotion to be expressed, and with a power or strength of voice sufficient to fill the room, so that every person in it may hear distinctly every word that is uttered.

4. Force of voice must be stronger in the school-room than in the parlor, and louder in the lecture-hall than in the school-room. If read to an assemblage of a thousand people, the most didactic and unimpassioned document must be read with considerable force.

5. Pupils should be cautioned against attempting any degree of force beyond the compass of their voices, and also against the conventional school-tone of loudness, which consists in raising the voice to so high a pitch that it grates on the ear like the filing of a saw.

6. "The command of all degrees of force of voice," says Prof. Russell, "must evidently be essential to true

and natural expression, whether in reading or speaking. Appropriate utterance ranges through all stages of vocal sound, from the whisper of fear and the murmur of repose, to the boldest swell of vehement declamation, and the shout of triumphant courage. But to give forth any one of these or the intermediate tones, with just and impressive effect, the organs must be disciplined by appropriate exercise and frequent practice. For every day's observation proves to us, that mere natural instinct and animal health, with all the aids of informing intellect, and inspiring emotion, and exciting circumstances, are not sufficient to produce the effects of eloquence, or even of adequate utterance.

7. "The overwhelming power of undisciplined feeling may not only impede but actually prevent the right action of the instruments of speech; and the novice who has fondly dreamed, in his closet, that nothing more is required for effective expression than a genuine feeling, finds, to his discomfiture, that it is perhaps the very intensity of his feeling that hinders his utterance; and it is not till experience and practice have done their work, that he learns the primary lesson, that force of emotion needs a practiced force of will to balance and regulate it, and a disciplined control over the organs to give it appropriate utterance.

8. "The want of due training for the exercise of public reading or speaking is evinced in the habitual undue loudness of some speakers, and the inadequate force of others—the former subjecting their hearers to unnecessary pain, and the latter to disappointment and uneasiness.

9. "Force of utterance, however, has other claims on the attention of students of elocution, besides those which are involved in correct expression. It is, in its various gradations, the chief means of imparting strength to the vocal organs, and power to the voice itself. The due

practice of exercises in force of utterance, does for the voice what athletic exercise does for the muscles of the body: it imparts the two great conditions of power—vigor and pliancy."

CAUTION.

10. In drill upon the following exercises, bear in mind the following direction from Prof. Monroe: "Seek to make the sounds always smooth and musical; and never lose sight of the fact that what is wanted in every-day use of the voice, in the school-room or elsewhere, is a pleasant and natural intonation. The practice of loud and sustained tones is an excellent means of improving the voice; but is to be the exception, not the rule, in ordinary reading. Still less should a shouting tone be used in conducting a recitation, or in the ordinary discipline of a class. Yet the softest tone must be elastic and full of life, not dull and leaden."

Concert Drill on Force.

1. Repeat, three times, the long vocals, ā, ē, ī, ō, ū, (1) with soft force; (2) with moderate force; (3) with loud force.

2. Count from one to twenty with very soft force; with soft force; with moderate force; with loud force; with very loud force.

3. Repeat, five times, the word "all," beginning with very soft force, and increasing the degree of force with each successive repetition of the word.

4. Repeat the following with increased force on each successive repetition: "loud, *louder*, LOUDEST."

5. Repeat, three times, ĕ, ŭ, ü, ạ, ŏ, ǫ, (1) with soft force; (2) moderate force; (3) loud force.

I. Very Soft Force.

Very soft force is appropriate to the expression of tenderness, sadness, or peaceful and tranquil feeling.

EXAMPLES.
1. DIRGE.

Softly! She is lying
With her lips apart.
Softly! She is dying
Of a broken heart.

Whisper! She is going
To her final rest.
Whisper! Life is growing
Dim within her breast.   EASTMAN.

2. LULLABY.

Sweet and low, sweet and low,
　Wind of the western sea,
Low, low, breathe and blow,
　Wind of the western sea!   TENNYSON.

3. ENOCH ARDEN.

　He therefore turning softly like a thief,
Lest the harsh shingle should grate underfoot,
And feeling all along the garden-wall,
Lest he should swoon and tumble and be found,
Crept to the gate, and opened it, and closed,
As lightly as a sick man's chamber-door,
Behind him, and came out upon the waste.
　And there he would have knelt, but that his knees
Were feeble, so that falling prone he dug
His fingers into the wet earth, and prayed.
                                        TENNYSON.

II. Soft or Subdued Force.

Soft force differs from very soft only in degree.

EXAMPLES.

1. TIME.

Touch us gently, Time!
   Let us glide adown thy stream
Gently, as we sometimes glide
   Through a quiet dream.
Humble voyagers are we,
   O'er life's dim, unsounded sea,
Seeking only some calm clime;
   Touch us gently, Time!   BARRY CORNWALL.

2. DEATH OF THE OLD YEAR.

Full knee-deep lies the winter-snow,
   And the wintry winds are wearily sighing,
Toll ye the church-bell, sad and slow,
And tread softly and speak low,
   For the old year lies a-dying.
   Old year, you *must* not die.   TENNYSON.

3. THE DEATH-BED.

We watched her breathing through the night,
   Her breathing soft and low,
As in her breast the wave of life
   Kept heaving to and fro.
Our very hopes belied our fears,
   Our fears our hopes belied—
We thought her dying when she slept,
   And sleeping when she died.   HOOD.

4. THE FAERIE QUEEN.

Eftsoons they heard a most melodious sound
Of all that might delight a dainty ear.
Such as, at once, might not on living ground,
Save in this paradise, be heard elsewhere:
Right hard it was for wight which did it hear

To weet what manner music that might be,
For all that pleasing is to living ear
Was there consorted in one harmony;
Birds, voices, instruments, winds, waters, all agree.

SPENSER.

5. THE ARSENAL.

Down the dark future, through long generations,
 The echoing sounds grow fainter and then cease;
And like a bell, with solemn, sweet vibrations,
 I hear once more the voice of Christ say, "Peace!"

LONGFELLOW.

6. THE LOST CHORD.

Seated one day at the organ,
 I was weary and ill at ease,
And my fingers wandered idly
 Over the noisy keys.

I do not know what I was playing,
 Or what I was dreaming then;
But I struck one chord of music,
 Like the sound of a great Amen!

It flooded the crimson twilight,
 Like the close of an angel's psalm,
And it lay on my fevered spirit,
 With a touch of infinite calm.

It quieted pain and sorrow,
 Like love overcoming strife;
It seemed the harmonious echo
 From our discordant life.

It linked all perplexed meanings
 Into one perfect peace,
And trembled away into silence,
 As if it were loath to cease.

ADELAIDE PROCTOR.

III. Moderate Force.

Moderate force is the prevailing tone in the reading of unimpassioned narrative, descriptive, or didactic composition, in a small room, or to a small number of persons. It is the degree of force used in conversation. The characteristic quality of moderate force is "pure tone," and the stress, "unimpassioned radical."

EXAMPLES.

1. There was a sound of revelry by night.

2. What constitutes a state?

3. Scrooge never painted out old Marley's name.

4. The history of England is emphatically the history of progress.

5. The eyes of men converse as much as their tongues.

6. Spake full well in language quaint and olden,
   One who dwelleth by the castled Rhine,
When he called the flowers, so blue and golden,
   Stars, that in earth's firmament do shine.

7. The way was long, the wind was cold,
   The minstrel was infirm and old.

8. I met a little cottage girl,
   She was eight years old, she said;
Her hair was thick with many a curl,
   That clustered round her head.

9. Blessings on thee, little man,
   Barefoot boy with cheeks of tan,
With thy turned-up pantaloon,
   And thy merry whistled tune.

10. I wrote some lines once on a time
    In wondrous merry mood,
And thought, as usual, men would say
    They were exceeding good.

They were so queer, so very queer,
    I laughed as I would die;
Albeit, in the general way,
    A sober man am I.

11. Listen, my children, and you shall hear
Of the midnight ride of Paul Revere,
    On the eighteenth of April, in seventy-five;—
    Hardly a man is now alive
Who remembers that famous day and year.

12. Around I see the powers that be;
    I stand by Empire's primal springs;
And princes meet in every street,
    And hear the tread of uncrowned kings!

13. Mrs. Siddons once had a pupil who was practicing for the stage. The lesson was upon the "part" of a young girl whose lover had deserted her. The rendering did not please that Queen of Tragedy, and she said: "Think how you would feel under the circumstances. What would you do if your lover were to run off and leave you?" "I would look out for another one," said that philosophic young lady; and Mrs. Siddons, with a gesture of intense disgust, cried out, "Leave me!" and would never give her another lesson.

14. READING AS AN ACCOMPLISHMENT.

We had rather have a child return to us from school a first-rate reader, than a first-rate performer on the piano-forte. We should feel that we had a far better pledge for the intelligence and talent of our child. The accomplishment, in its perfection, would give more pleasure. The voice of song is not sweeter than the voice of eloquence. And there may be eloquent readers, as well as eloquent speakers.

IV. Loud Force.

Loud force is the tone used to express courage, boldness, defiance, anger, grandeur, and sublimity. It is used by the public speaker in addressing a large audience, or when speaking under the sway of strong emotion.

This degree of force requires full and deep breathing, and a vigorous use of the vocal organs.

The middle pitch is the appropriate key of loud force. A high pitch weakens the effect of forcible reading or declamation.

EXAMPLES.

1. Joy! Joy! Shout, shout aloud for joy.
2. Hark to the brazen blare of the bugle!
   Hark to the rolling clatter of the drums.
3. Not in vain the distance beacons. Forward, forward, let us range;
   Let the great world spin forever down the ringing grooves of change.

4. ALEXANDER'S FEAST.

Now strike the golden lyre again;
A louder yet, and yet a louder strain.
Break his bands of sleep asunder,
And rouse him, like a rattling peal of thunder.
DRYDEN.

5. REVENGE.

And longer had she sung—but, with a frown,
    Revenge impatient rose.
He threw his blood-stained sword in thunder down,
    And, with a withering look,
    The war-denouncing trumpet took,
And blew a blast, so loud and dread,
Were ne'er prophetic sounds so full of woe:
    And ever and anon, he beat
    The doubling drum with furious heat. COLLINS.

6. MILTON'S "PARADISE LOST."

Now storming *fùry* rose,
And *clámor* such as heard in heaven till *nów*
Was *nèver;* arms on armor clashing, brayed
Horrible *discord,* and the madding wheels
Of brazen *cháriots* raged: dire was the noise
Of *cònflict;* overhead the dismal hiss
Of fiery darts in flaming *vòlleys* flèw,
And flýing vaulted either host with fìre.
So under fiery cópe, together rushed
Bòth battles màin, with ruinous *assáult*
And inextinguishable *ràge.* All *hèaven*
Resòunded; and had *èarth* been then, all *èarth,*
Had to her *cènter* shòok. What *wònder?* where
Millions of fierce encountering angels fought
On *éither sìde,* the *lèast* of whom could wield
These *élements,* and arm him with the force
Of all their *règions.*

7. THE BELLS.

Hear the loud *alarum* bells—
Brazen bells!
What a tale of *terror,* now, their turbulency tells!
In the startled ear of night
How they scream out their affright!
Too much horrified to speak,
They can only shriek, shriek,
Out of tune,
In the clamorous appealing to the mercy of the fire,
In a mad expostulation with the deaf and frantic fire.
Leaping higher, *higher,* HIGHER,
With a desperate desire,
And a resolute endeavor,
Now, now to sit or never
By the side of the pale-faced moon!   POE.

V. Very Loud or Declamatory Force.

Very loud force prevails in oratorical declamation before large audiences. It is also heard in the tones of anger, of passion, of command, in calling or shouting, and in intensely dramatic reading.

EXAMPLES.

1. Now for the *fĭght!* now for the *cánnon* peal,
    Forward! through blòod and tòil, and cloùd, and fìre!
    Glorious the *shòut*, the *shŏck*, the crash of *stèel*,
    The volley's roll, the rocket's blasting spìre.

2. To àrms! they còme! the Grèek! the Grèek!

3. Lìberty! Frèedom! Tyranny is *dèad*.

4. Thy threats, thy mercy I *defŷ*,
    I give thee in thy teeth the *lîe*.

5. He raised a shout as he drew on
    Till all the welkin rang again:
    "Elizabeth! Elizabeth!"

6. From every hill, by every sea,
    In shouts proclaim the great decree,
    "*All chains are burst, all men are free!*"
    Hurrah, hurrah, hurrah!

    7. SPARTACUS TO THE GLADIATORS.

[*Radical and vanishing stress, and strongly marked circumflex inflections.*]

Ye stand here now like *gĭants*, as ye *àre*. The strength of *brâss* is in your toughened *sìnews;* but *to-mŏrrow* some *Rŏman Adŏnis*, breathing sweet perfume from his *cŭrly lŏcks*, shall with his *lĭly fĭngers pât* your red *brăwn*, and bet his *sèsterces* upon your *blòod*. Hàrk! hear ye yon lion roaring in his *dén?* 'T is *three dàys* since he tasted *flèsh;* but *to-mŏrrow* he shall break his

fast upon *yoúrs*, and a *dáinty* meal for him ye will *bĕ*.
If ye are *bĕasts*, then stand here like fat *ŏxen*, waiting
for the *bútcher's knĭfe!* If ye are *mĕn*, follow *mĕ!*
Strike down yon *guárd*, gain the *mountain pásses*, and
thĕre do bloody *wŏrk*, as did your *sĭres* at old *Thermŏpylæ!* Is *Spárta dĕad?* Is the old Grecian spirit
frŏzen in your véins, that you do *crŏuch* and *cŏwer* like
a belabored *hŏund* beneath his master's *lăsh?* Oh, *cŏmrades! wárriors! Thrácians!* if we *mŭst* fight, let us
fight for *oursĕlves!* If we *mŭst* slaughter, let us slaughter
our *opprĕssors!* If we *mŭst* die, let it be under the
clear *skỹ*, by the bright *wáters*, in noble, honorable
báttle.

KELLOGG.

8. CATILINE'S DEFIANCE.

Conscript fáthers,
I do not rise to waste the night in *wórds:*
Let that *plebĕian* talk; 't is not *my* tráde;
But here I stand for *rĭght!*—Let him show *prŏofs!*
For *Rŏman* right; though none, it seems, dare stand
To take their share with *mĕ*. Ay, clùster thĕre!
Cling to your màster, jùdges, Ròmans, *sláves!*
His charge is *fálse.* I *dáre* him to his proofs.

CROLY.

9. RICHELIEU.

Who spake of *lĭfe?*
I bade thee grasp that treasure as thine *hŏnor*—
A *jéwel* worth whole *hécatombs* of lives!
Begòne! redéem thine honor! *Báck* to *Màrion*—
Or *Bàradas*—or *Orleans*—tràck the ròbber—
Regàin the *pácket*—or crawl on to *àge*—
Àge and gray *hàirs* like *mĭne*—and know thou 'st lost
That which had made thee *grèat* and saved thy *còuntry*.
See me *nòt* till thou 'st bought the *rĭght* to seek me.
Awày! Nay, *chèer* thee! thou hast not fail'd *yĕt*—
There 's no such *wôrd* as fàil.

BULWER.

10. FREEDOM.

8. If I could stand for a moment upon one of your high mountain tóps, far above all the kingdoms of the civilized wórld, and there might sée, coming úp, one after anóther, the brávest and wísest of the ancient wárriors, and státesmen, and kíngs, and monárchs, and priésts; and if, as they came úp, I might be permitted to ask from them an expression of opinion upon such a case as *thís*, with a *common vòice* and in *thunder tònes*, reverberating through a thousand válleys, and echoing down the áges, they would crý : " *Lìberty, Frèedom, the Universal Brotherhood of Màn !*" *I* join that shòut ; I swell that ánthem ; I echo that práise *forever*, and for *evermòre*.

11. THE WAR INEVITABLE.

They tell us, sir, that we are *wèak*—unable to *còpe* with so formidable an *àdversary*. But when shall we be *strònger?* Will it be the next *wéek*, or the next *yéar?* Will it be when we are totally *disármed*, and when a *British guárd* shall be stationed in *every hóuse?* Shall we gather strength by *irresolútion* and *ináction?* Shall we acquire the means of effectual | *resìstance* by lying supinely on our *bácks*, and hugging the delusive phantom of *hópe*, until our enemies shall have bound us *hánd* and *fóot?* Sír, we are *nòt* weak, if we make a proper use of those means which the God of nature hath placed in our pòwer. It is in vain, sir, to *extènuate* the matter. Gentlemen may cry *péace, péace!*—but there is *nó* peace. The war is actually *begún!* The next gale that sweeps from the *nórth* will bring to our ears the clash of *resounding àrms!* Our *bréthren* are *alréady* in the fièld! *Whỳ* stand we here *ìdle ?* What is it that gentlemen *wìsh?* What would they *hàve?* Is life so *dèar*, or peace so *swèet*, as to be purchased at the price of *cháins* and *slávery?* *Forbíd* it, Almighty

Gôd! I know not what course ŏ*thers* may take; but as for *mé*, give me *liberty*, or give me *déath!*

Patrick Henry.

VI. Recapitulation of Force.

1. *Force must be regulated by the thought or feeling to be expressed.*

2. *Soft force prevails in the expression of peaceful thought, of sentiment, of tranquillity, and of suppressed emotion.*

3. *Moderate force is the natural tone of conversation and of narrative, descriptive, and didactic composition.*

4. *Loud force prevails in the expression of anger, passion, sublimity, command, and strong feeling.*

5. *Very loud force prevails in calling and shouting; in cries of alarm, fear, and terror; and in intense dramatic expression.*

Examples of Force.

VERY SOFT.
Low, low, breathe and blow, wind of the western sea.

SOFT.
How sweet the moonlight sleeps upon this bank.

MODERATE.
Marley was dead, to begin with.

LOUD.
Hear the loud alarum bells—brazen bells!
How they clang, and clash, and roar.

VERY LOUD.
Liberty! freedom! Tyranny is dead.

Require each pupil to select, write out, and read in the class, a similar set of quoted illustrations.

SECTION II.
STRESS OF VOICE.

Stress denotes the manner of applying volume of voice to single words or sounds. The elocutionary divisions of stress are:

1. Radical >
2. Median <>
3. Vanishing >
4. Thorough =
5. Compound ×
6. Intermittent ∾∾

The radical and the median stress are the most important and the most used of these divisions; and to these the attention of school readers should be chiefly directed. The other forms of stress mainly concern the special elocutionist or the actor; and may, therefore, be treated very briefly.

I. RADICAL STRESS.

1. In *radical* stress, the force strikes abruptly upon the *radix*, or beginning of a word or a sound. It corresponds to the *diminuendo* in music.

2. It may be illustrated by exploding the full force of the voice upon the initial vowel in the following words: (1) āle, ärm, all, ōld, ōoze. (2) ăt, ĕnd, ĭn, ŏn, ŭp.

3. Of this stress, Dr. Rush says: "There are so few speakers able to give a radical stress with this momentary burst, and therefore so few who may comprehend the mere description of it, that I must draw an illustration from the effort of coughing. A single impulse of coughing is not in all points exactly like the abrupt voice on syllables, for that single impulse is a forcing out of almost all the breath, which is not the case in syllabic utterance; yet if the tonic element be employed as the vocality of coughing, its abrupt opening will truly represent the function of radical stress, when used in discourse.

4. "It is this stress which draws the cutting edge of words across the ear, and startles even stupor into attention; this, which lessens the fatigue of listening, and out-voices the murmur and unruly stir of an assembly; and a sensibility to this, through a general instinct of the animal ear, which gives authority to the groom, and makes the horse submissive to his angry accent.

5. "Besides the fullness, loudness, and abruptness of the radical stress, when employed for distinct articulation, the tonic sound itself should be a pure vocality. When mixed with aspiration, it loses the brilliancy that serves to increase the impressive effect of the explosive force."

DISTINCTIONS OF RADICAL STRESS.

1. Radical stress may be distinguished as *unimpassioned* and *impassioned*.

2. The *unimpassioned* radical is used in narrative, descriptive, and didactic reading, to give a clear, distinct, energetic style of expression. The *impassioned* radical is the strong, full, abrupt utterance which characterizes the voice when under the influence of strong passions, such as anger, hatred, etc. It is the stress of authoritative command, of strength, and of power.

I. THE UNIMPASSIONED RADICAL.

This form of the radical stress is generally combined with moderate force and middle pitch. In the unimpassioned radical the vowel and liquid sounds are cut short as in the *staccato* movement in music.

This stress is characteristic of vivacity, gayety, humor, and of clear, distinct, and definite statement.

UNIMPASSIONED RADICAL DRILL.

1. Repeat rapidly four times, with the falling inflec-

tion, the short vowel sounds, ă, ĕ, ĭ, ŏ, ŭ; the long vocals, ā, ē, ī, ō, ū.

2. Count from one to twenty with moderate force and falling inflection, cutting short the words as in *staccato* movement.

3. Is this a time to be gloomy and sad,
    When our mother nature laughs around?
  When even the deep blue heavens look glad,
    And gladness breathes from the blossoming ground?

4. Hear the sledges, with the bells—silver bells,
  What a world of merriment their melody foretells;
    How they tinkle, tinkle, tinkle,
      In the icy air of night!

Examples of Unimpassioned Radical.

1. Bob-o'-link, bob-o'-link,
    Spink, spank, spink;
      Chee! chee! chee!

2. Sometimes, with secure delight,
  The upland hamlets will invite,
  When the merry bells ring round,
  And the jocund rebecs sound
  To many a youth and many a maid,
  Dancing in the checkered shade.

3. HUDIBRAS.

In mathematics he was greater
Than Tycho Brahe or Erra Pater;
For he, by geometric scale,
Could take the size of pots of ale;
Resolve by sines and tangents, straight,
If bread or butter wanted weight;
And wisely tell what hour o' th' day
The clock does strike, by algebra.

4. RHYME OF THE RAIL.

Singing through the forests,
    Rattling over ridges,
Shooting under arches,
    Rumbling over bridges;
Whizzing through the mountains,
    Buzzing o'er the vale—
Bless me! this is pleasant,
    Riding on the rail!

5. SUMMER.

There's a dance of *lèaves* in that aspen *bòwer*,
  There's a titter of *wìnds* in that beechen *trèe*,
There's a smile on the *frùit*, and a smile on the *flòwer*,
  And a *làugh* from the *bróok* that runs to the *sèa!*
BRYANT.

6. SUMMER.

And what is so rare as a day in June?
  Then, if ever, come perfect days;
Then Heaven tries the earth if it be in tune,
  And over it softly her warm ear lays;
Whether we look or whether we listen,
We hear life murmur or see it glisten;
Every clod feels a stir of might,
  An instinct within it that reaches and towers,
And, groping blindly above it for light,
  Climbs to a soul in grass and flowers.
LOWELL.

7. SEA-WEED.

When descends on the Atlantic
    The gigantic
Storm-wind of the equinox,
Landward in his wrath he scourges
    The toiling surges,
Laden with sea-weed from the rocks:

Ever drifting, drifting, drifting
    On the shining
Currents of the restless main;
Till in sheltered coves, and reaches
    Of sandy beaches,
All have found repose again.   LONGFELLOW.

8. THE DRUM.

At a distance, down the street, making music with their feet,
Came the soldiers from the wars, all embellished with their scars,
To the tapping of a drum, of a drum;
To the pounding and the sounding of a drum!
Of a drum, of a drum, of a drum! drum, drum, drum!

9. COMPENSATION.

Experienced men of the world know very well that it is best to pay scot and lot as they go along, and that a man often pays dear for a small frugality. The borrower runs in his own debt. Has a man gained anything who has received a hundred favors and rendered none? Has he gained by borrowing, through indolence or cunning, his neighbor's wares, or horses, or money? There arises on the deed the instant acknowledgment of benefit on the one part, and of debt on the other; that is, of superiority and inferiority. The transaction remains in the memory of himself and his neighbor; and every new transaction alters, according to its nature, their relation to each other. He may soon come to see that he had better have broken his own bones than to have ridden in his neighbor's coach, and that "the highest price he can pay for a thing is to ask for it."
   EMERSON.

II. The Impassioned Radical.

1. The impassioned radical stress falls on the ear with abrupt, explosive force, like the beat of a bass drum. A good illustration of extreme radical stress is afforded by loud, explosive laughter.

2. The impassioned radical marks positive assertion, strong determination, and authoritative command. It is the abrupt stress of courage, boldness, anger, and hatred.

3. The absence of radical stress, so common in untrained readers and speakers, indicates feebleness, indecision, and confusion or timidity. A lack of radical stress may kill the most impressive sentiments, or may transform a gay, joyous, lively piece of composition into dull, joyless, or even melancholy expression.

4. Carried to excess, however, the radical stress becomes the mark of egotism, dogmatism, and undue self-assertion. It often characterizes the rant of the stump speaker who "tears a passion into tatters."

5. There is little tendency in school to excess of radical stress: on the contrary, there is generally a lack of it.

Impassioned Radical Stress Drill.

1. Repeat, three times, with abrupt, explosive force, the long vocals, ā, ē, ī, ō, ū.

2. Repeat, in the same manner, the following: ale, arm, all, ooze.

3. Repeat, four times, with explosive laughter: ha! ha! ha! ho! ho! ho! haw! haw! haw!

4. Tramp, tramp, tramp, the boys are marching.

5. *Awàke! arìse!* or be *forèver fàllen!*

6. Up, *dràwbridge*, groom, what, warder, *hò!*
Let the *portcùllis* fall.

7. To *àrms!* to *àrms!* to *àrms!* they cry.

8. Shoulder *àrms!* forward *màrch!* *hàlt!* Right about *fàce, màrch!*

9. Hold! hold! for your lives!

10. Back to thy punishment, false fugitive.

11. He was *struck*, struck like a *dog*.

12. Up! comrades, up! in Rokeby's halls
Ne'er be it said our courage falls.

13. Send out more horses! skirr the country round.
Awake! Awake!

14. Ring the alarum bell! Murder and treason!
Malcolm! awake! Malcolm! Banquo!

15. THE CLANSMAN TO HIS CHIEF.

"*Macláine!* you've scourged me like a *hòund;*—
You should have *strùck* me to the *gròund.*
You should have played a *chìeftain's* part;—
You should have *stàbbed* me to the *heàrt.*

"You should have *crùshed* me unto *dèath;*
But here I *swcár* with living *breáth,*
That for this *wróng* which you have dóne,
I'll wreak my vengeance on your *sòn.*

"I *scórn* forgiveness, haughty màn!
You've *ìnjured* me before the *clàn;*
And naught but *blóod* shall wipe away
The *shâme* I have *endùred* to-day."   MACKAY.

16. ALEXANDRA.

Wèlcome her, thunders of fort and of flèet!
Wèlcome her, thundering cheer of the strèet!
Wèlcome her, all things useful and swèet;
Scatter the *blòssoms* under her fèet!
Brèak, happy lànd, into earlier flòwers!
Make mùsic, O bìrd, in the new budded bòwers!

Blazon your mottoes | of blessing and pràyer!
Wèlcome her, *wélcome* her, all that is oùrs!
Wárble, O bùgle; and trúmpet, blàre!
Flàgs, flutter out | upon tùrrets and tòwers!
Flàmes, on the windy headland flàre!
Utter your *jùbilee*, stèeple and *spìre!*
Clásh, ye *bèlls*, in the merry March àir!
Flásh, ye *cìties*, in rivers of fìre!
Rush to the *ròof*, sudden ròcket, and hígher |
Melt into the *stàrs* for the land's *desìre!*

TENNYSON.

17. THE OLD CONTINENTALS.

And *grummer, grummer, grummer,*
Rolled the roll of the drummer,
   Through the morn!

And *louder, louder,* LOUDER,
Cracked the loud gunpowder,
   Cracked amain!

Then *higher, higher,* HIGHER,
Burned the old-fashioned fire
   Through the ranks!

And *rounder,* ROUNDER, ROUNDER,
Roared the iron six-pounder,
   Hurling death!

18. THE BRAZEN BELLS.

Hear the loud *alárum* bells,—
   Brazen bells!
What a tale of *terror*, now, their turbulency tells!
   In the startled ear of night
   How they scream out their affright!
     Too much horrified to speak,
     They can only shriek, shriek,
       Out of tune,

In the clamorous appealing to the mercy of the fire,
In a mad expostulation with the deaf and frantic fire
    Leaping higher, *higher*, HIGHER,
      With a desperate desire,
    And a resolute endeavor,
Now—*now* to sit or never,
By the side of the pale-face moon.
    O the bells, bells, bells,
      What a tale their terror tells
        Of despair!
  How they *clang* and *clash* and *roar !*
  What a *horror* they outpour
On the bosom of the palpitating air!
    Yet the ear, it fully knows,
      By the twanging
      And the clanging,
  How the danger ebbs and flows;
  Yet the ear distinctly tells,
    In the jangling
    And the wrangling,
  How the danger sinks and swells,
By the sinking or the swelling in the anger of the bells—
    Of the bells—
  Of the bells, bells, bells, bells,
    Bells, bells, bells—
In the clamor and clangor of the bells!   POE.

19. INDEPENDENCE.

Read this Declaration | at the head of the *àrmy:* every *swòrd* | will be drawn from its *scàbbard*, and the solemn vow | úttered, to *maintáin* it, or to *pèrish* | on the bed of *hònor*. Publish it from the *pùlpit; relìgion* | will *appróve* it, and the love of *religious líberty* | will cling *round* it, resolved ⸮ to *stánd* with it, or *fàll* with it. *Send* it to the *public hàlls; procláim* it thère; let *thĕm* | hear it, who heard the first roar | of the enemy's cánnon; let th*ĕ*m | see it, who saw their *brŏthers* and their *sŏns* | fall on the field of *Bunker Hill*, and in the streets of *Lèxington* and *Còncord*, and the *very wàlls* | will cry out | in its *suppòrt*. WEBSTER.

20. FREEDOM.

Many years long gone, I took my stand by *Frèedom*, and *where* | in my earliest youth | my *féet* | were plánted, *thére* | my *mánhood* | and my *àge* shall march. And for *óne*, I am not *ashámed* of Frèedom. I know her *pŏwer*. I *rejŏice* | in her *májesty*. I *wálk* | beneath her *bànner*. I *glóry* | in her *strèngth*. I have seen *Frèedom* | in history, *agáin* and *agáin*; with mine own *éyes* | I have watched her | agáin and agáin | *struck dówn* | on a hundred chosen *fiélds* of *bàttle*.

I have seen her *friénds* | fly *fròm* her; I have seen *fóes* | gather *rŏund* her; I have seen them | *bind* her to the *stàke*; I have seen them give her *áshes* to the *winds—regáthering* them agáin | that they might scatter them | yet *more widely*; but when her foes | turned to *exúlt*, I have seen her *agàin* | meet them | *fáce* to *fàce, respléndent in compléte stéel*, and brandishing | in her strong right *hánd* | a *flaming swórd, réd with insúfferable lìght*.

And I *take còurage*. The *pèople* | gather rŏund her. The *Genius of America* | will at last | lead her *sóns* to Frèedom. BAKER.

21. PERORATION OF BUZFUZ :—BARDELL vs. PICKWICK.

[*The following is an example of the bombastic style of ranting oratory, which is a burlesque of true art.*]

Of this man I will say little. The subject presents but few attractions; and *Í*, gentlemen, am not the *màn*, nor are *yoú*, gèntlemen, the *mèn*, to delight in the contemplation of revolting heártlessness, and of *systemátic villany*. I say *systemátic* villany, gèntlemen; and when

I say *systemătic* villainy, let me tell the defendant Pickwick, if he be in coúrt, as I am informed he *ís*, that it would have been more *děcent* in him, more becoming, if he had stopped *awáy*. Let me tell him, *fùrther*, that a counsel, in the discharge of his dùty, is neither to be intímidated, nor búllied, nor *put dòwn;* and that any attempt to do either the *óne* or the *òther* will recoil on the head of the attémpter, be he *pláintiff* or be he *defèndant,* be his name Píckwick, or Nóakes, or Stóakes, or Stíles, or Brówn, or Thòmpson.

But Píckwick, géntlemen, Píckwick, the ruthless destroyer of this domestic oasis in the desert of Goswell stréet,—Píckwick, who has choked up the well, and thrown ashes on the swárd,—Píckwick, who comes before you to-day with his heartless tomáto-sauce and wárming-pans,—Píckwick, still rears his head with unblushing effróntery, and gazes without a *sìgh* on the *rùin* he has made! *Dàmages,* gèntlemen, *hèavy* damages, is the only púnishment with which you can vìsit hìm,—the only *récompense* you can award to my clìent! And for *those dámages* she now appeals to an *enlíghtened,* a *highmìnded,* a *rìght-fèeling,* a *conscièntious,* a *dispàssionate,* a *sỳmpathizing,* a *contèmplative júry* of her *civilízed coùntrymen!*

DICKENS.

II. MEDIAN STRESS.

1. The *median stress* corresponds to the "swell" in music. It is strongest in the middle of a sound or a word. It is adapted to the expression of harmonious and poetic ideas.

2. "It is," says Russell, "the natural utterance of those emotions which allow the intermingling of reflection and sentiment with expression, and which purposely dwell on sound, as a means of enhancing their effect.

3. "This mode of *stress* is one of the most important

in its effect on language, whether in the form of speaking or of reading. Destitute of its ennobling and expansive sound, the recitation of poetry sinks into the style of dry prose, the language of devotion loses its sacredness, the tones of oratory lose their power over the heart.

4. "There is great danger, however, of this natural beauty of vocal expression being converted into a fault by being overdone. The habit recognized under the name of *mouthing* has an excessively increased and prolonged median swell for one of its chief characteristics. In this shape, it becomes a great deformity in utterance,—particularly when combined with what is no infrequent concomitant, the faulty mode of voice known as chanting or singing. Like sweetness among savors, this truly agreeable quality of sound becomes distasteful or disgusting when in the least degree excessive.

5. "The practice of median stress, therefore, requires very close attention. The spirit of poetry and the language of eloquence,—the highest effects of human utterance,—render it indispensable as an accomplishment in elocution. But a chaste and discriminating ear is requisite to decide the just degree of its extent.

6. "Median stress has the form of *effusive* utterance in *sublime, solemn,* and *pathetic* emotions: it becomes *expulsive,* in those which combine *force* with *grandeur,* as in *admiration, courage, authoritative command, indignation, and similar feelings.* But its effect is utterly incompatible with the abruptness of *explosion.* Its comparatively musical character adapts it, with special felicity of effect, to the melody of *verse,* and the natural *swell* of poetic expression."

7. Median stress requires a prolongation of vowel and liquid sounds; it is a contrast to the abruptness of the radical stress. It prevails in combination with "pure tone" and the "orotund."

Median Stress Drill.

1. Repeat, three times, the long vocals, ā, ē, ī, ō, ū: (1) With moderate force and effusive median stress. (2) With expulsive median stress. (3) With increased force and expulsive median stress.

2. In the same manner repeat, four times, the vocals, ĕ, ā, ŭ, a, ō, o.

3. Count from one to twenty, with soft force and effusive median stress; with loud force and expulsive median stress.

4. Repeat, three times, the following words with expulsive median stress: all, call, ball, tall, hall, pall.

5. Repeat four times, in monotone, with full swell on the prolonged *l*, the following: bēlls, bēlls, bēlls, bēlls, bēlls.

Examples of Median Stress.

1. Roll on, thou deep and dark blue ocean, roll!

2. Ye winds, ye unseen currents of the air,
   Softly ye played a few brief hours ago.

3. The curfew tolls the knell of parting day.

4. Hail! holy light, offspring of heaven, first-born.

5. The rivers, lakes, and ocean, all stood still.

6. Sweet Auburn! loveliest village of the plain.

7. Was it the chime of a tiny bell
   That came so sweet to my dreaming ear?
   Like the silvery tones of a fairy's shell
   That he winds on the beach, so mellow and clear.

8. Ring out the old, ring in the new,
   Ring, happy bells, across the snow.

9. O Lord, thou art clothed with honor and majesty.

10. And where her sweetest theme she chose,
A soft, responsive voice was heard at every close,
And Hope, enchanted, smiled and waved her golden hair.

11. These are thy glorious works, parent of good,
Almighty! Thine this universal frame.

12. Then the angel threw up his glorious hands to the heaven of heavens, saying: "End is there none to the universe of God. Lo! also, there is no beginning."

13.   Peal out evermore,
    Peal as ye pealed of yore,
Brave old bells, on each Sabbath day.

14. I heard the bells on Christmas Day
Their old, familiar carols play,
    And wild and sweet,
    The words repeat
Of peace on earth, good-will to men!

15. Thou, too, sail on, O Ship of State!
Sail on, O Union, strong and great!

16. These struggling tides of life that seem
    In wayward, aimless course to tend,
Are eddies of the mighty stream
    That rolls to its appointed end.   BRYANT.

17. From the wall into the sky,
    From the roof along the spire:
Ah, the souls of those that die
    Are but sunbeams lifted higher.   LONGFELLOW.

18. So shall our voice of sovereign choice
    Swell the deep bass of duty done,
And strike the key of time to be,
    When God and man shall speak as one!
                                      WHITTIER.

19. Ah, distinctly I remember, it was in the bleak December,
And each separate dying ember wrought its ghost upon the floor.
Eagerly I wished the morrow: vainly I had sought to borrow
From my books surcease of sorrow—sorrow for the lost Lenore—
For the rare and radiant maiden whom the angels name Lenore—
Nameless here for evermore. POE.

20. O Babie, dainty Babie Bell,
How fair she grew from day to day!
What woman-nature filled her eyes—
What poetry within them lay!
Those deep and tender twilight eyes,
So full of meaning, pure and bright,
As if she yet stood in the light
Of those oped gates of Paradise. ALDRICH.

21. The splendor falls on castle walls
And snowy summits old in story:
The long light shakes across the lakes,
And the wild cataract leaps in glory.
Blow, bugle, blow; set the wild echoes flying;
Blow, bugle; answer, echoes—dying, dying, dying.
TENNYSON.

22. By the rude bridge that arched the flood,
Their flag to April's breeze unfurled,
Here once the embattled farmers stood,
And fired the shot heard round the world.
EMERSON.

23. Down the dark future, through long generations,
The echoing sounds grow fainter, and then cease;
And like a bell, with solemn, sweet vibrations,
I hear once more the voice of Christ say, "Peace!"

Peace! and no longer from its brazen portals
  The blast of War's great organ shakes the skies!
But beautiful as songs of the immortals,
  The holy melodies of love arise. LONGFELLOW.

24. Youth longs and manhood strives, but age remembers—
  Sits by the raked-up ashes of the past;
Spreads its thin hands above the whitening embers
  That warm its creeping life-blood till the last.

But O my gentle sisters! O my brothers!
  These thick-sown snow-flakes hint of toil's release;
These feebler pulses bid me leave to others
  The tasks once welcome—evening asks for peace.

Time claims his tribute; silence now is golden;
  Let me not vex the too long-suffering lyre;
Though to your love untiring still beholden,
  The curfew tells me—*cover up the fire.* HOLMES.

25. O, a wonderful stream is the river Time,
  As it runs through the realm of tears,
With a faultless rhythm and a musical rhyme,
And a boundless sweep and surge sublime,
  As it blends with the Ocean of Years. TAYLOR.

26. THE WEDDING BELLS.

[*Read this stanza with pure tone, middle pitch, slow movement, and orotund quality.*]

Hear the mellow *wèdding*-bells—*gólden* bells!
What a world of *háppiness* their harmony foretèlls!
Through the balmy air of nìght, how they *ring out* their delìght!
    From the molten-golden nótes,
      All in túne,
    What a liquid ditty floats
To the turtle-dove that listens, while she glóats
      On the mòon!

Oh, from out the sounding célls,
What a gush of *eùphony* voluminously wèlls!
How it swells, how it dwells
On the Future! How it tells of the rapture that impels
To the swinging and the ringing of the bēlls, bēlls, bēlls,
Of the bēlls, bēlls, bēlls, bēlls, bēlls, bēlls, bēlls—
To the rhyming and the chiming of the bēlls. POE.

27. INVOCATION TO LIGHT.

[*Read the following selection with orotund quality, slow movement, and strong force.*]

Hail! holy Light—offspring of Heaven, first-born,
Or of the Eternal, co-eternal beam;
May I express thee unblamed? since God is light,
And never but in unapproachéd light,
Dwelt from eternity—dwelt then in thee,
Bright effluence of bright Essence increate!
Or hear'st thou, rather, pure ethereal stream,
Whose fountain who shall tell?—Before the sun,
Before the heavens thou wert, and, at the voice
Of God, as with a mantle, didst invest
The rising world of waters, dark and deep,
Won from the void and formless infinite. MILTON.

28. LIBERTY OF THE PRESS.

1. The liberty of the press is the highest safeguard to all free government. Ours could not exist without it. It is like a great, exulting, and abounding river. It is fed by the dews of heaven, which distill their sweetest drops to form it. It gushes from the rill, as it breaks from the deep caverns of the earth. It is augmented by a thousand affluents, that dash from the mountain top, to separate again into a thousand bounteous and irrigating streams around.

2. On its broad bosom it bears a thousand barks. There genius spreads its purpling sail. There poetry dips its silver oar. There art, invention, discovery,

science, morality, religion, may safely and securely float. It wanders through every land. It is a genial, cordial source of thought and inspiration, whatever it touches, whatever it surrounds. Upon its borders there grows every flower of grace, and every fruit of truth. BAKER.

29. FROM THE BOOK OF PSALMS.

Bless the Lord, O my soul. O Lord my God, Thou art very great; Thou art clothed with honor and majesty: who coverest thyself with light as with a garment; who stretchest out the heavens like a curtain; who layeth the beams of His chambers in the waters; who maketh the clouds His chariot; who walketh upon the wings of the wind; who laid the foundations of the earth, that it should not be removed forever.

30. OSSIAN'S ADDRESS TO THE SUN.

O thou that rollest above, round as the shield of my fathers! whence are thy beams, O sun! thy everlasting light? Thou comest forth in thy awful beauty; the stars hide themselves in the sky; the moon, cold and pale, sinks in the western wave. But thou thyself movest alone: who can be a companion of thy course?

III. VANISHING STRESS.

1. The *vanishing* or terminal stress is used when the force of voice hangs upon the final part of a word. It corresponds to the *crescendo* in music. It is a form of stress expressive of very strong emphasis, and is often combined with the rising or falling circumflex.

2. Used with a moderate degree of force, this stress is applied in the expression of petulance, of peevishness, of impatience, of willfulness, and of querulous complaint; combined with strong force, it is applied to express persistent determination, astonishment, amazement, and horror.

3. Concerning the use of this stress, Prof. Russell remarks: "Like all other forms of impassioned utterance which are strongly marked in the usages of natural habit, this property of voice is indispensable to appropriate elocution, whether in speaking or reading. Without 'vanishing stress,' declamation will sometimes lose its manly energy of determined will, and become feeble song to the ear. High-wrought resolution can never be expressed without it. Even the language of protest, though respectful in form, needs the aid of the right degree of vanishing stress, to intimate its sincerity and its firmness of determination, as well as its depth of conviction.

4. "But when we extend our views to the demands of lyric and dramatic poetry, in which high-wrought emotion is so abundant an element of effect, the full command of this property of voice, as the natural utterance of extreme passion, becomes indispensable to true, natural, and appropriate style."

EXAMPLES.

[*The italicized words have the vanishing stress, and are marked with the circumflex inflection.*]

1. I know we do *nôt* mean to submit. We never *shâll* submit.

2. Earth may hide, waves engulf, fire consûme us,
But they *shâll* not to *slâvery* doom us.

3. I'll have my *bônd;* I *will* not hear thee spêak:
I'll have my *bônd:* and therefore speak no *môre*.

4. But they *shâll* go to school. Don't tell me they *shŏuldn't*. (You are so *ăggravating*, Caudle, you'd spoil the temper of an *ângel!*) They *shâll* go to school: mark *thăt!* and if they get their *dêaths* of cold, it's not *mў* fault; *Ĭ didn't lend the umbrĕlla*.

5. "Be that word our sign of parting, bird or *fiênd*," I
shrieked, upstarting;

"Get thee *báck* into the tempest, and the night's
   Plutonian shòre!
Lèave no black plume as a token of that *lìe* thy
   soul hath spoken!
Lèave my loneliness *unbròken! quìt* the bust above
   my *dòor!*
Take thy *béak* from out my *héart*, and take thy form
   from off my *dôor!*"
   Quoth the Raven, "Nēvērmōre."

6. FROM GRATTAN'S SPEECH.

Here I stand for impeachment or trial. I *dáre* accusation! I *defý* the honorable gentleman! I defy the *gôvernment!* I defy their *whŏle phálanx! Let them come fórth!*

7. FROM WEBSTER.

On such occasions, I will place myself on the *extreme bóundary* of my right, and bid *defiance* to the arm that would push me from it.

8. THE SEMINOLE'S REPLY.

I *lŏathe* ye in my bosom,
   I *scôrn* ye with mine eye,
I'll taunt ye with my latest *bréath*,
   And *fight* ye till I *dìe*. PATTEN.

9. RIENZI.

I come not here to *tálk*. Ye know too well
The story of our *thrálldom*. We are *sláves!*
The bright sun rises to his course and lights
A *ráce* of slaves! He sets, and his last beam
Fálls on a slave. MITFORD.

10. BRUTUS TO CASSIUS.

Frèt, till your proud heart *breàk;*
Go, show your *sláves* how choleric you are,
And make your bondsmen tremble. Must *I* budge?

Must *I* observe *yŏu?* Must *I* stand and *croŭch*
Under your testy *hŭmor?* By the *gôds,*
You shall *digést* the venom of your spleen,
Though it do *splĭt* you; for, from this day forth,
I'll use you for my *mĭrth,* yea, for my *láughter,*
When you are *wáspish.*   SHAKESPEARE.

IV. THOROUGH STRESS.

Thorough or *through* stress corresponds to the organ tone in music. The force is powerful enough to pervade an entire word or sound — the beginning, the middle, and the end. It is indicated thus: (=).

Thorough stress prevails in vehement declamation and impassioned oratory when the speaker is under the sway of intense excitement. It is also used in calling or shouting, when the voice is rolled out in a full and steady stream.

Carried to excess, this stress is characteristic of rant, bombast, and the worst faults of untrained speakers.

EXAMPLES.

1. Vanguard! to right and left the front unfold.

2. Peal! peal! peal!
   Bells of brass and bells of steel.

3. "To all the truth we tell! we tell!"
   Shouted in ecstasies a bell.

4. And like a silver clarion rung,
   "*Excelsior.*"

5. Advance your standards! draw your willing swords.

6. Forward the light brigade!

7. Clang! clang! clang! the massive anvils rang.

8. "Ship *ahoy!* ship *ahoy!*" shouted the captain.

9. Shoulder—*arms!* For*ward march!* *Halt!*

10. *Charge* for the guns! *Charge! Charge!*

11. Then rose the awful cry, "*Fire! fire! fire!*"

12. *Halloo!* ho-o-o-o! come here! *Halloo!*

13. *Hurrah! hurrah!* for the fiery fort is ours;
Victory! Victory! Victory!

14. Liberty! freedom! Tyranny is dead;
Run hence, proclaim, cry it about the streets!

15. Rejoice, ye men of Angiers! ring your bells;
King John, your king and England's, doth approach.
Open your gates, and give the victors way!

16. "O, spare my child, my joy, my pride!
O, give me back my child!" she cried;
"*My child! my child!*" with sobs and tears,
She shrieked upon his callous ears.

17. "Nine," by the cathedral clock!
Chill the air with rising damps;
Drearily from block to block
In the gloom the bell-man tramps—
"*Child lost! Child lost!
Blue eyes, curly hair,
Pink dress—child lost!*"

18. Body of turkey, head of owl,
Wings a-droop like a rained-on fowl,
Feathered and ruffled in every part,
Skipper Ireson stood in the cart.
Scores of women, old and young,
Strong of muscle, and glib of tongue,
Pushed and pulled up the rocky lane,
Shouting and singing the shrill refrain:
"*Here's Flud Oirson, fur his horrd horrt,
Torr'd an' futherr'd an' corr'd in a corrt,
By the women o' Morble'cad!*"

SCHOOL ELOCUTION.

19. FITZ-JAMES'S DEFIANCE.

Come óne, come àll! this róck shall fly
From its firm base as soon as Ì. Scott.

20. THE AMERICAN FLAG.

Flag of the free heart's hópe and hòme!
 By angel hands | to vàlor given;
Thy stars | have lit the welkin dóme,
 And all thy húes | were born in hèaven.
Forèver float | that standard shèet!
 Where breathes the fóe | but falls befòre us,
With Frèedom's soil | beneath our féet,
 And Freedom's bánner | streaming ò'er us.! Drake.

21. MOLOCH.

He called so loud, that all the hollow deep
Of hell resounded.
  "Prínces! Pótentates!
Wàrriors! the flower of héaven, once yoúrs, now lòst,
If such astonishment as thìs can seize |
Etérnal spìrits; or have ye chosen this place
To rest your wearied virtue, for the éase | ye find |
To slumber here, as in the vales of hèaven?
Or | in this abject pósture | have you sworn |
To adòre the Cònqueror, who now beholds |
Cherub and seraph | rolling in the flood,
With scattered árms and ènsigns; till, anon,
His swift pursuers, from heaven's gates | discern |
The advántage, and descénding, trèad us dòwn |
Thus drōoping; or with linked thúnderbolts |
Transfìx us to | the bottom of this gùlf?
Awàke! arìse! or be foréver fàllen!" Milton.

22. PERORATION OF WEBSTER'S REPLY TO HAYNE.

The scene in the Senate Chamber of the United States, as Webster delivered this peroration, is thus described by C. W. March:
  The exulting rush of feeling with which he went through the

peroration threw a glow over his countenance, like inspiration—eye, brow, each feature, every line of his face seemed touched as with a celestial fire. The swell and roll of his voice struck upon the ears of the spell-bound audience, in deep and melodious cadence, as waves upon the shore of the far-sounding sea. The Miltonic grandeur of his words was the fit expression of his thought and raised his hearers up to his theme. His voice, exerted to its utmost power, penetrated every recess and corner of the Senate—penetrated even the ante-rooms and stair-ways, as he pronounced in the deepest tones of pathos these words of solemn significance:

I have not allowed myself, sir, to look *beyŏnd* the Union, to see what might lie hidden in the dark recess *behĭnd*. I have not coolly weighed the chances of *preserving lĭberty* when the bonds that unite us *togéther* shall be *broken asúnder*. I have not accustomed myself to hang over the *precipice of disúnion*, to see whether, with my short sight, I can fathom the depth of the *abýss belów;* nor could I regard him as a safe *cóunselor* in the affairs of *this góvernment* whose thoughts should be mainly bent on considering, *not* how the Union may be *best presĕrved*, but how *tólerable* might be the condition of the people when it shall be *brŏken up* and *destrŏyed*. While the *Union* lasts, we have hĭgh, excĭting, *grătifying* prospects spread out before us, for us and our children. Beyond *thăt* I seek not to penetrate the veil. God grant that, in my day at least, *that cúrtain may not rĭse!* *Gòd grànt* that on *mỳ vĭsion* never may be opened *what lies behĭnd!* When my eyes shall be turned to *behóld*, for the last tíme, the sun in *héaven*, may I *nòt* see him shining on the broken and dishonored fragments of a once *glorious Union';* on States dissévered, discórdant, *bellĭgerent;* on a land rent with civil *feŭds*, or drenched, it may be, in *fratérnal blóod!* Let their last feeble and lingering *glánce*, rather, behold the *gorgeous énsign* of the *repúblic*, now *known* and *honored* throughout the *éarth*, still *full high advánced*, its arms and trophies streaming in their *original lúster*, not a *strĭpe erásed* or *pollŭted*, nor a single *stȧr obscúred;* bearing for its motto, *nȯ* such *mĭserable interrógatory* as " What is all this *wŏrth?*" nor those *ŏther* words of *delŭsion* and folly, " Liberty *fĭrst*, and Union *ȧfterwards;* but *ėverywhere, spread all over* in characters of *living lĭght, blazing on all its ample fŏlds*, as they float over the *séa* and over the *lȧnd*, and in *every wĭnd* under the whole *héavens*, that *ŏther* sentiment, dear to *èvery trúe Américan héart*—Liberty *and* Union, *nȯw* and *forèver, óne* and *insèparable.*

23. PERORATION OF BURKE'S SPEECH ON THE IMPEACHMENT OF WARREN HASTINGS.

Of this famous speech Macaulay says : "The energy and pathos of the great orator extorted expressions of unwonted admiration from all ; and, for a moment, seemed to pierce even the resolute heart of the defendant. The ladies in the galleries, unaccustomed to such displays of eloquence, excited by the solemnity of the occasion, and perhaps not unwilling to display their taste and sensibility, were in a state of uncontrollable emotion. Handkerchiefs were pulled out ; smelling-bottles were handed round ; hysterical sobs and screams were heard, and some were even carried out in fits. At length, the orator concluded. Raising his voice, till the old arches of Irish oak resounded, he said :

" I impeach him in the name of the *Commons of Great Brĭtain* in *Parliament assèmbled*, whose parliamentary trust he has *abŭsed.*

" I impeach him in the name of the Commons of Great Britain, whose *national chȧracter* he has dishónored.

" I impeach him in the name of the *people of Ĭndia*, whose *lȧws, rĭghts*, and *lĭberties* he has *subvèrted.*

" I impeach him in the name of the people of India, whose *prŏperty* he has destroyed, whose *coùntry* he has laid waste and *dèsolate.*

" I impeach him in the name of *human nȧture ĭtself*, which he has cruelly *oùtraged, ĭnjured*, and *oppréssed*, in both séxes. And I impeach him *in the nȧme and by the vírtue* of those *etèrnal làws of jùstice*, which ought equally to pervade every *àge*, *condìtion*, *rànk*, and *situátion*, in the *wòrld*."

V. COMPOUND STRESS.

Compound stress is a combination of the *radical* and the vanishing stress upon the same word. Indeed, it may be considered as a very emphatic form of the emotional circumflex inflection. It is applied, like the circumflex, to express extreme astonishment, irony, sarcasm, mockery, and contempt. It is the stress of extreme emotion.

In the following examples, the words upon which the compound stress falls are marked with the circumflex inflection.

EXAMPLES.

1. Repeat, three times, with extreme astonishment: *ăh ! indĕed !*

2. Repeat, three times, with strong emphasis and the falling circumflex: êve, âle, ârm, âll, ôld, ôoze.

3. Repeat, with strong force and the rising circumflex: ā̌, ē̌, ī̌, ō̌, ū̌ ; the same with the falling circumflex.

4. *Bănished* from *Rŏme !* What's banished but set free
From daily contact of the things I *lôathe ?*
He *dâres* not touch a *hâir* of Catiline.

5. KING JOHN.

Gŏne to be *mărried ! gŏne* to swear a *pĕace !*
Fălse blood to false blood *jŏined ! gŏne* to be *friĕnds !*
Shall Louis have *Blănche*, and Blanche these *prŏvinces ?*
SHAKESPEARE.

6. SPARTACUS.

Is Sparta *dĕad ?* Is the old Grecian spirit *frŏzen* that you do *croŭch* and *cŏwer* like a belabored *hoŭnd* beneath his master's *lăsh ?*

7. JULIUS CÆSAR.

Must I *bŭdge?*
Must *I* observe *yŏu?* Must *I* stand and crouch
Under your testy *hŭmor?* By the *gôds,*
You shall digest the venom of your spleen
Though it do *splĭt* you; for, from this day forth,
I'll use you for my *mĭrth,* yea, for my *láughter*
When you are *wáspish!*   SHAKESPEARE.

8. FROM CICERO'S ACCUSATION OF VERRES.

Is it come to *thĭs?* Shall an inferior *măgistrate,* a *góvernor,* who holds his whole power from the Roman *pĕople,* in a Roman *prŏvince,* within sight of Italy, *bĭnd, scŏurge, tŏrture* with *fĭre* and red-hot plates of *ĭron,* and at last put to the infamous death of the *crŏss,* a *Rŏman cĭtizen?*

VI. INTERMITTENT STRESS, OR THE TREMOR.

1. *Intermittent* stress, or the tremor, is the tremulous force of voice upon a sound or a word. The tremor is characteristic of the tottering feebleness of old age, of the weakness of sickness, or of the tones of a person shivering and trembling with cold, or with fear.

2. It naturally occurs in the utterance of fear, grief, joy, sobbing, and laughter, when the emotions are so strong as to enfeeble the flow of breath. In extreme pathos, the voice often trembles or quickens with emotion.

3. This form of stress must be very delicately applied, for, in excess, it becomes ridiculous.

4. Concerning the appropriate application of this form of stress, Prof. Russell remarks: "In the reading or the recitation of lyric and dramatic poetry, this function of voice is often required for full, vivid, and touching expression. Without its appeals to sympathy, and its peculiar power over the heart, many of the most beau-

tiful and touching passages of Shakespeare and Milton become dry and cold. Like the *tremolo* of the accomplished vocalist in operatic music, it has a charm, for the absence of which nothing can atone—since nature suggests it as the genuine utterance of the most delicate and thrilling emotion.

5. "The perfect command of tremor requires often-repeated practice on elements, syllables, and words, as well as on appropriate passages of impassioned language."

Drill on Tremor.

1. Inhale; give the tremulous sound of long *a*, thus: ā—ā—ā—ā, etc., prolonged until the breath is exhausted.

2. In a similar manner, take each of the remaining long vowel sounds, ē, ī, ō, ū.

3. Take a similar drill on ä; on ạ; on ọ.

Examples of Tremor.

1. OLD AGE.

Pity the sorrows of a poor old man,
  Whose trembling limbs have borne him to your door,
Whose days are dwindled to the shortest span;—
  Oh! give relief; and Heaven will bless your store!

2. GAFFER GRAY.

"Ho! why dost thou shiver and shake, Gaffer Gray?
  And why does thy nose look so blue?"
  "'Tis the weather that's cold,
   'Tis I'm grown very old,
And my doublet is not very new; Well-a-day!"
WORDSWORTH.

3. OLD AGE.

And still there came that silver tone,
  From the shriveled lips of the toothless crone—

Let me never forget to my dying day
The tone or the burden of her lay—
"*Passing away! passing away!*" PIERPONT.

4. LAUGHING UTTERANCE.

1. A fool, a fool, I met a fool in the forest;
A motley fool, a miserable varlet.

2. Oh! then I see Queen Mab hath been with you.

5. SOBBING.

So Mary said, and Dora hid her face
By Mary. There was silence in the room;
And all at once the old man burst in sobs:—
"*I have been to blame—to blame! I have killed my son!
I have killed him—but I loved him—my dear son!
May God forgive me!—I have been to blame.
Kiss me, my children!*" TENNYSON'S *Dora*.

6. GOODY BLAKE AND HARRY GILL.

She prayed, her withered hand uprearing,
  While Harry held her by the arm—
"*God! who art never out of hearing,
  O may he never more be warm!*"
The cold, cold moon above her head,
  Thus on her knees did Goody pray:
Young Harry heard what she had said,
  And icy cold he turned away.

No word to any man he utters,
  Abed or up, to young or old;
But ever to himself he mutters,
  "*Poor Harry Gill is very cold.*"
Abed or up, by night or day,
  His teeth may chatter, chatter still:
Now think, ye farmers all, I pray,
  Of Goody Blake and Harry Gill. WORDSWORTH.

7. RIP VAN WINKLE.

The honest man could contain himself no longer. He caught his daughter and her child in his arms. "*I am your father!*" cried he, "*young Rip Van Winkle once— old Rip Van Winkle now!—Does nobody know poor Rip Van Winkle?*"

IRVING.

8. ENOCH ARDEN.

"Enoch, poor man, was cast away and lost."
He, shaking his gray head pathetically,
Repeated muttering, "*Cast away and lost;*"
Again in deeper inward whispers, "*Lost!*"

TENNYSON.

9. LITTLE GRETCHEN.

They lifted her up tearfully, they shuddered as they said,
"It was a bitter, bitter night! the child is frozen dead."
The angels sang their greeting for one more redeemed from sin.
Men said, "It was a bitter night; would no one let her in?"

RECAPITULATION OF STRESS.

1. *The radical is the stress of animation, of earnestness, of assertion, of command, and of passion.*

2. *The median is the stress of sentiment, of pathos and tenderness, of awe, reverence, sublimity, and enthusiasm.*

3. *Vanishing stress is the stress of very strong emphasis, of contempt and disdain, of willfulness, petulance, and impatience.*

4. *Thorough stress is the stress of impassioned oratory, and intense dramatic expression.*

5. *The compound is the stress of the circumflex inflection, of irony, sarcasm, contempt, and astonishment.*

6. *The tremor is the stress of feebleness, of childishness, and of grief.*

STRESS DRILL.

1. *Radical.* Attention, *all*.
2. *Median.* All in one mighty sepulcher.
3. *Vanishing.* All, all is *lost!* All *lost!*
4. *Thorough.* Come *one*, come *all!*
5. *Compound.* What ăll, are they ăll lost?
6. *Intermittent.* All my sons are *dead, all, all dead!*

EXAMPLES OF STRESS.

RADICAL.
Hear the loud alarum bells—*brázen* bells!

MEDIAN.
Hear the mellow wedding bells—*gólden* bells!

VANISHING.
I'll have my *bónd*, and therefore speak no more.

THOROUGH.
Awàke! *Arise!* or be *foréver fàllen.*

COMPOUND.
Gŏne to be *mărried! gŏne* to *sweăr* a *peăce!*

INTERMITTENT.
Pity the sorrows of a poor old man
Whose trembling limbs have borne him to your door.

CHAPTER III.

MOVEMENT.

INTRODUCTORY.

1. The three leading divisions of movement, rate, or time, in reading, are slow, moderate, and fast. These distinctions are, for convenience, subdivided as follows: 1. Moderate (corresponding, in music, to *andante*). 2. Fast (*allegro*). 3. Very fast (*presto*). 4. Slow (*adagio*). 5. Very slow (*largo*).

2. Different kinds of prose and verse require different rates of movement, but the general principle that governs all reading or speaking may be stated as follows: *Read slowly enough for your hearers to comprehend, fully and easily, what is read.*

3. *Good extemporaneous speakers generally have a slow and deliberate utterance, because they take time to think what to say. They, also, give their hearers time to think of what is said by the speaker.*

4. The habit of slow reading may be acquired, not by a drawling, hesitating utterance, but by observing rhetorical and grammatical pauses; by prolonging vocal and liquid sounds; and by taking time to think of the meaning of what is read.

5. The general principles governing movement are well expressed in the following extract from Russell's "American School Reader:" "Everything tender, or solemn, plaintive, or grave, should be read with great moderation. Everything humorous or sprightly, every-

thing witty or amusing, should be read in a brisk and lively manner.

6. "Narration should be generally equable and flowing; vehemence, firm and accelerated; anger and joy, rapid; whereas dignity, authority, sublimity, reverence, and awe should, along with deeper tone, assume a slower movement.

7. "The movement should, in every instance, be adapted to the sense, and free from all hurry on the one hand, or drawling on the other.

8. "The pausing, too, should be carefully proportioned to the movement or rate of the voice; and no change of movement from slow to fast, or the reverse, should take place in any clause, unless a change of emotion is implied in the language of the piece."

Movement Drill.

1. Repeat, three times, the long vocals, ā, ē, ī, ō, ū: (1) With low pitch and very slow movement. (2) With middle pitch and slow movement. (3) With moderate movement. (4) With fast movement. (5) With very fast movement.

2. Count from one to twenty: (1) With slow movement. (2) With moderate movement. (3) With fast movement.

3. Repeat, with moderate movement—

    The day is done, and the darkness
      Falls from the wings of night
    As a feather is wafted downwards
      From an eagle in his flight.

I. Moderate Movement.

Moderate movement is the characteristic rate in the reading of didactic, descriptive, or narrative composition, and of the poetry of sentiment.

EXAMPLES.

1. ENGLISH SCENERY.

The great charm, however, of English scenery, is the moral feeling that seems to pervade it. It is associated in the mind with ideas of òrder, of quíet, of sober, well-established prínciples, of hoary úsage, and reverend cùstom. Everything seems to be the growth of ages of regular and peaceful exìstence. The neighboring víllage, with its venerable cóttages, its public gréen, sheltered by trées, under which the forefathers of the present race have spórted; the antique family mánsion, standing apart in some little rural domáin, but looking down with a protecting air on the surrounding scéne; all these common features of English lándscape evince a calm and settled secúrity, a hereditary transmission of home-bred virtues and local attáchments, that speak déeply and tòuchingly for the moral cháracter of the nàtion. IRVING.

2. THE SEASONS IN SWEDEN.

I must not forget the suddenly changing seàsons of the northern clime. There is no long and lingering spríng unfolding leaf and blossom one by óne; no long and lingering aútumn, pompous with many-colored leaves and the glow of Indian súmmers. But wínter and súmmer are wònderful, and pass into each òther. The quail has hardly ceased piping in the córn, when wínter, from the folds of trailing clóuds, sows broadcast over the land, snów, ícicles, and rattling hàil.

The days wane apace. Ere long the sun hardly rises above the horízon, or does not rise at àll. The moon and the stars shine through the dày; only, at noon, they are pale and wàn, and in the southern sky a red, fiery glòw, as of sùnset, burns along the horízon, and then goes òut. And pleasantly, under the silver móon, and under the silent, solemn stárs, ring the steel shoes of the skaters on the frozen sèa, and vòices, and the sound of bèlls. LONGFELLOW.

II. Fast Movement.

Fast, or quick, movement, is the characteristic rate in the expression of mirth, fun, humor, gladness, joy, and haste.

EXAMPLES.

1. PAUL REVERE'S RIDE.

A hurry of *hóofs* in a village strèet,
A shape in the *moonlight*, a bulk in the *dárk*,
And beneath, from the pebbles, in passing, a *spárk*
Struck out by a *stéed* that flies fearless and fléet:
That was *ăll!* And yet, through the gloom and the light,
The fate of a *nàtion was rìding* that night;
And the *spárk* struck out by that steed, in his *flíght*,
Kindled the land into *flàme* with its hèat.   LONGFELLOW.

2. L'ALLEGRO.

    Haste thee, nymph, and bring with thee
Jèst and youthful *Jòllity*,
Qùips, and *crànks*, and wanton *wìles*,
Nòds, and *bècks*, and wreathéd *smíles*
Such as hang on *Hèbe's* cheek,
And love to live in dimple slèek;
Spòrt that wrinkled Care *derìdes*,
And *Làughter* holding both his sides.
Come, and trip it as ye go
On the light fantastic tòe;
And in thy right hand lead with thee
The mountain *nỳmph*, sweet *Lìberty*.   MILTON.

3. ONCE MORE.

"Will I *cŏme?*" That *ĭs* pleasant! I beg to inquire
If the gun that I carry has *éver* missed fìre?
And which was the muster-roll—mention but *ónc*—
That missed your old comrade who carries the gùn!

You see me as always, my hand on the lock,
The cap on the nipple, the hammer full cock.

It is rŭsty, some tell me; I heed not the scŏff;
It is battered and brŭised, but it always goes ôff!
"Is it lŏaded?" I'll bét you! What dôcsn't it hold?
Rammed full to the muzzle with mèmories untòld;
Why, it scares me to fìre, lest the pieces should fly
Like the cànnons that burst on the Fourth of July!
HOLMES.

4. RHYME OF THE RAIL.

Singing through the fórests,
   Rattling over rĭdges,
Shooting under árches,
   Rumbling over brĭdges;
Whizzing through the móuntains,
   Buzzing o'er the vále,
Blèss me! this is pléasant,
   Rĭding on the ráil!
SAXE.

5. THE MAY QUEEN.

You must wake and call me early, call me early, mother dear;
To-morrow 'll be the happiest time of all the glad New Year;
Of all the glad New Year, mother, the maddest, merriest day;
For I'm to be Queen o' the May, mother, I'm to be Queen o' the May.
TENNYSON.

6. THE MESSAGE.

The muster-place is Lanrick mead;
Speed forth the signal! Norman, *speed!*
The summons dread brooks no delay.
Stretch to the race—away! away!
SCOTT.

7. THE SUMMONS.

Come as the winds come, when forests are rended;
Come as the waves come, when navies are stranded.
Faster come, faster come, faster and faster:
Chief, vassal, page, and groom, tenant and master.

Fast they come, fast they come; see how they gather!
Wide waves the eagle plume, blended with heather.
Cast your plaids, draw your blades, forward each man set;
Pibroch of Donuil Dhu, knell for the onset! SCOTT.

8. THE SMILING LISTENER.

Precisely. I see it. You all want to say
That a tear is too sad and a smile is too gay;
You could stand a faint smile, you could manage a sigh,
But you value your ribs, and you don't want to cry.

It's awful to think of—how year after year
With his piece in his pocket he waits for you here;
No matter who's missing, there always is one
To lug out his manuscript, sure as a gun.

III. VERY FAST MOVEMENT.

Very fast movement is expressive of hurry, alarm, confusion, flight, ecstatic joy, and ungovernable rage and fury.

EXAMPLES.

1. MAZEPPA.

Awáy!—awày!—and on we *dàsh!*—
Torrents less rapid and less ràsh.
    Awáy, awày, my steed and I,
Upon the pinions of the *wìnd*,
All *húman* dwellings left behìnd;
    We sped like *méteors* through the *skỳ*,
When with its crackling sound the night
Is chequered with the northern light. BYRON.

2. HURRY.

Sísters! *hènce*, with spurs of *spèed!*
    Each her thundering *fàlchion* wield;
Each bestride her sable *stèed;*
    Hùrry! hurry to the *fièld.*

3. FLIGHT.

Forth from the pass in tumult driven,
Like chaff before the wind of heaven,
    The *àrchery* appeár;
For lífe! for lífe! their flight they plý;
While shriék, and shóut, and báttle-cry,
And pláids and bónnets waving hígh,
And bróadswords flashing to the ský,
    Are maddening in the rèar.   SCOTT.

4. GOOD NEWS.

I sprang to the stìrrup, and Jòris, and hè;
I galloped, Dírck galloped, we galloped all thrèe;
"*Good spèed!*" cried the watch as the gate-bolts undrèw;
"*Spèed!*" echoed the wall to us galloping thròugh.
Behind shut the pòstern; the lights sank to rèst,
And into the midnight we galloped abrèast.

Not a word to each óther; we kept the great páce,
Néck by néck, stríde by strídc, never changing our pláce;
I turned in my saddle and made its girths tíght,
Then shortened each stirrup and set the pique ríght,
Rebuckled the chéck-strap, chained slacker the bít,
Nor galloped less steadily Róland a whít.   BROWNING.

5. HOW THE OLD HORSE WON THE BET.

"*Bring forth the horse!*" Alas! he showed
Not like the one Mazeppa rode;
Scant-maned, sharp-backed, and shaky-kneed,
The wreck of what was once a steed;
Lips thin, eyes hollow, stiff in joints,
Yet not without his knowing points.
"*Gò!*"—Through his ear the summons stung,
As if a battle-trump had rung;
The slumbering instincts long unstirred
Start at the old familiar word;
It thrills like flame through every limb—
What mean his twenty years to him?

The savage blow his rider dealt
Fell on his hollow flanks unfelt;
The spur that pricked his staring hide
Unheeded tore his bleeding side;
Alike to him are spur and rein—
He steps a five-year-old again!
Before the quarter-pole was passed,
Old Hiram said, "He's going fast."
Long ere the quarter was a half,
The chuckling crowd had ceased to laugh;
Tighter his frightened jockey clung
As in a mighty stride he swung,
The gravel flying in his track,
His neck stretched out, his ears laid back,
His tail extended all the while
Behind him like a rat-tail file!
Off went a shoe—away it spun,
Shot like a bullet from a gun;
The quaking jockey shapes a prayer
From scraps of oaths he used to swear;
He drops his whip, he drops his rein,
He clutches fiercely for a mane;
He'll lose his hold—he sways and reels—
He'll slide beneath those trampling heels!
But like the sable steed that bore
The spectral lover of Lenore,
His nostrils snorting foam and fire,
No stretch his bony limbs can tire;
And now the stand he rushes by,
And "Stop him! stop him!" is the cry,
Stand back! he's only just begun—
He's having out three heats in one!
Now for the finish! At the turn,
The old horse—all the rest astern—
Comes swinging in, with easy trot;
By Jove! he's distanced all the lot!   HOLMES.

IV. Slow Movement.

Slow movement prevails in the utterance of praise and adoration, and in all expression when the mind is under the influence of meditation, grief, melancholy, grandeur, sublimity, vastness, or power. It is the characteristic rate of thoughtful and powerful oratory. In slow movement, the rhetorical pauses are long, and the voice dwells on the liquid and the long vowel sounds.

EXAMPLES.

1. ASTRONOMY.

Generation after generation has *rolled awày*, age after age has swept *silently bỳ;* but each has swèlled, by its contribútions, the stream of discòvery. Mysterious *móvements* have been unràveled; *mighty láws* have been revèaled; *ponderous órbs* have been wèighed; *óne* barrier after *anòther* has given way to the force of intellect; until the mind, majestic in its stréngth, has moúnted, stép by stép, up the rocky height of its self-built pýramid, from whose star-crowned súmmit it looks out upon the grandeur of the úniverse self-clothed with the *prescience of a Gòd.*

MITCHELL.

2. THE RAVEN.

Ah, distinctly I remember, it was in the bleak December,
And each separate dying ember wrought its ghost upon
    the floor:
Eagerly I wished the morrow;—vainly I had sought to
    borrow
From my books surcease of sorrow—sorrow for the lost
    Lenore—
For the rare and radiant maiden whom the angels name
    Lenore—
        Nameless here for evermore.

POE.

3. THE ANCIENT MARINER.

Alone, alone, all, all alone,
  Alone on the wide, wide sea;
And never a saint took pity on
  My soul in agony.

The many men, so beautiful!
  And they all dead did lie!
And a thousand thousand slimy things
  Lived on—and so did I.

I closed my lids and kept them close,
  Till the balls like pulses beat;
For the sky and the sea, and the sea and the sky
Lay like a load on my weary eye,
  And the dead were at my feet.   COLERIDGE.

4. THE HOUR OF DEATH.

Leaves have their time to fall,
And flowers to wither at the north-wind's breath,
  And stars to set—but all,
Thou hast all seasons for thine own, O Death!
                      MRS. HEMANS.

5. TO A WATERFOWL.

Whither, midst falling dew,
  While glow the heavens with the last steps of day,
Far through their rosy depths dost thou pursue
  Thy solitary way?

Vainly the fowler's eye
  Might mark thy distant flight to do thee wrong,
As, darkly painted on the crimson sky,
  Thy figure floats along.   BRYANT.

V. VERY SLOW MOVEMENT.

Very slow movement prevails in the expression of deep emotions, such as awe, reverence, horror, melancholy, and grief.

In this movement the rhetorical and grammatical pauses are very long, and the vowel and liquid sounds are dwelt upon and prolonged.

The prevailing inflection in this movement is the monotone.

EXAMPLES.

1. Air, earth, and sea resound his praise abroad.
2. Roll on, thou deep and dark blue ocean, roll.
3. Old ocean's gray and melancholy waste.
4. Childless and crownless in her voiceless woe.
5. It thunders! Sons of dust, in reverence bow.
6. Unto Thee I lift up mine eyes, O Thou that dwellest in the heavens.
7. Thou hast all seasons for thine own, O Death!
8. Now o'er the one half world
Nature seems dead; and wicked dreams abuse
The curtained sleeper.
Thou sure and firm-set earth,
Hear not my steps which way they walk, for fear
The very stones prate of my whereabouts,
And take the present horror from the time
Which now suits with it.

9. CARDINAL WOLSEY.

Farewell, a long farewell, to all my greatness.
This is the state of man; to-day he puts forth
The tender leaves of hope, to-morrow blossoms,
And bears his blushing honors thick upon him;
The third day comes a frost, a killing frost;
And when he thinks, good easy man, full surely
His greatness is a-ripening—nips his root,
And then he falls, as I do. I have ventured,
Like little wanton boys that swim on bladders,
This many summers in a sea of glory—

But far beyond my depth; my high-blown pride
At length broke under me; and now has left me,
Weary, and old with service, to the mercy
Of a rude stream, that must forever hide me.
SHAKESPEARE.

10. DREAM OF DARKNESS.

The crowd was famished by degrees. But two
Of an enormous city did survive,
And they were enemies. They met beside
The dying embers of an altar-place,
Where had been heaped a mass of holy things
For an unholy usage. They raked up,
And, shivering, scraped with their cold, skeleton hands,
The feeble ashes; and their feeble breath
Blew for a little life, and made a flame,
Which was a mockery. Then they lifted
Their eyes as it grew lighter, and beheld
Each other's aspects—saw, and shrieked, and died;
Even of their mutual hideousness they died,
Unknowing who he was, upon whose brow
Famine had written Fiend.
BYRON

11. HIAWATHA.

O the long and dreary Winter!
O the cold and cruel Winter!
Ever thicker, thicker, thicker
Froze the ice on lake and river;
Ever deeper, deeper, deeper
Fell the snow o'er all the landscape,
Fell the covering snow, and drifted
Through the forest, round the village.
LONGFELLOW.

EXAMPLES OF MOVEMENT.

VERY SLOW.

Farewell, a long farewell to all my greatness.

SLOW.

Alone, alone, all, all alone.

MODERATE.

There was a sound of revelry by night.

FAST.

Come and trip it as ye go
On the light fantastic toe.

VERY FAST.

Hurry! hurry to the field!

Require each pupil to make out and read in the class a similar set of quoted illustrations.

CHAPTER IV.

PITCH OF VOICE.

I. INTRODUCTORY.

1. *Pitch*, or key, denotes the highness or lowness of the voice in tone. The range of the voice from the lowest to the highest tone is called its *compass*.

2. The compass of the voice among readers corresponds, in some degree, to the tenor, soprano, contralto, and bass, among singers; but every voice has its own relatively low, middle, and high tones.

3. For every one, the middle pitch is that tone to which the voice inclines in conversation, or in unimpassioned reading.

4. The three main divisions of pitch are the low, the middle, and the high; but these, for convenience, are subdivided into very low, low, middle, high, and very high.

5. The general key in which a selection should be read is determined by the general sentiment or character of the piece.

6. In order to avoid monotony, there should be some slight variation of pitch at the beginning of each successive paragraph that marks a new topic of discourse, or a change of idea.

7. *Low* pitch is the tone expressive of serious thought, of awe, of reverence, of adoration, of horror, and of despair.

8. *Middle* pitch is the tone of conversation, and of unimpassioned narrative or descriptive reading.

9. *High* pitch is the tone of gayety, joy, and gladness; of courage and exultation; and of shouting and calling.

10. Of the importance of drill exercises in pitch, Prof. Monroe says: "One of the commonest faults in school reading, and in the delivery of many public speakers, is a dull monotony of tone. This sameness is still more disagreeable to the ear when the voice is kept strained upon a high key. Not less unpleasant is an incessant repetition of the same cant or sing-song. Elocutionary rules will do little or nothing toward removing these faults. Faithful drill is needed, under the guidance of good taste and a correct musical ear. To this must be added an appreciation of the sentiment of the piece at the moment of utterance.

11. "When the organs have been trained to freedom and facility in all degrees of the musical scale, the pupil will find it easy to modulate his voice in reading. Vowels, words, and sentences should be practiced with high, middle, and low pitch. Having these tones at his command, the expressive reader will vary the pitch with every shade of thought or emotion, so that a foreigner who did not understand a word might listen with pleasure to the play of intonation. Next to sweetness of voice, a proper melody of delivery has the greatest charm to the hearer."

II. Concert Drill on Pitch.

1. Sing the scale, up and down: dō, re, mï, fä, sōl, lä, sï, dō.

2. Sing the scale with the long vowel sounds, instead of note names: ā, ē, ī, ō, ū, ā, ē, ī.

3. Sound, not sing, the long vowels, ā, ē, ī, ō, ū, on the key of dō; of mï; of sōl; of dō.

4. Sound the long vowels, ā, ē, ī, ō, ū: (1) With low

pitch. (2) With middle pitch. (3) With high pitch. (4) With very high pitch.

5. Count from one to twenty: (1) In middle pitch. (2) With low pitch. (3) With high pitch.

6. Repeat, five times, the word "all," beginning with very low pitch, and rising higher with each successive repetition.

III. Faults in Pitch.

1. The most common fault in school reading is the high pitch known as the conventional "school tone," which grates on the ear like the filing of a saw. It arises from an effort to read in a loud tone, and from a habit of reading without any regard to thought or feeling. This fault must be corrected by vocal drill on a low key.

2. A common fault, particularly of girls, is that of reading with feeble force and low pitch.

3. The failure to adapt the pitch to the sentiment or emotion of what is read.

IV. Examples of the Middle Pitch.

The middle pitch is the natural tone of ordinary conversation. It is the appropriate key for the reading of unimpassioned narrative, descriptive, and didactic composition.

1. Give a boy address and accomplishments, and you give him the mastery of palaces and fortunes where he goes.

2. Wisdom is better than riches.

3. Good morning, Mr. Brown. How do you do this morning?

4. For all a rhetorician's rules
   Teach nothing but to name his tools.

5. Marley was dead, to begin with; there is no doubt whatever about that. Old Marley was as dead as a door-nail.

6. CONCORD RIVER.

We stand now on the river's brink. It may well be called the Concord—the river of peace and quietness,—for it is certainly the most unexcitable and sluggish stream that ever loitered imperceptibly towards its eternity, the sea. Positively, I had lived three weeks beside it, before it grew quite clear to my perception which way the current flowed. It never has a vivacious aspect, except when a north-western breeze is vexing its surface, on a sunshiny day.

From the incurable indolence of its nature, the stream is happily incapable of becoming the slave of human ingenuity, as is the fate of so many a wild, free, mountain torrent. While all things else are compelled to subserve some useful purpose, it idles its sluggish life away in lazy liberty, without turning a solitary spindle, or affording even water-power enough to grind the corn that grows upon its banks. HAWTHORNE.

7. WOUTER VAN TWILLER.

This, by the way, is a casual remark, which I would not, for the universe, have it thought I apply to Governor Van Twiller. It is true he was a man shut up within himself, like an oyster, and rarely spoke except in monosyllables; but then it was allowed he seldom said a foolish thing. So invincible was his gravity that he was never known to laugh, or even to smile, through the whole course of a long and prosperous life. Nay, if a joke were uttered in his presence, that set light-minded hearers in a roar, it was observed to throw him into a state of perplexity. Sometimes he would deign to inquire into the matter, and when, after much explanation, the joke was made as plain as a pike-staff, he would continue to smoke his pipe in silence, and at length, knocking out the ashes, would exclaim, "Well, I see nothing in all that to laugh about." IRVING.

V. EXAMPLES OF HIGH PITCH.

Joy, mirth, and gayety incline the voice to pure tone and high pitch. Calling to persons at a distance inclines the voice to high pitch and pure tone. Anger, courage, boldness, and exultation incline the voice to high pitch and loud force.

1. Sound drums and trumpets, boldly and cheerfully.

2. Ring joyous chords! ring out again
   A swifter still and a wilder strain.

3. And dar'st thou, then,
   To beard the lion in his den,
   The Douglas in his hall?

4. But thou, O Hope, with eyes so fair,
   What was thy delighted measure?

5. ANGER.

Call me their *traitor!*—Thou *injúrious* tribune!
Within thine eyes sat *twenty thóusand deaths,*
In thine hands clutched as many *míllions,* in
Thy lying tongue *bóth* numbers, I would say
Thou *liest,* unto thee, with a voice as free
As I do pray the gods. *From Coriolanus.*

6. VICTORY.

They strike! hurrah! the foe has surrendered!
Shout! shout! my warrior boy,
And wave your cap, and clap your hands for joy.
Cheer answer cheer, and bear the cheer about.
Hurrah! hurrah! for the fiery fort is ours.
   Victory! victory! victory!

7. CALLING.

I'm with you once again!—I *call* to you
With all my *voice*, I hold my *hànds* to you,
To show they still are *frèe*. I *rùsh* to you
As though I could *embràce* you.
Tell's Address to the Mountains.

8. CALLING THE COWS.

When over the hill the farm-boy goes,
  Cheerily calling,
"*Co' boss! co' boss! co'! co'! co'!*"
  Farther, farther, over the hill,
  Faintly calling, calling still,
"*Co' boss! co' boss! co'! co'! co'!*"   TROWBRIDGE.

9. THE WATCHMAN'S CALL.

Ho! watchman, ho!
  Twelve is the clock!
God keep our town
  From fire and brand
  And hostile hand!
Twelve is the clock!

10. THE SILVER BELLS.

Hear the sledges with the bells—
  Silver bells
What a world of merriment their melody foretells!
  How they tinkle, tinkle, tinkle,
    In the icy air of night!
  While the stars that oversprinkle
  All the heavens, seemed to twinkle
    With a crystalline delight;
  Keeping time, time, time,
  In a sort of Runic rhyme,
To the tintinnabulation that so musically wells
  From the bells, bells, bells, bells,
    Bells, bells, bells—
From the jingling and the tinkling of the bells.   POE.

11. EXULTATION.

Joy! joy forever! my task is done;
The gates are passed, and heaven is won.   MOORE.

12. COMMAND AND SHOUTING.

Advance your *standards*, draw your willing *swords!*
Sound *drums* and *trumpets*, boldly and cheerfully!
God, and *Saint George! Richmond* and *victory!*

13. THE CHARCOAL MAN.

Though rudely blows the wintry blast,
And sifting snows fall white and fast,
Mark Haley drives along the street,
Perched high upon his wagon-seat;
His somber face the storm defies,
And thus from morn till eve he cries:—
  "*Charco'! charco'!*"
While echo faint and far replies:—
  "*Hark, O! hark, O!*"
"*Charco'!*"—"*Hark, O!*"—Such cheery sounds
Attend him on his daily rounds.   TROWBRIDGE.

14. THE LOST HEIR.

One day, as I was going by
  That part of Holborn christened High,
I heard a loud and sudden cry
  That chilled my 'very blood;
"O Lord! oh, dear, my heart will break, I shall go stick stark staring wild!
Has ever a one seen anything about the streets like a crying, lost-looking child?
The last time as ever I see him, poor thing, was with my own blessed motherly eyes,
Sitting as good as gold in the gutter, a-playing at making little dirt pies.
Billy—where are you, Billy?—I'm as hoarse as a crow, with screaming for ye, you young sorrow!

And sha'n't have half a voice, no more I sha'n't, for
    crying fresh herrings to-morrow.
Billy—where are you, Billy, I say? come Billy, come
    home to your best of mothers!
I'm scared when I think of them cabroleys, they drive
    so, they'd run over their own sisters and brothers.
Or may be he's stole by some chimbly-sweeping wretch,
    to stick fast in narrow flues and what not,
And be poked up behind with a picked pointed pole, when
    the soot has ketched, and the chimbly's red hot.
Oh, I'd give the whole wide world, if the world was
    mine, to clap my two longin' eyes on his face;
For he's my darlin' of darlin's, and if he don't soon come
    back, you'll see me drop stone-dead on the place.
I only wish I'd got him safe in these two motherly
    arms, and wouldn't I hug him and kiss him!
Lawk! I never knew what a precious he was—but a
    child don't feel like a child till you miss him.
Why, there he is! Punch and Judy hunting, the young
    wretch; it's that Billy as sartin as sin!
But let me get him home, with a good grip of his hair,
    and I'm blest if he shall have a whole bone in his
    skin!"

HOOD.

15. EXTRACTS FROM HOOD'S "TALE OF A TRUMPET."

Of all old women hard of hearing,
The deafest, sure, was Dame Eleanor Spearing!
    On her head, it is true,
    Two flaps there grew,
That served for a pair of gold rings to go through;
But for any purpose of ears in a parley,
They heard no more than ears of barley.

However, in the peddler came,
And the moment he met the eyes of the dame,
Popped a trumpet into her ear:—

"There, ma'am! *trỳ it!*
You need n't *búy it*—
The last new patent—and nothing comes nigh it,
For affording the deaf, at little expense,
The sense of *hearing*, and hearing of *sense!*
A real bléssing—and no mistáke,
Invented for poor *humanity's* sáke;
I would n't tell a *lĭe*, I *wŏuld n't*,
But *mý* trumpets have heard what *Sòlomon's* could n't;
Only a *gúinea*—and can't take *léss.*"
("*That's very déar,*" says Dame Eleanor Ś.)
"There was Mrs. F.,
So very déaf,
That she might have worn a percussion-*càp*,
And been knocked on the *hèad* without hearing it *snàp.*
Wêll, I sold her a hórn, and the very *néxt dày*
She heard from her husband at *Botany Bày!*
Come—speak your mind—it's '*Nŏ* or Yês.'"
("*I've half a mĭnd,*" said Dame Eleanor S.)
"*Trỳ it—bùy it!*
Bùy it—trỳ it!
The last new patent, and nothing comes *nĭgh it.*"
In short, the peddler so besét her—
Lord *Bàcon* could n't have gammoned her bétter—
With flatteries plump and indirect,
And plied his tongue with such efféct—
A tongue that could almost have buttered a crúmpet—
The deaf old woman bought the trumpet.

16. CONVERSATION UNDER DIFFICULTIES.

[*Each supposes the other to be very deaf, the pitch at times running into screaming.*]

Jones. (*Speaking shrill and loud.*) Miss, will you accept these flowers? I plucked them from their slumber on the hill.

Pru. (*In an equally high voice.*) Really sir, I—I—

Jones. (*Aside.*) She hesitates. It must be that she does not hear me. (*Increasing his tone.*) Miss, will you accept these flowers—FLOWERS? I plucked them sleeping on the hill—HILL.

Pru. (*Also increasing her tone.*) Certainly, Mr. Jones. They are beautiful—BEAU-U-TIFUL.

Jones. (*Aside.*) How she screams in my ear. (*Aloud.*) Yes, I plucked them from their slumber—SLUMBER, on the hill—HILL.

Pru. (*Aside.*) Poor man, what an effort it seems for him to speak. (*Aloud.*) I perceive you are poetical. Are you fond of poetry? (*Aside.*) He hesitates. I must speak louder. (*In a scream.*) Poetry—POETRY—POETRY!

Jones. (*Aside.*) Bless me, the woman would wake the dead! (*Aloud.*) Yes, Miss, I ad-o-r-e it.

Snob. Glorious! glorious! I wonder how loud they *can* scream. Oh, vengeance, thou art sweet!

Pru. Can you repeat some poetry—POETRY?

Jones. I only know one poem. It is this—

> You'd scarce expect one of my age—AGE,
> To speak in public on the stage—STAGE.

Pru. Bravo—bravo!

Jones. Thank you! THANK——

Pru. Mercy on us! Do you think I'm DEAF, sir?

Jones. And do you fancy *me* deaf, Miss? (*Natural tone.*)

Pru. Are you not, sir? You surprise me!

Jones. No, Miss. I was led to believe that you were deaf. Snobbleton told me so.

Pru. Snobbleton! Why, he told me that you were deaf.

Jones. Confound the fellow! he has been making game of us.

Beadle's Dime Speaker.

VI. Examples of Low Pitch.

Low pitch is the characteristic key of the voice when the mind is under the influence of serious, grave, and impressive thoughts; and *very low* pitch is the appropriate key for the expression of reverence, adoration, horror, and despair.

1. FROM THE "RIME OF THE ANCIENT MARINER."

An orphan's curse would drag to hell
  A spirit from on high;
But oh! more horrible than that
  Is the curse in a dead man's eye!
Seven days, seven nights I saw that curse,
  And yet I could not die.

2. FROM THE "RAVEN."

Deep into that darkness peering, long I stood there, wondering, fearing,
Doubting, dreaming dreams no mortal ever dared to dream before;
But the silence was unbroken, and the stillness gave no token,
And the only word there spoken was the whispered word "Lenore!"
This I whispered, and an echo murmured back the word "Lenore!"
      Merely this, and nothing more.

3. LAUS DEO.

  Let us knèel;
God's own voice is in that pèal,
And this spot is *hòly* ground.
  Lord, forgive us! What are wè,
  That our eyes this glòry see,
That our ears have heard the sòund!   WHITTIER.

4. FROM THE PSALMS.

He bowed the heavens, also, and came down; and darkness was under his feet; and he rode upon a cherub, and did fly; and he was seen upon the wings of the wind; and he made darkness pavilions round about him, dark waters, and thick clouds of the skies.

5. THE CHANDOS PICTURE.

The bell far off beats midnight; in the dark
  The sounds have lost their way, and wander slowly
Through the dead air; beside me things cry, "Hark!"
  And whisper words unholy.   EDWARD POLLOCK.

6. THE IRON BELLS.

    Hear the tolling of the bells—
      Iron bells!
What a world of solemn thought their monody compels!
      In the silence of the night,
      How we shiver with affright
    At the melancholy menace of their tone!
      For every sound that floats
      From the rust within their throats
        Is a groan.
    And the people—ah, the people—
    They that dwell up in the steeple,
      All alone!
    And who tolling, tolling, tolling,
      In that muffled monotone,
    Feel a glory in so rolling
      On the human heart a stone;
    They are neither man nor woman—
    They are neither brute nor human—
      They are ghouls;
    And their king it is who tolls—
    And he rolls, rolls, rolls, rolls,
      A pæan from the bells!

And his merry bosom swells
With the pæan of the bells!
And he dances and he yells;
Keeping time, time, time,
In a sort of Runic rhyme,
To the pæan of the bells—
    Of the bells!
Keeping time, time, time,
In a sort of Runic rhyme,
To the throbbing of the bells—
    Of the bells, bells, bells—
To the sobbing of the bells;
Keeping time, time, time,
  As he knells, knells, knells,
In a happy Runic rhyme,
To the rolling of the bells—
    Of the bells, bells, bells,
To the tolling of the bells—
    Of the bells, bells, bells, bells,
      Bells, bells, bells—
To the moaning and the groaning of the bells!

Poe.

VII. Examples of Very Low Pitch.

1. Concerning the application of very low pitch in reading and speaking, Prof. Russell remarks: "This lowest form of pitch is one of the most impressive means of powerful natural effect, in the utterance of all deep and impressive emotions. The pervading and absorbing effect of *awe, amazement, horror*, or any similar feeling, can never be produced without low pitch and deep successive notes; and the depth and reality of such emotions are always in proportion to the depth of voice with which they are uttered. The grandest descriptions in the 'Paradise Lost,' and the profoundest meditations in the 'Night Thoughts,' become trivial in their effect on the

ear, when read with the ineffectual expression inseparable from the pitch of ordinary conversation or discourse.

2. "The vocal deficiency which limits the range of expression to the middle and higher notes of the scale is not, by any means, the unavoidable and necessary fault of organization, as it is so generally supposed to be. Habit is in this, as in so many other things, the cause of defect. There is truth, no doubt, in the remark so often made in defense of a high and feeble voice, that it is natural to the individual, or that it is difficult for some readers to attain to depth of voice without incurring a false and forced style of utterance. But in most cases it is habit, not organization, that has made certain notes natural or unnatural—in other words, familiar to the ear or the reverse.

3. "The neglect of the lower notes of the scale, and, consequently, of the organic action by which they are produced, may render a deep-toned utterance less easy than it would otherwise be. But most teachers of elocution are, from day to day, witnesses to the fact that students, from the neglect of muscular action, and from all the other enfeebling causes involved in sedentary habits and intellectual application, sometimes commence a course of practice with a high-pitched, thin, and feminine voice, which seems at first incapable of expressing a grave or manly sentiment, and, in some instances, appears to forbid the individual from ever attempting the utterance of a solemn thought, lest his treble tone should make the effect ridiculous; but that a few weeks' practice of vocal exercise on bass notes and deep emotions, as embodied in rightly selected exercises, often enables such readers to acquire a round and deep-toned utterance, adequate to the fullest effects of impressive eloquence.

4. "The exercise of singing bass, if cultivated as an habitual practice, has a great effect in imparting com-

mand of deep-toned expression in reading and speaking. Reading and reciting passages from Milton and from Young, and particularly from the Book of Psalms, or from hymns of a deeply solemn character, are exercises of great value for securing the command of the lower notes of the voice."

5. In the following exercises the movement is very slow, the pauses are very long, and the prevailing inflection the grave monotone.

1. THE GRAVE.

Hōw frīghtful the *gràve!* how desērted and *drèar!*
With the hōwls of the stōrm-wind, the crēaks of the bier,
 And the whīte bōnes āll clāttering tōgèther!

2. THE BELL OF THE ATLANTIC.

Tōll, tōll, tōll, thōu bēll bȳ bīllows swūng;
And, nīght and dāy, thy wārning wōrds repēat wīth
 moūrnful tòngue;
Tōll for the quēenly bōat, wrēcked on yōn rōcky shòre!
Sēa-wēed is in her pālace wālls; she rīdes the sūrge nō
 mòre.   Mrs. Sigourney.

3. THE GHOST IN HAMLET.

I cōuld a tāle unfōld, whōse līghtest wōrd
Would hārrow up thy sōul, frēeze thy yoūng blōod,
Māke thy twō eȳes like stārs stārt from their sphēres,
Thy knōtted and combīned lōcks to pārt,
And ēach partīcular hāir to stānd on ēnd,
Like quīlls upon the frētful porcupīne.   Shakespeare.

4. DARKNESS.

 The world was vòid:
The pōpulous | and the pōwerful | was a lūmp,
Sēasonless, hērbless, trēeless, mānless, līfeless;
A lūmp of dēath, a chāos of hārd clày.
The rīvers, lākes, and ōcean, āll | stōod | stīll,

And nŏthing | stĭrred | withĭn thēir sīlent dèpths.
Shĭps, sāilorless, lāy rōtting ōn the sēa,
And their māsts | fĕll dōwn | pīecemèal; as they drōpped |
They slĕpt on the abȳss, withōut a sùrge—
The wāves | were dèad; the tīdes | wēre in thēir gràve;
The mōon, their mĭstress, had expīred befòre;
The wĭnds | wēre wĭthered | in the stāgnant āir,
And the clōuds | pērished: Dārkness | had nō nĕed |
Of āid | from thēm—shē | was the *ùniverse*. BYRON.

VIII. RECAPITULATION OF PITCH.

1. *Very low is the pitch of awe, of reverence, of solemnity, of melancholy, horror, and despair.*

2. *Low is the pitch of serious, grave, solemn, and impressive thoughts and feelings.*

3. *Middle is the pitch of ordinary conversation, and of unimpassioned narrative, descriptive, or didactic composition.*

4. *High pitch is the pitch of courage, boldness, exultation, wonder, and anger, and of shouting or calling.*

5. *Very high is the pitch of rapturous emotion, of uncontrollable passion, of terror, and pain.*

CHAPTER V.

QUALITY OF VOICE.

Introductory.

1. *Quality* of voice relates to the kind of tone used in reading or speaking in order to express varied thoughts and emotions.

2. The ever-varying intonations of a rich and cultivated voice constitute one of the greatest charms of a good reader or speaker.

3. "In poetical and impassioned language," says Prof. Russell, "tones are often the most prominent and the most important qualities of voice; and to give these with propriety, force, and vividness, is the chief excellence of good reading or recitation.

4. "The language of prose, being generally less imaginative and exciting, does not require the extent and power of tone used in poetry. But as true feeling is, in both cases, the same in kind, though not in degree, and as no sentiment can be uttered naturally without the tone of its appropriate emotion, and no thought, indeed, can arise in the mind without a degree of emotion, a great importance is attached, even in the reading or speaking of prose composition, to those qualities of voice comprehended under the name of tones.

5. "Without these, utterance would degenerate into a merely mechanical process of articulation. It is these that give impulse and vitality to thought, and which constitute the chief instruments of eloquence."

Kinds of Tone.

The different qualities of tone may be classed as follows:

    1. Pure tone.   4. The Guttural.
    2. The Orotund.   5. The Falsetto.
    3. The Aspirated.   6. The Semitone.

Of these divisions, the *pure tone* and the *orotund* are the most important, because they are most used in reading.

Faults in Quality.

1. Perhaps the most common fault in school reading consists in using one uniform tone for all kinds of selections.

2. This hard, thin, high, grating quality is appropriately termed the "school tone."

3. The faulty habits of pupils in this respect are best corrected by requiring pupils to repeat in concert, after the teacher, short extracts which include great variations of quality. Many timid pupils are, at first, frightened at the sound of their own voices in any other tone than the conventional school tone.

4. Another fault is the tendency to the *nasal tone*. This high, thin, sharp, disagreeable tone is produced by forcing the breath into the nose before it leaves the mouth, and this fault in reading is the result of not opening the mouth sufficiently in reading. It may be broken up by persistent drill on the open vowel sounds, and by exercises that keep the voice down to a low pitch.

I. Pure Tone.

1. *Pure* tone, or head tone, is a clear, smooth sound, so formed as to have a slight resonance in the head or through the nasal passages. A good illustration of this quality is afforded by giving the sound of *oo* as in moon,

prolonged for ten seconds, in a thin, clear, gentle vocal sound, on a moderately high pitch.

2. Pure tone is used in all quiet, gentle, subdued forms of utterance; in the expression of pathos and tenderness; in ordinary conversation; in unimpassioned reading; and in the prolonged tones of shouting or calling, when the voice, raised to a high pitch, flows in a thin, clear, penetrating volume.

3. "The production of pure and full tone," says Prof. William Russell, "is the common ground on which elocution and vocal music unite, in elementary discipline. Both arts demand attention to appropriate healthful attitude, and to free, expansive, energetic action in the organs.

4. "Both require erect posture, free opening of the chest, full and regular breathing, power of producing and sustaining any degree of volume of voice, and, along with these, the habit of vivid, distinct articulation.

5. "Both equally forbid that imperfect and laborious breathing which mars the voice, exhausts the organs, and produces disease. Both tend to secure that healthy vigor of organ which makes vocal exercise, at once, a source of pleasure and a source of health."

EXAMPLES.

1. Straight mine eye hath caught new pleasures,
   While the landscape round it measures.
2. O that this lovely vale were mine!
3. O then I see Queen Mab hath been with you!
4. Rejoice, ye men of Angiers; ring your bells;
   Open your gates to give the victors way.
5. Joy! joy forever! my task is done!
6. Ring, joyous chords! ring out again!
7. Hear the sledges with the bells—*silver* bells!

8. Marley was dead, to begin with. There is no doubt whatever about that.

9. Studies serve for delight, for ornament, and for ability.

10. Has there any *old* fellow got mixed with the *boys?*

11. Listen, my children, and you shall hear
Of the midnight ride of Paul Revere.

12. BUGLE SONG.

O hark, O hear! how thin and clear,
  And thinner, clearer, farther going;
O sweet and far, from cliff and scar,
  The horns of Elf-land faintly blowing!
Blow; let us hear the purple glens replying;
Blow, bugle; answer, echoes, dying, dying, dying.

TENNYSON.

13. THE BELLS.

Hear the sledges with the bells—
  Silver bells!
What a world of merriment their melody foretells!
  How they tinkle, tinkle, tinkle,
    In the icy air of night!
  While the stars that oversprinkle
  All the heavens seem to twinkle
    With a crystalline delight;
  Keeping time, time, time,
  In a sort of Runic rhyme,
To the tintinnabulation that so musically wells
    From the bells, bells, bells, bells,
      Bells, bells, bells;
From the jingling and the tinkling of the bells.   POE.

14. SONG ON MAY MORNING.

Now the bright morning Star, day's harbinger,
Comes dancing from the East, and leads with her

The flowery May, who from her green lap throws
The yellow cowslip and the pale primrose.
  Hail, bounteous May, that dost inspire
  Mirth, and youth, and warm desire:
  Woods and groves are of thy dressing,
  Hill and dale doth boast thy blessing.
Thus we salute thee with our early song,
And welcome thee, and wish thee long.   MILTON.

15. DRIFTING.

The day so mild is Heaven's own child,
With Earth and Ocean reconciled;
The airs I feel around me steal
Are murmuring to the murmuring keel.

Over the rail my hand I trail
Within the shadow of the sail;
A joy intense—the cooling sense—
Glides down my drowsy indolence.   READ.

16. TO A SKYLARK.

  Hail to thee, blithe spirit—
  Bird thou never wert—
  That from heaven, or near it,
  Pourest thy full heart
In profuse strains of unpremeditated art.

  Higher still and higher,
  From the earth thou springest;
  Like a cloud of fire
  The blue deep thou wingest,
And singing still dost soar, and soaring ever singest.
   SHELLEY.

17. PASSING AWAY.

Was it the chime of a tiny *bell*
  That came so sweet to my dreaming *ear*,
Like the silvery tones of a fairy's *shell*,
  That he winds, on the beach, so mellow and *clear*,

When the winds and the waves lie together *asleep*,
And the Moon and the Fairy are watching the *deep*,
She dispensing her silvery *light*,
And he his notes as *silvery quite*,
While the boatman listens and ships his *óar*,
To catch the music that comes from the *shóre?*
Hàrk! the notes on my ear that *pláy*,
Are set to *wòrds:* as they flóat, they *sáy*,
   "*Pássing awáy! pássing awáy!*"   PIERPONT.

18. EVE OF ELECTION.

From gold to gray, our mild, sweet day
   Of Indian summer fades too soon;
But tenderly, above the sea,
   Hangs, white and calm, the hunter's moon.

In its pale fire the village spire
   Shows like the zodiac's spectral lance;
The painted walls, whereon it falls,
   Transfigured stand in marble trance!   WHITTIER.

CONCERT DRILL ON PURE TONE.

1. Repeat, four times, the long vowels, ā, ē, ī, ō, ū: (1) With moderate force, pure tone, and rising inflection. (2) With soft or gentle force. (3) With high pitch, pure tone, and sustained force.

2. Count from one to fifty: (1) With quiet conversational tone and rising inflection. (2) Falling inflection. (3) Circumflex inflection. (4) The monotone.

3. Give the sound of long *o*, prolonged for ten seconds; of ü; of ē.

4. In high pitch, and thin, clear, pure tone, call as to persons at a distance: ho! ho! ho!

II. THE OROTUND.

1. The *orotund* is a round, deep, full, clear, resonant

chest tone of voice. It has the flow and fullness of an organ-peal. It is the tone of emotion, excitement, and passion.

2. The orotund has the smoothness of pure tone, but combines it with a much heavier volume of sound. The swelling tones of the orotund are the appropriate means of expressing reverence, awe, sublimity, grandeur, and strong feeling or passion. It prevails in oratorical declamation and in the reading of lyric or dramatic poetry.

3. The prevailing stress of the orotund is the median, changing, however, under excitement, into the radical.

4. In the orotund utterance, the breathing must be full and deep, to insure a good supply of breath; the mouth must be well opened; all the vocal organs must be called into full play; and then, in harmony with strong emotions, the voice swells out like the blast of a bugle or the resonant swell of an organ.

5. The three degrees of the orotund may be distinguished as the effusive, the expulsive, and the explosive.

Orotund Drill.

1. Repeat, four times, in monotone, the long vocals, ā, ē, ī, ō, ū.

2. Inhale to the utmost capacity of the lungs and then give, with strong swell and round tone, the sound of long *o*, prolonged as long as the breath will allow.

3. Repeat four times the following vocals: ē, ā, ä, ạ, ō, o.

4. Lo! the mighty sun looks forth!
Arm! thou leader of the north.

5. Awake! Arise! or be forever fallen!

6. Air, earth, and sea, resound his praise abroad.

7. Roll on, thou deep and dark blue ocean, roll,
Ten thousand fleets sweep over thee in vain.

8. Farewell, a long farewell to all my greatness.

9. Hail! holy light, offspring of Heaven first-born!

10. Liberty! freedom! Tyranny is dead!

11. It thunders! sons of dust, in reverence bow!

12. Hear the mellow wedding bells—*golden* bells.

13. Hear the loud alarum bells—*brazen* bells.

14. O thou Eternal One! whose presence bright
All space doth occupy, all motion guide,
Unchanged through time's all-devastating flight;
Thou only God! There is no God beside!

Examples of Effusive Orotund.

1. THE ARSENAL.

This is the Àrsenal. From floor to céiling,
 Like a huge òrgan, rise the burnished àrms;
But from their silent pípes no anthem péaling,
 Startles the vìllages | with strange alàrms.

Àh! what a sòund will rise—how wild and *dreary*—
 When the death-angel touches those swift *kèys!*
What loud lament | and dismal *Miserére*
 Will mingle | with their awful *sỳmphonies!*

I héar even nòw | the infinite fierce *chòrus*,
 The cries of *àgony*, the endless *gròan*,
Which, through the *àges* | that have gone befóre us,
 In long *reverberàtions* | reach our òwn. LONGFELLOW.

2. THE OCEAN.

The *àrmaments* | which thunderstrike the walls |
 Of rock-built cíties, bidding *nàtions* quake,
And *mónarchs* | tremble in their *cápitals;*
 The oak *levíathans*, whose *huge ríbs* make |
 Their clay creàtor | the vain title take |

Of lord of thee, and arbiter of *wár*—
    Thése | are thy *tòys*, and, as the snowy *flàke*,
They melt into thy yeast of wàves, which mar |
Alike | the *Armada's* príde, or spoils of *Trafalgàr*.
BYRON.

3. HYMN TO MONT BLANC.

Ye *ìce*-falls! ye that from the mountain's brow |
Adown *enormous ràvines* slope amain—
Torrents, methinks, that heard a mighty vóice,
And stopped at ònce amid their maddest plùnge!
Mòtionless tòrrents! *sìlent* càtaracts!
Who made you *glòrious* as the gates of *hèaven* |
Beneath the keen full moon? Who bade the sùn |
Clothe you with ràinbows? Who, with living *flòwers*
Of loveliest blúe, spread *gàrlands* at your feet?—
Gôd! let the torrents like a shout of *nàtions* |
Answer! and let the *ìce*-plains echo: *Gôd!*
Gôd! sing, ye meadow-streams, with gladsome vòice!
Ye *pìne*-groves, with your soft and soul-like sòunds!
And *thèy* too have a *vòice*, yon piles of snòw,
And in their perilous fall | shall thúnder: *Gôd!*
COLERIDGE.

4. THE CHAMBERED NAUTILUS.

Build thee more *stàtely* mansions, O my soul,
    As the swift seasons ròll!
      Lèave thy low-vaulted *pàst!*
Let each new *témple*, nobler than the lást,
Shut thee from heaven with a dome more vást,
    Till thou at length art *frèe,*
Leaving thine outgrown *shéll* by life's unresting sèa!
HOLMES.

5. FROM THE PSALMS.

Praise ye the *Lòrd*. Praise ye the Lord from the *hèavens;* praise him in the *hèights*. Praise ye him, all his *àngels:* praise ye him, all his *hòsts*. Praise ye him, *sùn* and *mòon:* praise him, all ye *stàrs* of *lìght*. Praise him, ye heavens of *hèavens*, and ye *wáters* that be *abòve* the heavens. Let them *práise* the name of the *Lòrd:* for he commánded, and they were creáted. He hath also established them for *éver* and *èver:* he hath made a decree which shall not pass. Praise the Lord from the earth, ye *drȧgons*, and all *dèeps: fíre*, and *hȧil; snów*, and *vȧpors;* stormy *wind* fulfilling his *wȯrd: mȯuntains*, and all *hȧlls;* fruitful *trèes*, and *all cèdars: bèasts*, and *all cȧttle; crėeping* things, and *flying fȯwl: kíngs* of the earth, and *all pèople: prínces*, and *all jȧdges* of the earth: both *young mėn* and *mȧidens;* old *mėn* and *chȧldren.* Let them *praise the name of the Lòrd:* for *hís* name alone is excèllent; *hís glory* is above the earth and hèaven.

6. EVE OF ELECTION.

Our hearts grow cold, we lightly hold
  A right which brave men died to gain;
The stake, the cord, the ax, the sword,
  Grim nurses at its birth of pain.

The shadow rend, and o'er us bend,
  O martyrs, with your crowns and palms!
Breathe through these throngs, your battle-songs,
  Your scaffold prayers and dungeon psalms!

WHITTIER.

EXAMPLES OF EXPULSIVE OROTUND.

These examples are to be rendered with a stronger swell than those under the head of effusive orotund.

1. LAUS DEO.

It is *dòne!*
Clang of *bell* and roar of *gun*
Send the tidings *úp* and *dòwn.*
How the belfries *róck* and *rèel*,
How the great *gúns*, peal on *péal*,
Fling the joy from *tówn* to *tòwn !*

WHITTIER.

2. CHRISTMAS.

Ring òut, ye crystal *sphèrcs!*
Once bless our *hùman* ears,
 If ye have power to touch our *sènses* so;
And let your silver chime
Move in melodious time,
 And let the bass of heaven's deep òrgan blow;
And with your ninefold harmony
Make up full consort to the angelic symphony.
MILTON.

3. THE OCEAN.

Rōll on, thōu dēep and dārk blūe Ocean—rōll!
Tèn thòusand flĕets | sweep over thee in vàin;
Mán | marks the *éarth* with *rùin,*—his contról |
Stóps with the *shòre;* upon the watery plain |
The *wrécks* are all *thy̆* deed, nor doth remain |
A *shàdow* of man's ravage, save his ówn,
When for a móment, like a drop of ráin,
Hē sīnks into thy̆ dēpths | wīth būbbling grōan,
Without a grāve, unknēlled, uncōffined, and unknōwn.
BYRON.

4. THE ORGAN.

Suddenly the notes of the deep-laboring *òrgan* burst upon the èar, falling with doubled and redoubled inténsity, and rolling, as it wére, huge billows of sòund. How *wèll* do their volume and grandeur accord with this mighty búilding! With what pòmp do they swell through its vast vàults, and breathe their awful harmony through these caves of dèath, and make the silent sépulcher vòcal! And now they rise in triumph and acclamàtion, heaving *hígher* and *hígher* their accordant nótes, and piling *sòund* on *sòund.* And now they *pàuse,* and the soft voices of the choir break out into sweet gushes of mèlody; they soar *alóft,* and warble along the róof, and seem to play about these lofty vaults like the pure airs of *hèaven.* Again the pealing organ heaves its thrilling *thùnders*, compressing *áir* into *mùsic*, and *rolling it forth* upon the *sòul*. What long-drawn *cádences!* What solemn, *swèeping còncords!* It grows more and more *dense* and *pòwerful;* it fills the *vast pìle*, and seems to jar the *véry wàlls;* the ear is *stùnned*, the senses are *overwhèlmed*. And now it is winding up in *full jùbilee;* it is rising from the *éarth* to *hèaven;* the *very sòul* seems rapt away and *floated úpwards* on this swelling tide of *hármony*.

IRVING.

5. PERORATION OF WEBSTER'S PLYMOUTH ROCK ORATION.

Advance, then, ye *future generátions!* We would *hàil* you, as you rise in your long succéssion, to fill the places which *wè* now fill, and to taste the blessings of existence, where *we are passing*, and soon shall have passed, our own human durátion. We bid you *wèlcome* to this pleasant land of the fàthers. We bid you *wèlcome* to the healthful *skìes* and the verdant *fìelds* of New England. We greet your accession to the *great inhéritance* which *wè* have enjoyed. We welcome you to the blessings of *good gòvernment* and *religious lìberty*. We welcome you to the treasures of *scìence*, and the delights of *lèarning*. We welcome you to the *transcéndent swéets* of *domestic lìfe*, to the happiness of *kìndred*, and *párents*, and *chìldren*. We welcome you to the *imméasurable blessings* of *rational exístence*, the *immortal hópe* of *Christiánity*, and the light of *everlasting Trùth!*

6. GOD IN NATURE.

"God," sing ye meadow streams, with gladsome voice!
Ye pine groves, with your soft and soul-like sounds!
Ye living flowers that skirt the eternal frost!
Ye wild goats sporting round the eagle's nest!
Ye eagles, playmates of the mountain storm!
Ye lightnings, the dread arrows of the clouds!
Ye signs and wonders of the elements!
Utter forth "God," and fill the hills with praise!

From COLERIDGE'S *Hymn to Mont Blanc*.

7. A NEW YEAR'S CHIME.

Ho! ye wardens of the bells,
    Ring! ring! ring!
Ring for winter's bracing hours,
Ring for birth of spring and flowers,
Ring for summer's fruitful treasure,
Ring for autumn's boundless measure,
Ring for hands of generous giving,
Ring for vows of nobler living,
Ring for truths of tongue or pen,
Ring, "Peace on earth, good-will toward men."
    Ring! ring! ring!
Ring, that this glad year may see
Earth's accomplished jubilee!
    Ring! ring! ring!

8. REVERENCE.

O Lord, my God, Thou art very great! Thou art clothed with honor and majesty; who coverest thyself with light as with a garment; who stretchest out the heavens like a curtain; who layeth the beams of his chambers in the waters; who maketh the clouds his chariot; who walketh upon the wings of the wind; who laid the foundations of the earth, that it should not be removed forever. *The Bible.*

EXAMPLES OF EXPLOSIVE OROTUND.

1. THE BATTLE OF IVRY.

Now *glòry* to the Lord of Hosts, from whom *àll* glories are!
And glory to our *Sovereign Lìege, King Hènry* of Navarre!
Now let there be the merry sound of *mùsic* and the *dànce*,
Through thy cornfields grèen, and sunny vàles, *O pleasant land of Frànce!*

And *thòu*, Rochèlle, our *òwn* Rochelle, proud city of the wáters,
Again let *ràpture* light the eyes of all thy mourning dàughters;
As thou wert constant in our *ílls*, be *jòyous* in our *jòy*,
For cóld and stíff and stíll are they who wrought thy walls annòy.
Hurràh! *hurràh!* a single field hath turned the chance of wàr.
Hurràh! hurràh! for Ivry and *King Hénry* of *Navàrre!*
MACAULAY.

2. RICHMOND TO HIS TROOPS.

Fíght, gentlemen of *Èngland! fight*, bold *yèomen!*
Dràw, archers, draw your arrows to the *hèad*:
Spur your proud horses *hàrd*, and ride in *blòod;*
Amaze the *wèlkin* with your broken stàves.
A *thòusand* hearts are great within my bòsom:
Advance our *stàndards*, set upon our *fòes!*
Our ancient word of *còurage*, fair St. George,
Inspire us with the spleen of fiery dràgons!
Upon them! *Víctory* sits on our hèlms. SHAKESPEARE.

3. INDEPENDENCE.

The great bell swung as ne'er before:
It seemed as it would never cease;
And every word its ardor flung
From off its jubilant iron tongue
  Was, "War! WAR! WAR!" READ.

4. INDEPENDENCE.

Sír, before Gòd, I believe the hour is *còme!* My *júdgment appróves* this measure, and my whole *hèart* is *ìn* it. All that I *háve*, and all that I *ám*, and all that I *hòpe*, in *thís* life, I am now ready here to *stàke* upon it; and I *leave óff*, as I *begàn*, that, *líve* or *díe*, survive or

pĕrish, I am for the *declarâtion!* It is my *lĭving* sentiment, and, by the blessing of God, it shall be my *dy̆ing* sentiment—*Independence nŏw*, and *indepéndence | forĕver!*
WEBSTER.

EXPLOSIVE AND EXPULSIVE OROTUND.

These two forms of the orotund are often combined in the same piece, and it is not easy to draw a marked line of division. In impassioned declamation the utterance changes from one to the other, according to the degree of feeling or passion. The following extract affords an illustration:

1. WEBSTER'S TRIBUTE TO MASSACHUSETTS.

Mr. Président, I shall enter on no encòmium upon Massachúsetts; she *nècds* none. There she ís; behòld her, and judge for yoursèlves. There is her *history;* the *wòrld* knows it by heart. The *pást*, at least, is *secùre*. There is Bòston, and Còncord, and Lèxington, and Bunker Hĭll; and there they will remain *forèver*. The bones of her sóns, fallen in the great struggle for Indepéndence, now lie mingled with the soil of every State, from New Éngland to Geòrgia; and *there* they will lie *forèver*.

And, sir, where American Liberty raised its first vóice, and where its youth was nurtured and *sustáincd*, there it *still lĭves*, in the strength of its *mánhood*, and full of its *original spĭrit*. If discord and disunion shall *wóund* it; if party strife and blind ambition shall *hawk at* and *tćar* it; if folly and *mádness*, if uneasiness under salutary and *necessary restráint*, shall succeed in separating it from *that Union* by which *alóne* its existence is *made súre*—it will stand, in the end, by the side of *that crádle* in which its *infancy was rŏcked;* it will stretch forth its árm, with whatever of vigor it may still retáin, over the *friĕnds* who *gather rŏund* it; and it will fall *at làst*, if fall it *mŭst*, amid the *proudest mònuments* of its own *glóry*, and on the very *spot* of its *òrigin*.

III. Aspirated Quality.

Aspirated quality means, in general, a combination of tone with whisper, causing the huskiness and harshness produced by a superabundance of breath under the influence of powerful emotions, such as anger, rage, terror, and horror. The whisper represents the extreme of aspirated quality.

The Whisper.

The pure whisper lies half way between breathing and vocality. The half-whisper is a combination of tone and whisper. The forcible whisper is a most valuable vocal exercise. It requires full, deep, and frequent breathing, and the vigorous use of the lips, tongue, and other vocal organs. The degrees of force in the whisper are indicated by the terms effusive, expulsive, and explosive.

The pure whisper is rarely used in reading, the effect being generally *suggested* by the half-whisper, or by aspirated quality. The following exercises and examples are given for the purposes of vocal training.

Table of Aspirates.

[*First whisper the words, then the aspirates, and then give the phonic spelling of each word in a forcible whisper.*]

p	p-i-pe,	li-p	t	t-en-t,	t-as-te
wh	wh-en,	wh-y	ch	ch-ur-ch,	bir-ch
f	f-i-fe,	lea-f	sh	sh-all,	la-sh
th	th-ick,	my-th	h	h-ow,	h-ail
s	s-ale,	le-ss	k	ea-ke,	la-ke

SCHOOL ELOCUTION.

WHISPER DRILL.

Practice each exercise with three degrees of force: (1) *Effusive, or soft.* (2) *Expulsive, or forcible.* (3) *Explosive, or intense.*

1. With effusive force, repeat as many times as possible without taking breath: ā–ē–ī–ō–ū.

2. To ā, ē, ī, ō, ū, join *f*, and repeat as above; join *t*; join *h*.

3. Count, in a whisper, from one to ten, with one breath; from one to twenty; one to thirty, or more.

EXAMPLES OF EFFUSIVE WHISPER.

1. Step softly, and speak low.

2. Whisper! she is going to her final rest.
   Whisper! life is growing dim within her breast.

3. Hark! hist! around I list.
   The bounds of space all trace efface
   Of sound.

4. And his little daughter whispered,
   As she took his icy hand:
   "Isn't God upon the water,
   Just the same as on the land?"

5. And again to the child I whispered:
   "*The snow that husheth all,
   Darling, the merciful Father
   Alone can make it fall!*"

6. And the bridemaidens whispered: "'*Twere better by far,
   To have matched our fair cousin with young Lochinvar.*"

7. The red rose cries, "She is near, she is near;"
   And the white rose weeps, "She is late;"
   The larkspur listens, "I hear, I hear;"
   And the lily whispers, "I wait."

Examples of Expulsive Whisper.

1. Or whispering with white lips, "The foe! they come! they come!"

2. To bed, to bed; there's knocking at the gate.
Come, come, come, give me your hand.

3. Soldiers! You are now within a few steps of the enemy's outposts. Let every man keep the strictest silence, under pain of instant death.

Examples of Explosive Whisper.

1. Hark! I hear the bugles of the enemy. *For the boats! Forward! Forward!*

2. *Hamlet. Săw! whô?*
Horatio. The kìng, your fàther.
Hamlet. The kĭng, my făther?

3. Art thou some *gód*, some *ăngel*, or some *dévil*,
That mak'st my blood run cold and my hair to stand!

Whisper and Tone.

In some of the following illustrations of aspirated quality, the *whisper* predominates over *tone;* in others, the aspiration only affects the tone with a marked roughness, huskiness, or aspirated harshness. The extent to which aspirated quality may be applied is often a matter of taste on the part of the reader.

EXAMPLES.

1. But hush! hark! a deep sound strikes like a rising knell.

2. THE CURFEW BELL.

"Sexton," Bessie's white lips faltered, pointing to the prison old,
With its walls so dark and gloomy—walls so dark, and damp, and cold—

"I've a lover in that prison, doomed this very night to die,
At the ringing of the Curfew, and no earthly help is nigh.
Cromwell will not come till sunset," and her face grew strangely white,
As she spoke in husky whispers, "*Curfew must not ring to-night.*"

3. MACBETH TO THE GHOST.

Avàunt! and quit my sìght! Let the èarth hĭde thee!
Thy bones are màrrowless, thy blood is còld:
Thou hast no *speculàtion* in those eyes
Which thou dost glàre with!
      Hènce, horrible shàdow!
Unreal móckery, hènce!

4. HAMLET TO THE GHOST.

[*Aspirated quality and occasional half-whisper.*]

Angels and ministers of gràce defènd ùs!
Be thou a spirit of héalth, or gòblin dàmned—
Bring with thee airs from héaven, or blasts from hèll—
Be thy intents wícked, or chàritable—
Thou com'st in such a questionable shăpe
That I *wĭll* speak to thee. I'll call thee, Hàmlet,
Kìng, fàther, royal Dàne: Oh, ànswer me:
Let me not bùrst in ígnorance! but tell
Whỳ thy canonized bones, hearséd in death,
Have burst their cèrements! whỳ the sepulcher,
Wherein we saw thee quietly inurned,
Hath oped his pónderous and marble jaws,
To cast thee up again? What may this mean,
That thou, dead corse, again, in cómplete steel,
Revisit'st thus the glimpses of the moon,
Making night hideous: and we fools of nature,
So horribly to shake our disposition,
With thoughts beyond the reaches of our souls?
Say, *whỳ* is this? whèrefore? what should we dó?

5. FROM "EUGENE ARAM."

[*Horror and remorse. Aspirated pectoral and guttural quality.*]

And, lo! the universal air
　Seemed lit with ghastly flame;—
Ten thousand thousand dreadful eyes
　Were looking down in blame:
I took the dead man by his hand,
　And called upon his name!

O God! it made me quake to see
　Such sense within the slain!
But when I touched the lifeless clay,
　The blood gushed out amain!
For every clot, a burning spot
　Was scorching in my brain!

And now, from forth the frowning sky,
　From the heaven's topmost height,
I heard a voice—the awful voice
　Of the blood-avenging sprite:—
"*Thou guilty man! take up thy dead
　And hide it from my sight!*"　　　Hood.

6. MACBETH.

[*Horror and fear. Intense suppressed force; prevailing monotone; very slow movement; strong aspirated quality.*]

Nōw ō'er the ōne hālf wōrld
Nāture sēems dĕad; and wĭcked drēams abūse
The cūrtained slĕep; nōw wĭtchcraft cĕlebrates
Pale Hēcate's ŏfferings; and wĭthered *murder*,
Alārumed by his sĕntinel, the wōlf,
Whōse hōwl's his wătch, thūs wĭth his stēalthy pāce,
Tōwards his dēsign
Moves like a ghòst.—Thōu sūre and fīrm-sĕt ēarth!
Hēar nōt mȳ stĕps, whĭch wāy thĕy wălk; fōr fĕar
The very *stònes* prāte of my whereabout,
And tāke the prĕsent hŏrror frōm the tīme
Whĭch nōw sūits wĭth it.

7. DARIUS GREEN AND HIS FLYING MACHINE.

[*Secrecy. Forcible whisper and half-whisper.*]

And one by one, through a hole in the wall,
In under the dusty barn they crawl,
Dressed in their Sunday garments all;
And a very astonishing sight was that,
When each in his cobwebbed coat and hat
Came up through the floor like an ancient rat.
    And there they hid;
    And Reuben slid
The fastenings back, and the door undid.
    "Keep dark!" said he,
"While I squint an' see what the' is to see."
    "Hush!" Reuben said,
    "He's up in the shed!
He's opened the winder—I see his head!
He stretches it out, an' pokes it about,
Lookin' to see 'f the coast is clear,
    An' nobody near;—
Guess he don' o' who's hid in here!
He's riggin' a spring-board over the sill!
Stop laffin', Solomon! Burke, keep still!
He's a-climbing out now—Of all the things!
What's he got on? I van, it's wings!
An' that 't other thing? I vum, it's a tail!
An' there he sets like a hawk on a rail!
Steppin' careful, he travels the length
Of his spring-board, and teeters to try its strength.
Now he stretches his wings, like a monstrous bat;
Peeks over his shoulder, this way an' that,
Fer to see 'f there's any one passin' by;
But there's on'y a ca'f an' a goslin' nigh.
    Flop—flop—an' plump
    To the ground with a thump,
Flutterin' and flounderin' all in a lump."   TROWBRIDGE.

Special Aspirate Drill.

[In pronouncing the following words having the combination **hw**, *the aspiration is often very feebly given or not given at all. Sound the* **hw** *with marked force.]*

way	*whey*	wet	*whet*
wear	*where*	wit	*whit*
weal	*wheel*	wot	*what*
wen	*when*	wig	*whig*
were	*whir*	wield	*wheeled*
wine	*whine*	witch	*which*
wight	*white*	wist	*whist*
wile	*while*	weather	*whether*

Pronunciation Drill.

[Keep the lungs well filled with air and exhaust the breath upon each word.]

whale	whalebone	whatever
whap	whapper	whatsoever
wharf	wharfage	wheelbarrow
wheat	what-not	wheel-horse
wheeze	wheezing	wheelwright
whelp	whereas	whensoever
whelm	wherever	wheresoever
whence	whenever	whereabout
whew	whereby	whereunto
whiff	wherefore	wherewithal
whim	whiffle	whimper
whip	whinny	whipsaw
whir	whirlwind	whirligig
whirl	whistle	whisper
whisk	whittle	whizzing
white	whither	whoa

IV. Guttural Quality.

The *guttural*, or throat, quality is the harsh, grating, rasping utterance to which the voice tends in the expression of hatred, contempt, revenge, and loathing. It is often combined with aspirated quality in the expression of extreme impatience or disgust, intense rage, and extreme contempt.

EXAMPLES.

1. OTHELLO.

Oh, that the slave had *forty thousand lives,*
My great revenge had stomach for them all.

2. THE SPY.

You shall *die,* base *dog!* and that before
Yon *cloud* has passed over the *sun!*

3. SHYLOCK TO ANTONIO.

Signior Antonio, màny a time and óft,
On the Riálto you have ràted me
About my môneys and my úsances;
Still have I bórne it with a patient shrúg,
For sùfferance is the badge of *all our trìbe:*
You call me—misbeliever, cût-throat, dôg,
And *spìt* upon my Jewish gàberdine,
And all for use of that which is *mìne òwn.*
Well, thén, it now appears, you need mý hèlp.
Go to, thèn; you cóme to me, and you sáy,
"Shýlock, we would have môneys;" yôu say sò;
Yôu, that did void your rheum upon my bèard,
And fòot me as you spurn a stranger cûr
Over your thrèshold; môneys is your sùit.
What should I sáy to you? Should I not sáy,
"Hath a dŏg mŏney? is it possible
A cûr can lend thrée thóusand dúcats?" or
Shall I bend lôw, and in a bôndman's key,
With bated breath, and whispering humbleness,

Say this:—

"Fair sír, you *spát* on me on Wednesday lást;
You *spúrned* me such a dáy; another time
You called me—*dóg;* and for *these cóurtesies*
I'll *lènd* you—*thus much—mòneys.*"

V. THE FALSETTO.

The falsetto is the thin, sharp, high-pitched tone produced when the voice *breaks,* or gets above its natural compass. It is used by men when they imitate the voices of women and children. It is the tone suitable for the expression of old age, sickness, feebleness, pain, and helpless terror.

1. "*My child! my child!*" with sobs and tears,
    She shrieked upon his callous ears.

2. "Billy—where are you, Billy, I say? Come, Billy, come home to your best of mothers!"

3. And even Tiny Tim, excited by the two young Cratchits, beat on the table with the handle of his knife, and feebly cried, "*Hurrah!*"

4. Mr. Orator Puff had two tones in his voice,
    The one squeaking *thus,* and the other down *so;*
    In each sentence he uttered he gave you your choice;
    For one half was B alt, and the rest G below.
        Oh! oh! Orator Puff,
        One voice for an orator's surely enough!

"Oh! save!" he exclaimed, in his he-and-she tones,
"Help me out! help me out! I have broken my bones!"
"Help you out!" said a stranger, who passed, "what
    a bother!
Why, there's two of you there; can't you help one
    another?"
        Oh! oh! Orator Puff,
        One voice for an orator's surely enough!

5. And in a coaxing tone he cries,
"*Charco'! charco'!*"
And baby with a laugh replies,
"*Ah, go! Ah, go!*"
"*Charco'!*"—"*Ah, go!*"

VI. THE SEMITONE.

When the voice slides through the interval of a semitone only, it gives the plaintive tones expressive of sadness, grief, or pathetic entreaty. If the inflection runs through the interval of a tone and a half—a minor third in music—it becomes more plaintive, and marks a stronger degree of pathos or sadness; and when the inflection extends into the minor fifth, it denotes still stronger pathetic feeling.

The semitone, then, is the plaintive tone in reading, corresponding to the minor key in music. It should be used delicately, for, in excess, it runs into the whine, or becomes the affectation of cant.

SEMITONE DRILL.

1. Sound the vocals, ā, ē, ī, ō, ū, three times, on the interval between C and C sharp; then on the minor third; then on the minor fifth.

2. Count from one to twenty on the same notes as above.

EXAMPLES OF SEMITONE.

1. O come in life, or come in death,
   O lost! my love, Elizabeth.

2. For I am poor and miserably old.

3. How many hired servants of my father's have bread enough and to spare, and I perish with hunger! I will arise and go to my father and will say to him,

"Father, I have sinned against heaven and before thee, and am no more worthy to be called thy son: make me as one of thy hired servants!"

4. MY CHILD.

I can not make him *déad!*
His fair sunshiny *héad*
Is ever bounding round my study chàir;
Yet, when my eyes, now dim
With tears, I turn to him,
The vision vánishes, he is *not thére!*

I walk my parlor flòor,
And, through the open dóor,
I hear a fòotfall on the chamber stàir;
I'm stepping toward the hall
To give the boy a cáll;
And then bethink me that he is *not thére!*

PIERPONT.

5. HIAWATHA.

O the long and dreary Winter!
O the cold and cruel Winter!
Ever thicker, thicker, thicker
Froze the ice on lake and river;
Ever deeper, deeper, deeper
Fell the snow o'er all the landscape,
Fell the covering snow, and drifted
Through the forest, round the village.

O the famine and the fever!
O the wasting of the famine!
O the blasting of the fever!
O the wailing of the children!
O the anguish of the women!
All the earth was sick and famished;
Hungry was the air around them,
Hungry was the sky above them,

And the hungry stars in heaven
Like the eyes of wolves glared at them!

"Give your children food, O Father!
Give us food, or we must perish!
Give me food for Minnehaha,
For my dying Minnehaha!"
Through the far-resounding forest,
Through the forest vast and vacant
Rang that cry of desolation;
But there came no other answer
Than the echo of his crying,
Than the echo of the woodlands,
"*Minnehaha! Minnehaha!*" LONGFELLOW.

6. BABIE BELL.

It came upon us by degrees,
  We saw its shadow ere it fell,
The knowledge that our God had sent
  His messenger for Babie Bell.
We shuddered with unlanguaged pain,
And all our thoughts ran into tears,
  Like sunshine into rain.
We cried aloud in our belief,
"*Oh, smite us gently, gently, God!*
Teach us to bend and kiss the rod,
  And perfect grow through grief."
Ah, how we loved her, God can tell;
  Her heart was folded deep in ours;
Our hearts are broken, Babie Bell. ALDRICH.

7. MACBETH.

To-morrow, and to-morrow, and to-morrow,
Creeps in this petty pace from day to day
To the last syllable of recorded time,
And all our yesterdays have lighted fools
The way to dusty death. SHAKESPEARE.

8. NEW YEAR'S EVE.

You'll bury me, my mother, just beneath the hawthorn shade;
And you'll come sometimes and see me where I am lowly laid.
I shall not forget you, mother; I shall hear you when you pass,
With your feet above my head in the long and pleasant grass.

Good-night, good-night! When I have said good-night for evermore,
And you see me carried out from the threshold of the door,
Don't let Effie come to see me till my grave be growing green—
She'll be a better child to you than ever I have been.

TENNYSON'S May Queen.

9. FROM "BERTHA IN THE LANE."

[*This extract should be read with subdued force, slow movement, and prevailing poetic monotone and semitone.*]

Colder grow my hands and feet;—
 When I wear the shroud I made,
Let the folds lie straight and neat,
 And the rosemary be spread;—
That if any friend should come
(To see thee, sweet!), all the room
 May be lifted out of gloom.

And, dear Bertha, let me keep
 On my hand this little ring—
Which at nights, when others sleep,
 I can still see glittering.
Let me wear it out of sight,
In the grave—where it will light
 All the dark up, day and night.

On that grave drop not a tear!
  Else, though fathom-deep the place,
Through the woolen shroud I wear
  I shall feel it on my face.
Rather smile there, blessed one,
Thinking of me in the sun;
Or forget me—smiling on!   E. B. BROWNING.

VII. RECAPITULATION OF QUALITY.

1. Pure tone is the tone of ordinary conversation, and of unimpassioned didactic, narrative, or descriptive reading.

2. The orotund is the tone expressive of deep feeling, of reverence, of sublimity, and of grandeur. It prevails in oratorical declamation, and in the reading or recitation of lyric or dramatic poetry.

3. Aspirated quality is expressive of secrecy, feebleness, terror, horror, and amazement.

4. Guttural quality is expressive of disgust, impatience, hatred, and revenge.

5. The semitone is the plaintive expression, in the minor key, of pathos, pity, grief, or entreaty.

EXAMPLES OF QUALITY.

PURE TONE.

Was it the chime of a tiny bell
That came so sweet to my dreaming ear?

OROTUND.

1. Build thee more stately mansions, O my soul!
2. And let the bass of heaven's deep organ blow.

WHISPER.

To bed, to bed; there's knocking at the gate.
Come, come, come, give me your hand.

ASPIRATED.

Angels, and ministers of grace, defend us.

GUTTURAL.

How like a fawning *públican* he looks!

SEMITONE.

For Heaven's sake, Hubert, let me not be bound.

VIII. GENERAL REVIEW DRILL.

1. Repeat, three times, the long vowel sounds, ā, ē, ī, ō, ū: (1) With moderate rising inflection. (2) Moderate falling inflection. (3) High rising inflection. (4) Emphatic falling inflection. (5) High rising circumflex. (6) Emotional falling circumflex. (7) Low monotone.

2. Repeat, three times, ā, ē, ī, ō, ū: (1) With very soft force. (2) With soft force. (3) With moderate force. (4) Loud force. (5) Very loud force.

3. Repeat, three times, ā, ē, ī, ō, ū: (1) With the median stress. (2) With the radical stress. (3) With compound stress. (4) With vanishing stress. (5) Thorough stress. (6) With intermittent stress.

4. Repeat, three times, ā, ē, ī, ō, ū: (1) With slow movement. (2) With moderate movement. (3) With fast movement.

5. Repeat, three times, ā, ē, ī, ō, ū: (1) With very high pitch. (2) With high pitch. (3) With middle pitch. (4) With low pitch. (5) With very low pitch.

6. Repeat, three times, ā, ē, ī, ō, ū: (1) With the whisper. (2) With pure tone. (3) With the orotund.

CHAPTER VI.

MODULATION AND STYLE OF EXPRESSION.

SECTION I.

MODULATION.

1. *Modulation* is the variation in the tones of the voice in order to express the ever-varying thought, feeling, emotion, or passion to be expressed.

2. These changes depend largely upon the perception, taste, and judgment of readers; upon the extent to which readers are capable of entering into the spirit of what they read; and upon the flexibility of the voice in expressing different shades of emotion by appropriate tones.

3. There are certain general principles that control modulation, but there are no fixed rules of detail which can be applied in the exercise of "good taste."

4. "The importance of this principle of adaptation of voice," says Prof. William Russell, "may be perceived by adverting to the fact, that nothing so impairs the effect of address, as the want of spirit and expression in elocution.

5. "No gravity of tone, or intensity of utterance, or precision of enunciation, can atone for the absence of that natural change of voice, by which the ear is enabled to receive and recognize the tones of the various emotions accompanying the train of thought which the speaker is expressing. These, and these only, can indi-

cate his own sense of what he utters, or communicate it by sympathy to his audience.

6. "The adaptation of the voice to the expression of sentiment is not less important, when considered in reference to meaning, as dependent on distinctions strictly intellectual, or not necessarily implying a vivid or varied succession of emotions.

7. "The correct and adequate representation of continuous or successive thought, requires its appropriate intonation; as may be observed in those tones of voice which naturally accompany discussion and argument, even in their most moderate forms.

8. "The modulation or varying of tone is important, also, as a matter of cultivated taste. It is the appropriate grace of vocal expression; it has a charm founded in the constitution of our nature; it touches the finest and deepest sensibilities of the soul; it constitutes the spirit and eloquence of the human voice, whether regarded as the noblest instrument of music, or the appointed channel of thought and feeling."

I. GENERAL PRINCIPLES.

1. A *low key* is the natural expression of awe, reverence, solemnity, sadness, and melancholy; a *high key*, of violent passions, such as anger and rage, joy and exultation. The *middle key* is the natural pitch of conversation, and of unimpassioned narrative, descriptive, or didactic writing.

2. *Soft* or *gentle force* is expressive of subdued feeling, pathos, and tenderness; *loud force*, of strong passions and oratorical declamation; *moderate force*, of unimpassioned thought.

3. *Slow movement* is appropriate to the expression of deep thought, power, grandeur, sublimity, solemnity; *fast movement* is characteristic of vivacity, joy, and uncon-

trolled passion; *moderate movement*, of unimpassioned narrative, descriptive, or didactic pieces.

4. The *whisper* is expressive of secrecy, silence, or extreme fear; *guttural quality*, of revenge, hatred, despair, horror, or loathing; the *orotund*, of power, grandeur, vastness, sublimity; the *falsetto*, of puerility or weakness; the *semitone*, of sadness and pathetic entreaty.

5. The *radical stress* is expressive of command, assertion, force, power, and excited feelings; the *median stress*, of peace, tranquillity, solemnity, grandeur, sublimity, reverence, and awe.

6. Then there is the variety that arises from imitative reading, or the suiting of the sound to the word, phrase, or sentence; and that of *personation*, or the changes of expression to denote the different characters in a dialogue or play.

II. STYLE OF READING.

1. The following analysis of a good style of reading is taken from Russell's "American School Reader": "If we observe attentively the voice of a good reader or speaker, we shall find his style of utterance marked by the following traits. His voice pleases the ear by its very sound. It is wholly free from affected suavity; yet, while perfectly natural, it is round, smooth, and agreeable. It is equally free from the faults of feebleness and of undue loudness.

2. "It is perfectly distinct, in the execution of every sound, in every word. It is free from errors of negligent usage and corrupted style in pronunciation. It avoids a measured, rhythmical chant, on the one hand, and a broken, irregular movement, on the other.

3. "It renders expression clear, by an attentive observance of appropriate pauses, and gives weight and effect to sentiment, by occasional impressive cessations of voice. It sheds light on the meaning of sentences,

by the emphatic force which it gives to significant and expressive words.

4. "It avoids the 'school' tone of uniform inflections, and varies the voice upward or downward, as the successive clauses of a sentence demand. It marks the character of every emotion, by its peculiar traits of tone; and hence its effect upon the ear, in the utterance of connected sentences and paragraphs, is like that of a varied melody, in music, played or sung with ever-varying feeling and expression."

SECTION II.

THE READING OF POETRY.

I. INTRODUCTORY.

1. Pupils are sometimes told to read verse as if it were prose. Such a direction may be given to counteract the tendency to sing-song, or it may be applied in the reading of doggerel rhymes; but it cannot be applied to the reading of *poetry*.

2. Poetry, being the language of imagination, sentiment, or passion, requires, as compared with prose, a greater variety of expression. Moreover, poetry is rhythmical and melodious, and, in reading it, attention must be given to movement and harmony.

3. "The modulation of the voice," says Prof. Russell, "in adaptation to *different species of metrical composition*, is indispensable to the appropriate or effective reading of verse. The purest forms of poetry become, when deprived of this aid, nothing but awkward prose. A just and delicate observance of the effect of meter, on the other hand, is one of the surest means of imparting that inspiration of feeling which it is the design of poetry to produce."

4. In the reading of poetry, the pupil should bear in mind the following hints: (1) The movement, or time, in verse, is generally slower than in prose, the vowel and liquid sounds being slightly prolonged. (2) In poetry, as compared with prose, the *force* is somewhat softened for the sake of melody. (3) The existence of meter in poetry requires a rendering of verse different from the reading of prose. The meter should not be made prominent, but should be delicately indicated. As in prose, attention must be given to the sense, to emphasis, and to inflection.

II. Cæsural Pauses.

The cæsural pause is a slight rest occurring somewhere near the middle of the line in certain kinds of verse. In heroic and blank verse, it commonly falls at the end of the fourth syllable. In smoothly written verse, the grammatical pause marking a phrase or a clause is often made to coincide with the cæsural pause.

EXAMPLES.

1. This is the place, | the centre of the grove:
   Here stands the oak, | the monarch of the wood.
   How sweet and solemn | is this midnight scene!
   The silver moon, | unclouded, holds her way
   Through skies where I | could count each little star;
   The fanning west wind | scarcely stirs the leaves.

2. A man he was | to all the country dear,
   And passing rich | with forty pounds a year;
   Remote from towns | he ran his godly race,
   Nor e'er had changed, | nor wished to change, his place;
   Unpracticed he | to fawn, or seek for power,
   By doctrines fashioned | to the varying hour;
   Far other aims | his heart had learned to prize,
   More skilled to raise | the wretched than to rise.

III. Meter, or Rhythmical Accent.

1. *Meter* is the measure of rhythm, or metrical feet, in poetry. One difference between the reading of prose and of poetry consists in the distinctive marking of the rhythm in verse. If read without regard to rhythm, the sonorous harmony of the higher forms of poetry is lost.

2. As some knowledge of prosody is generally obtained from the school text-books on rhetoric, only an allusion to the subject is necessary in a manual of elocution.

3. In reading poetry, the measure should be delicately indicated, but not made so prominent as to run into sing-song, or to break the grammatical relation of words.

4. The melody of verse often depends on making some word, or successive words, slightly emphatic, as in the following line from Longfellow's "Psalm of Life:"

"*And* things | *are* not | *what* they | *seem.*"

If "not" is emphasized, the rhythm is broken. So in the successive stanzas of Bryant's "Planting of the Apple-tree," the emphasis in the last line of the successive stanzas falls as follows:

1. "So *plant* we | the *apple-tree.*"
2. "When *we* plant | the *apple-tree,*" etc.

IV. Kinds of Verse.

1. The following summary from Prof. Russell's "American Elocutionist" may be of interest to the critical student: "The influence of the various kinds of verse on the voice may be considered as affecting generally the *rate,* or *movement,* and the *time,* of utterance.

2. "Thus, *blank verse* is remarkably *slow* and *stately* in the character of its tone; and the timing of the pauses requires attention chiefly to *length. Heroic verse* is commonly in the *same prevailing strain,* but not to such an extent as the preceding.

3. "The *octo-syllabic meter* is generally more *quick* and *lively* in its movement, and the pauses are comparatively brief. But, under the influence of *slow time*, it gives intensity to grief, and tenderness to the pathetic tone.

4. "The *quatrain*, or four-lined stanza, in the common form (called sometimes *common meter*), has a comparatively musical arrangement of the lines, and a peculiar character in its cadence, which admits of its expressing the *extremes of emotion whether grave or gay*. It prevails, accordingly, in *hymns* and in *ballads* alike, whether the latter are *pathetic* or *humorous*. It derives the former character from the observance of *slow rate*, and the latter from *quick rate*.

5. "*Trochaic* verse has a peculiar energy, from the abruptness of its character—the foot commencing either with a long or an accented syllable. In *gay pieces*, and with *quick time* in utterance, it produces a *dancing* strain of voice, peculiarly adapted to the expression of *joy;* while in *grave* and *vehement* strains, with *slow time*, it produces the utmost *force* and *severity* of tone. These two extremes are strikingly exemplified in Milton's 'L'Allegro' and 'Il Penseroso.'

6. "*Anapæstic meter* has a peculiar *fullness* and *sweetness* of melody. *Slow* time accordingly renders it deeply *pathetic*, and *quick* time renders it the most graceful expression of *joy*. This, as well as iambic and trochaic verse, becomes well fitted to express the mood of *calmness* and tranquillity, when the *rate* is rendered *moderate*."

V. Accent of Words.

The accent of a word is sometimes changed to prevent breaking the measure, as in the following examples:

1. Ye icefalls! ye that from your dizzy heights
   Adown enormous *rav'*ines slope amain.

2. That thou, dead corse, arrayed in *com'*plete steel.

3. And these few precepts in thy memory, see thou charac′ter.

4. Then lend the eye a terrible as*pect′*.

5. I must be patient till the heavens look with an as*pect′* more favorable.

VI. Final -ed.

The final -*ed* is often sounded as a separate syllable, to prevent a break in the meter.

EXAMPLES.

1. To live with her and live with thee
In unreprov*éd* pleasures free.

2. Of link*éd* sweetness long drawn out.

3. Rode arm*éd* men adown the glen.

4. Through this the well-belov*éd* Brutus stabbed.

5. And as he plucked his curs*éd* steel away.

6. To wear an undeserv*éd* dignity.

7. That orb*éd* maiden with white fire laden.

8. Whereat she smil*éd* with so sweet a cheer.

9. While that the arm*éd* hand doth fight abroad,
The advis*éd* head defends itself at home.

VII. Rhyme.

In reading poetry, the words that rhyme must sometimes be specially emphasized. Sometimes, also, the pronunciation of a word may be changed to make it rhyme with another word, as wīnd for wĭnd.

In reading the following couplet from Hudibras,

"And pulpit, drum ecclesiastic,
He beat with drum instead of *a* stick,"

it becomes necessary to emphasize the *a*, or rather to

sound the two words "a stick" like a word of two syllables accented on the first, thus—*a′stick*.

In reading the following lines from the same poem, the word "coloneling" is pronounced exactly as it is spelled, *col′o nel ing*, in four syllables:

"Then did Sir Knight abandon dwelling,
And out he rode *a-coloneling*."

Also, in the following,

"And wisely tell what hour o' th' day
The clock does strike, by algebrā,"

the long sound is given to final *a* in *algebra*, to make the word rhyme with *day*.

In the following couplets from Holmes, the rhyming words are italicized for emphasis:

"It is a pity and a shame—alas! alas! I *know* it is,
To tread the trodden grapes again, but so it *has* been,
  so it *is*."

In this example the three words, "know it is," are pronounced like a word of three syllables, accented on the first, thus—*know′*-it-is; so, also, *so′*-it-is.

VIII. Examples of Rhyme.

1. AT THE ATLANTIC DINNER.

I suppose it's myself that you're making allusion to,
And bringing the sense of dismay and confusion to.
Of course *some* must speak—they are always selected to,
But pray what's the reason that I am expected to?
I'm not fond of wasting my breath as those fellows do
That want to be blowing forever as bellows do;
Their legs are uneasy, but why will you jog any
That long to stay quiet beneath the mahogany?

HOLMES.

2. CLASS MEETING, 1875.

It is a pity and a shame—alas! alas! I know it is,
To tread the trodden grapes again, but so it has been,
  so it is;

The purple vintage long is past, with ripened clusters
    bursting so
They filled the wine-vats to the brim—'t is strange you
    will be thirsting so!

For who can tell by what he likes what other people's
    fancies are?
How all men think the best of wives their own par-
    ticular Nancies are!
If what I sing you brings a smile, you will not stop
    to catechise,
Nor read Bœotia's lumbering line with nicely scanning
    Attic eyes.

Though on the once unfurrowed brows the harrow-teeth
    of Time may show,
Though all the strain of crippling years the halting
    feet of rhyme may show,
We look and hear with melting hearts, for what we all
    remember is
The morn of Spring, nor heed how chill the sky of
    gray November is.

Thanks to the gracious powers above from all mankind
    that singled us,
And dropped the pearl of friendship in the cup they
    kindly mingled us,
And bound us in a wreath of flowers with hoops of
    steel knit under it;—
Nor time, nor space, nor chance, nor change, nor death
    himself shall sunder it!

            HOLMES.

SECTION III.
IMITATIVE READING.

The extent to which imitative reading, or the suiting of sound to sense, may properly be carried, in certain classes of selections, is a matter in regard to which there is a diversity of opinion among elocutionists. It is one of those questions of taste that cannot be regulated by definite directions applicable to all cases. Some general principles, however, may be laid down, from which there is no intelligent dissent.

The style of reading should be imitative in the sense of making it conform to the spirit and meaning of the piece.

In the utterance of words in which the sound seems to approximate to the sense, such as *buzz, hiss, thunder, groan, sigh, scream*, etc., the tone may be suggestive of the idea. Thus, in reading such passages as,

"From his lips escaped a *groan*,"

though an actual groan would be ridiculous, the word "groan" may be uttered so as to *suggest* a groan.

EXAMPLES.

1. Hear the loud *alárum* bells—*brázen bells*.
2. *Clang! clang!* the massive anvils *ring*.
3. *Blow*, bugle; answer echoes, *dying, dying, dying*.
4. Oh! the *bells!* what a tale their terror tells
   Of despair!
   How they *clang*, and *clash*, and *roar*,
   What a *horror* they *outpour*
   On the bosom of the *palpitating air!*

Wherever the author distinctly suggests an imitation, it should be given so far as is consistent with good taste. Thus, when Longfellow writes,

"And *loud* that *clarion* voice replied,"

it is evident that the refrain, "Excelsior!" should be given in a loud, clear, resonant manner.

Examples for Practice.

1. A voice replied far up the height, "*Excelsior!*"
2. She seemed in the same silver tones to say,
   "Passing away, passing away!"
3. What this grim, ungainly, ghastly, gaunt, and ominous bird of yore
   Meant in croaking, "Nevermore."
4. An ancient time-piece says to all,
   "*Forever—never! Never—forever!*"
5. "To all the truth we tell, we tell,"
   Shouted in ecstasies a bell.

6. Bunker Hill.

How the bayonets gleamed and glistened, as we *looked far down and listened*
To the *trampling* and the *drum-beat* of the belted grenadiers.
Over heaps all torn and gory—shall I tell the fearful story,
How they *surged above the breastwork* as a sea breaks o'er a deck;
How, driven, yet scarce defeated, our worn-out men retreated,
With their powder-horns all emptied, like the swimmers from a wreck! Holmes.

Imitation should not be too literal. The attempt is sometimes made in reading Tennyson's "Bugle Song," to give a realistic imitation of the notes of a bugle. While the professional reader may attempt such a feat of vocal gymnastics, it is certainly outside of the limits of good taste in school reading. The words, "Blow, bugle, blow," may be given with a prolonged swell, and in a thin, clear, pure tone, so as to *suggest* the bugle note.

So in reciting Poe's "Bells," the imitative rendering is often carried to a ridiculous extreme. In these and similar cases it is not a literal reproduction of the sound that should be attempted, but an artistic and idealized suggestion of it.

EXAMPLES.

1. And grummer, grummer, grummer,
Rolled the drum of the drummer,
Through the morn.

And rounder, rounder, rounder,
Roared the iron six-pounder,
Hurling death.

2. I hear them marching o'er the hill;
I hear them fainter, fainter still.

3. CHURCH BELLS.

"In deeds of love, excel! excel!"
Chimed out from ivied towers a bell.

"O heed the ancient landmarks well!"
In *solemn* tones exclaimed a bell.

"Ye purifying waters swell!"
In *mellow* tones rung out a bell.
"To all the truth we tell! we tell!"
Shouted in ecstasies a bell.

4. WHEN THE COWS COME HOME.

When klingle, klangle, klingle,
Far down the dusty dingle,
The cows are coming home;
Now sweet and clear, now faint and low,
The airy tinklings come and go,
Like chimings from the far-off tower,

Or patterings of an April shower
That makes the daisies grow.
Ko-ling, ko-lang, kolinglelingle,
Far down the darkening dingle,
The cows are coming home.

5. CHARCOAL.

And thus from morn to eve he cried,
"Charco'! charco'!"
While echo faint and far replied,
"Charco'!"—"Hark, O!"
And in a *coaxing* tone he cries,
"Charco'! charco'!"
And baby with a *laugh* replies,
"Ah, go!"—"Ah, go!"
"Charco'!"—"Ah, go!" TROWBRIDGE.

6. FIRE.

Fire! fire! fire!
See the red flames leaping higher.

Peal! peal! peal!
Bells of brass and bells of steel.

Crash! crash! crash!
See the fiery surges lash!

Fire! fire! fire!
Bristles every throbbing wire.

7. EXCELSIOR.

And like a *silver clarion* rung—"*Excelsior!*"
And from his lips escaped a *groan*—"*Excelsior!*"
But still he answered with a *sigh*—"*Excelsior!*"
A voice replied far up the height—"*Excelsior!*"

8. THE BELLS.

Hear the sledges with the *bèlls—sílver* bells!
What a world of *mèrriment* their melody foretells!

Hear the mellow *wèdding* bells—*gólden* bells!
What a world of *háppiness* their harmony foretells!

Hear the loud *alárum* bells—*brázen* bells!
What a tale of *tèrror* now their turbulency tells!

Hear the *tòlling* of the bells—*íron* bells!
What a world of solemn *thòught* their monody compels!
Poe.

SECTION IV.

EXERCISES IN MODULATION.

Modulation is the variation of voice according to the sentiment, thought, or emotion to be expressed. In impassioned reading, tones are the most prominent qualities of voice.

Thorough drill on the following examples will break up the tendency of pupils to read all kinds of selections in one formal "school-tone." It is left for teachers and pupils to exercise their own judgment and taste in the rendering of these extracts, which embrace a wide range of expression.

EXAMPLES.

1. Blow, bugle, blow, set the wild echoes flying,
   Blow, bugle, answer echoes, dying, dying, dying.

2. The loud wind dwindled to a whisper low.

3. There is a silence where no sound may be.

4. I hear them marching o'er the hill,
   I hear them fainter, fainter still.

5. "Cusha, cusha, cusha," calling.

6. *To arms! to arms! to arms!* they cry.

7. *Arm! arm!*—it is—it is the cannon's opening roar.

8. Advance your standards, draw your willing swords!

9. Pity the sorrows of a poor old man.

10. Ring, joyous chords!—ring out again!

11. Roll on, thou deep and dark blue ocean, roll.

12. Come and trip it, as ye go,
On the light fantastic toe.

13. But hush! hark! a deep sound strikes like a rising knell.

14. Away! away! and on we dash.

15. *Forward the light brigade!*

16. All's hushed as midnight yet.

17. Hail! holy light, offspring of Heaven, first born.

18. Liberty! Freedom! Tyranny is dead!

19. Silence how dead! and darkness how profound!

20. Or whispering with white lips, "The foe! they come, they come!"

21. Joy! joy! Shout, shout aloud for joy!

22. Strike! till the last armed foe expires!

23. How like a fawning publican he looks!

24. Thou hast all seasons for thine own, O Death!

25. Ring the alarm-bell! Murder! and treason!

26. Ride softly! ride slowly! the onset is near!
Move slowly! move softly! the sentry may hear.

27. No! by St. Bride of Bothwell, no!

28.   On a sudden open fly
The infernal gates, and on their hinges grate
Harsh thunder!

29.   Heaven opened wide
Her ever-during gates, harmonious sound,
On golden hinges turning.

30. But gentler now the small waves glide,
   Like playful lambs on a mountain side.

31. With many a weary step, and many a groan,
   Up the high hill he heaves a huge round stone.

32. When Ajax strives some rock's vast weight to throw,
   The line, too, labors, and the words move slow.

33. Soft is the strain when zephyr gently blows,
   And the smooth stream in smoother numbers flows.
   But when loud surges lash the sounding shore,
   The hoarse rough verse should like the torrent roar.

34. Clang! clang! the massive anvils ring,
   Clang! clang! a hundred hammers swing;
   Like the thunder rattle of a tropic sky,
   The mighty blows still multiply.

35. SONG OF THE SHIRT.

Work! work! work!
Till the brain begins to swim;
Work! work! work!
Till the eyes are heavy and dim!
   Seam, and gusset, and band,
   Band, and gusset, and seam,
      Till over the buttons I fall asleep,
      And sew them on in a dream! — *Hood.*

36. THE TWO VOICES FROM THE GRAVE.

First Voice.

How frightful the grave! how deserted and drear!
With the howls of the storm-wind, the creaks of the bier,
   And the white bones all clattering together!

Second Voice.

How peaceful the grave! its quiet how deep!
Its zephyrs breathe calmly, and soft is its sleep,
   And flow'rets perfume it with ether.

37. MILITARY COMMAND.

"Forward the Light Brigade!
Charge for the guns!" he said.
Shoulder arms! Forward march! Halt!
Charge! Chester, charge! On! Stanley, on!

38. THE HERALD'S CALL.

Rejoice, ye men of Angiers, ring your bells,
King John, your king and England's, doth approach.
Open your gates and give the victor way.

SECTION V.

DIALECT READING AND PERSONATION.

In dialect reading, the peculiarities of speech should be reproduced with fidelity, but should not be exaggerated. In the reading of dialogues there is, of necessity, a marked change of tone and manner when the reader personates two or more characters.

EXAMPLES OF DIALECT READING.

1. SKIPPER IRESON'S RIDE.

Scores of women, old and young,
Strong of muscle, and glib of tongue,
Pushed and pulled up the rocky lane,
Shouting and singing the shrill refrain:
"*Here's Flud Oirson, fur his horrd horrt,
Torr'd an' futherr'd an' corr'd in a corrt
By the women o' Morble'cad!*" —Whittier.

2. THE DEACON'S MASTERPIECE.

But the Deacon swore, as deacons do,
With an "*I dew vum,*" or an "*I tell yeou,*"
He would build one shay to beat the *taown*,
'n' the *kaounty* 'n' all the *kentry raoun'*;
It should be so built that it *couldn'* break *daown*.

"Fur," said the Deacon, "'t's mighty plain
Thut the weakes' place mus' stan' the strain;
'n' the way t' fix it, uz I maintain,
    Is only jest
T' make that place uz stroug uz the rest."
HOLMES.

3. SPRING.

O little city-gals, don't never go it
Blind on the word o' noospaper or poet!
They're apt to puff, an' May-day seldom looks
Up in the country ez it doos in books;
They're no more like than hornets'-nests an' hives,
Or printed sarmons be to holy lives.
I, with my trouses perched on cow-hide boots,
Tuggin' my foundered feet out by the roots,
Hev seen ye come to fling on April's hearse
Your muslin nosegays from the milliner's—
Puzzlin' to find dry ground your queen to choose,
An' dance your throats sore in morocker shoes;
I've seen ye an' felt proud, thet, come wut would,
Our Pilgrim stock wuz pithed with hardihood.
Pleasure does make us Yankees kind o' winch,
Ez though 'twuz sumthin' paid for by the inch;
But yit we du contrive to worry thru—
Ef Dooty tells us thet the thing's to du—
An' kerry a hollerday, ef we set out,
Ez stiddily ez though 'twuz a redoubt.
LOWELL.

4. THE GRIDIRON.

Patrick. I beg pardon, sir; but maybe I'm under a mistake, but I thought I was in France, sir. An't you all furriners here? Parley voo frongsay?

Frenchman. Oui, monsieur.

Patrick. Then, would you lind me the loan of a gridiron, if you plase? I know it's a liberty I take, sir; but it's only in the regard of bein' cast away; and if you plase, sir, parley voo frongsay?

Frenchman. Oui, monsieur, oui.

Patrick. Then would you lind me the loan of a gridiron, sir, and you'll obleege me?

Frenchman. Monsieur, pardon, monsieur—

Patrick. Then lind me the loan of a gridiron, I say.

Frenchman. Oui, oui, monsieur.

Patrick. Then lind me the loan of a gridiron, and howld your prate. Well, I'll give you one chance more, you owld thafe! Are you a Christian, at all, at all? Are you a furriner that all the world calls so p'lite? Bad luck to you! do you understand your mother tongue? Parley voo frongsay? *(Very loud.)* Parley voo frongsay?

Frenchman. Oui, monsieur, oui, oui.

Patrick. *(Screaming.) Thin lind me the loan of a gridiron!*

5. AFTER-DINNER SPEECH BY A FRENCHMAN.

"Milors and Gentlemans—You excellent chairman, M. le Baron de Mount-Stuart, he have say to me, 'Make de toast.' Den I say to him dat I have no toast to make; but he nudge my elbow ver soft, and say dat dere is von toast dat nobody but von Frenchman can make proper; and, derefore, wid your kind permission, I vill make de toast. 'De brevete is de sole of de feet,' as you great philosophere, Dr. Johnson, do say, in dat amusing little vork of his, de Pronouncing Dictionnaire; and, derefore, I vill not say ver moch to de point.

"Ah! mes amis! ven I hear to myself de flowing speech, de oration magnifique of you Lor' Maire, Monsieur Gobbledown, I feel dat it is von great privilege for von étranger to sit at de same table, and to eat de same food, as dat grand, dat majestique man, who are de terreur de voleurs and de brigands of de metropolis; and who is also, I for to suppose, a halterman and de chief of you common scoundrel. Milors and gentlemans, I feel dat I can perspire to no greatare honneur dan to be von common scoundrelman myself; but, hélas! dat plaisir are not for me, as I are not freeman of your great cité, not von liveryman servant of von of you compagnies joint-stock. But I must not forget de toast.

"Milors and Gentlemans! De immortal Shakispeare he have write, 'De ting of beauty are de joy for nevermore.' It is de ladies who are de toast. Vat is more entrancing dan de charmante smile, de soft voice, de vinking eye of de beautiful lady! It is de ladies who do sweeten de cares of life. It is de ladies who are de guiding stars of our existence. It is de ladies who do cheer but not inebriate, and, derefore, vid all homage to dere sex, de toast dat I have to propose is, 'De Ladies! God bless dem all!'"

6. DUNDREARY IN THE COUNTRY.

1. Diwectly after the season is over in town, I always go into the countwy. To tell you the twuth, I hate the countwy—it's so awful dull—there's such a howid noise of nothing all day; and there is nothing to see but gween twees, and cows, and buttercups, and wabbits, and all that sort of cattle—I don't mean exactly cattle either, but animals, you know.

2. And then the earwigs get into your hair-bwushes if you leave the bed-woom window open; and if you lie down on the gwass, those howid gwasshoppers, all legs, play at leap-frog over your nose, which is howible torture, and makes you weady to faint, you know, if it is not too far to call for assistance.

3. And the howid sky is always blue, and everything bores you; and they talk about the sunshine, as if there was more sunshine in the countwy than in the city—which is abthurd, you know—only the countwy sun is hotter, and bwings you all out in those howid fweckles,

and turns you to a fwiteful bwicky color, which the wetches call healthy.

4. As if a healthy man must lose his complexion, and become of a bwicky wed color—ha, ha!—bwicky—howid—bwicky wed color—cawoty wed color!

7. THE HEATHEN CHINEE.

Which I wish to remark—
 And my language is plain—
That for ways that are dark,
 And for tricks that are vain,
The heathen Chinee is peculiar,
Which the same I would rise to explain.

 Ah Sin was his name;
  And I shall not deny,
 In regard to the same,
  What that name might imply;
But his smile it was pensive and child-like,
As I frequently remarked to Bill Nye.

 It was August the third,
  And quite soft was the skies—
 Which it might be inferred
  That Ah Sin was likewise;
Yet he played it that day upon William
And 'me in a way I despise.

 Which we had a small game,
  And Ah Sin took a hand;
 It was Euchre. The same
  He did not understand;
But he smiled as he sat by the table,
With a smile that was child-like and bland.

 Yet the cards they were stocked
  In a way that I grieve,
 And my feelings were shocked
  At the state of Nye's sleeve.

Which was stuffed full of aces and bowers,
And the same with intent to deceive.

    But the hands that were played
      By that heathen Chinee,
    And the points that he made,
      Were quite frightful to see;
Till at last he put down a right bower,
Which the same Nye had dealt unto me.

    Then I looked up at Nye,
      And he gazed upon me;
    And he rose with a sigh,
      And said, "Can this be?
We are ruined by Chinese cheap labor"—
And he went for that heathen Chinee.

    In the scene that ensued
      I did not take a hand;
    But the floor it was strewed,
      Like the leaves on the strand,
With the cards that Ah Sin had been hiding,
In the game he "did not understand."

    In his sleeves, which were long,
      He had twenty-four packs—
    Which was coming it strong,
      Yet I state but the facts;
And we found on his nails, which were taper,
What is frequent in tapers—that's wax.

    Which is why I remark—
      And my language is plain—
    That for ways that are dark,
      And for tricks that are vain,
The heathen Chinee is peculiar,
Which the same I am free to maintain.

                          BRET HARTE

8. MARK TWAIN AND THE REPORTER.

"Hoping it's no harm, I've come to interview you. I am connected with *The Daily Thunderstorm.*"

"Come to what?"

"*Interview* you."

"Ah! I see. Yes—yes. Um! Yes—yes."

"Are you ready to begin?"

"Ready."

"How old are you?"

"Nineteen in June."

"Indeed! I would have taken you to be thirty-five or six. Where were you born?"

"In Missouri?"

"When did you begin to write?"

"In 1836."

"Why, how could that be, if you are only nineteen now?"

"I don't know. It does seem curious, somehow."

"It does indeed. Whom do you consider the most remarkable man you ever met?"

"Aaron Burr."

"But you never could have met Aaron Burr, if you are only nineteen years—"

"Now, if you know more about me than I do, what do you ask me for?"

"Well, it was only a suggestion; nothing more. How did you happen to meet Burr?"

"Well, I happened to be at his funeral one day; and he asked me to make less noise, and—"

"But, good heavens! If you were at his funeral, he must have been dead; and, if he was dead, how could he care whether you made a noise or not?"

"I don't know. He was always a particular kind of a man that way."

"Still, I don't understand it at all. You say he spoke to you, and that he was dead?"

"I did n't say he was dead."

"But was n't he dead?"

"Well, some said he was, some said he was n't."

"What do *you* think?"

"Oh, it was none of my business. It was n't any of my funeral."

"Did you— However, we can never get this matter straight. Let me ask about something else. What was the date of your birth?"

"Monday, October 31, 1693."

"What! Impossible! That would make you a hundred and eighty years old. How do you account for that?"

"I do n't account for it at all."

"But you said at first you were only nineteen, and now you make yourself out to be one hundred and eighty. It is an awful discrepancy."

"Why, have you noticed that? (*Shaking hands.*) Many a time it has seemed to me like a discrepancy; but some how I could n't make up my mind. How quick you notice a thing!"

"Thank you for the compliment, as far as it goes. Had you, or have you, any brothers or sisters?"

"Eh! I—I—I think so—yes—but I do n't remember."

"Well, that is the most extraordinary statement I ever heard."

"Why, what makes you think that?"

"How could I think otherwise? Why, look here! Who is this a picture of on the wall? Is n't that a brother of yours?"

"Oh, yes, yes, yes! Now you remind me of it, that *was* a brother of mine. That's William, *Bill* we called him. Poor old Bill!"

"Why, is he dead, then?"

"Ah, well, I suppose so. We never could tell. There was a great mystery about it."

"That is sad, very sad. He disappeared, then?"

"Well, yes, in a sort of general way. We buried him."

"*Buried* him! Buried him without knowing whether he was dead or not?"

"Oh, no! Not that. He was dead enough."

"Well, I confess that I can't understand this. If you buried him, and you knew he was dead—"

"No, no! We only thought he was."

"Oh, I see! He came to life again?"

"I bet he did n't."

"Well, I never heard anything like this. *Somebody* was dead. Somebody was buried. Now, where was the mystery?"

"Ah, that's just it! That's it exactly! You see we were twins—defunct and I; and we got mixed in the bath-tub when we were only two weeks old, and one of us was drowned. But we did n't know which. Some think it was Bill; some think it was me."

"Well, that *is* remarkable. What do *you* think?"

"Goodness knows! I would give whole worlds to know. This solemn, this awful mystery has cast a gloom over my whole life. But I will tell you a secret now, which I never have revealed to any creature before. One of us had a peculiar mark, a large mole on the back of his left hand; that was *me*. *That child was the one that was drowned.*"

"Very well, then, I do n't see that there is any mystery about it, after all."

"You do n't? Well, *I* do. Anyway, I do n't see how they could ever have been such a blundering lot as to go and bury the wrong child. But, 'sh! Do n't mention it where the family can hear of it. Heaven knows they have heart-breaking troubles enough without adding this."

"Well, I believe I have got material enough for the

present; and I am very much obliged to you for the pains you have taken. But I was a good deal interested in that account of Aaron Burr's funeral. Would you mind telling me what particular circumstance it was that made you think Burr was such a remarkable man?"

"Oh, it was a mere trifle! Not one man in fifty would have noticed it at all. When the sermon was over, and the procession all ready to start for the cemetery, and the body all arranged nice in the hearse, he said he wanted to take a last look at the scenery; and so he *got up, and rode with the driver.*"

9. PRINCE HENRY AND FALSTAFF.

Falstaff. I call thee cŏward? I'll see thee hânged ere I call thee coward: but I would give a thŏusand pôund I could run as fast as thŏu canst. You are straight enough in the shŏulders, you care not who sees your bâck. Call you thăt backing your friĕnds? A plâgue upon such backing! give me them that will fâce me.— Give me a cup of sack: I am a rogue, if I have drunk to-day.

P. Henry. O vĭllain! thy lips are scarce wiped since thou drank'st last.

Fal. All's one for that. A plâgue on all cowards, still say I!

P. Henry. What's the mâtter?

Fal. What's the mătter? here be four of us have taken a thousand pound this morning.

P. Henry. Where is it, Jack? where is it?

Fal. Where ĭs it? taken frôm us, it is; a hŭndred upon poor fôur of us.

P. Henry. What! a hŭndred, mán?

Fal. I am a rogue, if I were not at half-sword with a dozen of them, for two hours together. I have 'scaped by miracle. I am eight times thrust through the doublet; four, through the hose; my buckler cut through and through; my sword hacked like a hand-saw. I never dealt better since I was a man; all would not do. A plague of all cowards! Let them speak; if they speak more or less than truth, they are villains and the sons of darkness.

P. Henry. Speak, sirs; how *wàs* it?

Gadshill. We four, set upon some dozen—

Fal. Sĭxteen, at least, my lord.

Gad. And bound them.

Peto. No, no, they were not bound.

Fal. You rogue, they were bound, every man of them, or I am a Jew, else—an Ebrew Jew.

Gad. As we were sharing, some six or seven fresh men set upon us—

Fal. And unbound the rest; and then come in the other.

P. Henry. What! fought ye with them ăll?

Fal. All? I know not what ye call ăll; but if I fought not with *fĭfty* of them, I am a bunch of radish: if there were not two or three and fifty upon poor old Jack, then I am no two-legged creature.

Poins. Pray heaven, you have not murdered some of them.

Fal. Nay, that's past praying for; for I have peppered two of them; two I am sure I have paid; two rogues in buckram suits. I tell thee what, Hal, if I tell thee a lie, spit in my face, and call me a horse. Four rogues in buckram let drive at me—

P. Henry. What! fŏur? Thou saidst but *two* even now.

Fal. Fŏur, Hal; I told thee *fŏur*.

Poins. Ay, ay, he said *fŏur*.

Fal. These four came all afront, and mainly thrust at me. I made no more ado, but took all their seven points on my target thus.

P. Henry. Sĕven! why, there were but *fôur*, even now.

Fal. In buckram?

P. Henry. Ay, four in buckram suits.

Fal. Sĕven, by these hilts, or I am a *vîllain* else. Dost thou *hĕar* me, Hal?

P. Henry. Ay, and *mȧrk* thee too, Jack.

Fal. Do so, for it is worth listening to. These *nine* in buckram that I told thee of—

P. Henry. So, two more already.

Fal. Their points being broken,—began to give me ground; but I followed me close, came in foot and hand, and with a thought, *seven* of the *eleven* I paid.

P. Henry. O *mônstrous!* elĕven buckram men grown out of *twô!*

Fal. But, as ill luck would have it, three misbegotten knaves, in Kendal green, came at my back, and let drive at me;—for it was so dark, Hal, that thou couldst not see thy hand.

P. Henry. These lies are like the father that begets them; gross as a mountain, open, palpable. Why, thou knotty-pated fool; thou greasy tallow-tub.

Fal. What, art thou *mȧd?* art thou *mȧd?* is not the truth the *trŭth?*

P. Henry. Why, how couldst thou know these men in Kendal green, when it was so dark thou couldst not see thy hand? Come, tell us your *rėason;* what sayest thou to *thîs?* Come, your *rėason,* Jack, your *rėason.*

Fal. What, upon *compŭlsion? Nô.* Were I at the strappado, or all the racks in the world, I would not tell you on *compŭlsion.* Give you a *rĕason* upon *compŭlsion!* If reasons were as plenty as *blȧckberries,* I would give no man a reason upon *compŭlsion.*

P. Henry. I'll be no longer guilty of this sin. This sanguine coward, this bed-presser, this horse-back breaker, this huge hill of flesh—

Fal. Awây, you stârvĕling, you êel-skin, you dried *nêat's*-tongue, you *stôck*-fish! O for *brĕath* to utter what is *like* thee! you *tâilŏr's* yard, you *shêath*, you *bŏw*-case, you vile standing tuck—

SHAKESPEARE.

HINTS ABOUT ADDITIONAL SELECTIONS.

Dialogues, dialect pieces, and humorous selections are useful in school for the purpose of breaking up the tendency to stiffness, formality, and monotony in reading. There are times when the ripple of laughter is music in the school-room, and when the sunlight of humor is needed to dispel the mists of a gloomy day. There seems to be no good reason why the flashes of wit and humor that delight a whole nation should be altogether shut out from the school-room, because they do not form a part of "classic literature." Though such humorous and dialect selections might not seem appropriate for a drill-book like this volume, the wise and cheerful teacher will make good use of them, taking care, of course, to exclude objectionable selections. Teachers will do well to bear in mind that the taste of boys and girls from fourteen to eighteen years of age is not so critical as that of men and women of middle age.

These extracts should be read *at sight*, the book being passed from hand to hand, and one book serving for the whole class.

Many excellent selections can be found in such books as Lowell's "Biglow Papers," Dickens's "Pickwick Papers," Bret Harte's "Poems," Saxe's "Poems," Hood's "Poems," Mark Twain's books, Monroe's "Humorous Readings," Garrett's "Speaker's Garland," Shoemaker's "Elocutionist's Annual," and many other books of "Selections."

PART III.

PART III.

MISCELLANEOUS SELECTIONS.

SECTION I.

PROSE SELECTIONS.

1. ELOCUTIONARY TRAINING.

1. Elocutionary training should be begun in early life, because then the vocal organs are flexible. It is a serious defect in our school methods of instruction, that the expressive faculties, comprising feeling, affection, emotion, passion, imagination, fancy, association, imitation, and description, are called so little into action. Elocution, when properly taught, calls into active exercise the expressive faculties, and tends to educate the child as a social being.

2. In most ungraded schools in the country, and in many city schools, an hour of the closing afternoon of each week may be usefully devoted to declamation, dialogue, and select readings. It is not advisable to compel every child in school to take part in these exercises, for there are some who never can become good readers, and others who are so awkward and diffident that it is cruel to force them upon the school stage with a declamation.

3. Appropriate selections should at first be made by

the teacher; for the uncultivated taste of pupils will lead them to choose pieces altogether too difficult, or utterly worthless when committed to memory. Select at times, for the boys, short prose declamations, which, when learned, remain in the memory as models of pure prose and patriotic feeling. If they learn a poem, let it not be one made up of doggerel rhymes, or of painful attempts at a low order of wit.

4. A careful selection of pieces will be the surest safeguard against the ranting, tearing, overstrained, theatrical style of florid oratory which so painfully mars many school exhibitions. The teacher can take odd moments at the intermission, or recess, or before and after school, for the purpose of hearing rehearsals, and giving special instructions.

5. Teachers should instruct pupils in the elements of gesture. Gestures spring naturally from the close sympathy of mind and body. A look of the eye, an expression of the countenance, a movement of the hand, often convey more than words can express. The principles of gesture may be easily learned from any one of several excellent works on elocution.

6. The reading and recitation of poetry by girls is an indispensable part of the education of woman, as one of the most efficient modes of discipline for the taste and imagination. Many of the most exquisite passages of the poets can never be fully appreciated until repeated by the voice of woman.

7. It requires no close observer to perceive the effects of poetry on the youthful mind. Childhood delights in the melody of verse, and is pleased with its flowing harmony of sound. In poetry are embodied some of the most beautiful lessons of morality; and they are presented in a manner which arrests the attention and impresses the character. What teacher has not seen the dull eye kindle, the vacant countenance take expression,

the face glow with emotion, and the whole boy become lost in the sentiment of his declamation?

8. Introduce elocution into school to cultivate a taste for reading, to exercise and strengthen memory, to awaken feeling, to excite imagination, and to train those who are to enter the professions, to become graceful and pleasing speakers. Introduce it as a relief from study, a pleasing recreation, and a source of intellectual enjoyment. Introduce it as a part of the æsthetic education so peculiarly appropriate for woman. Make it as a part of the education of man as an expressive being.

2. GOOD READING.

1. There is *óne* accomplishment, in particular, which I would earnestly *recommènd* to you. Cultivate assiduously the ability to *rèad* well. I stop to *particularize* this, because it is a thing so very much *negléctcd*, and because it is such an elegant and charming *accòmplishment*. Where *óne* person is really interested by *músic*, *twènty* are pleased by *good rèading*. Where *óne* person is capable of becoming a skillful *musícian*, *twènty* may become *good rèaders*. Where there is *óne* occasion suitable for the exercise of *músical* talent, there are *twènty* for that of *good rèading*.

2. The culture of the voice necessary for *rèading* well, gives a delightful charm to the same voice in *conversàtion*. Good *réading* is the natural exponent and vehicle of *àll good thìngs*. It seems to bring dead aúthors to lífe again, and makes us sit down familiarly with the gréat and góod of all àges.

3. What a *fascinátion* there is in really *good rèading!* What a *pòwer* it gives one! In the *hòspital*, in the chamber of the *ìnvalid*, in the *nùrsery*, in the *doméstic* and in the *sòcial* circle, among chosen *friénds* and *compánions*, how it enables you to minister to the *amùse-*

ment, the còmfort, the plèasure of déar ones as no ŏther art or accomplishment cȧn. No instrument of man's devìsing can reach the héart as does that most wónderful instrument, the húman vòice.

4. If you would double the value of all your ŏther acquisítions, if you would add immeasurably to your ówn enjoyment and to your power of promoting the enjoyment of ȯthers, cultivate, with incessant care, this divíne gỳft. No music below the skȉes is equal to that of pure, silvery spéech from the lips of a man or woman of high cùlture. JOHN S. HART.

3. THE MUSIC OF THE HUMAN VOICE.

1. Willis, in his essay on "unwritten music," has placed the appropriate sound of the female voice among the most beautiful of its forms; and there is, unquestionably, a fine analogy between the sound of the running brook, the note of the wood-bird, the voice of a happy child, the low breathing of a flute, and the clear, soft tone of a woman's voice, when it utters the natural music of home—the accents of gentleness and love.

2. To a well-tuned ear, there is a rich, deep melody in the distinctive bass of the male voice, in its subdued tones. But the key-note of poetry seems to have been lent to woman. On the ear of infancy and childhood, her voice was meant to fall as a winning prelude to all the other melodies of nature; the human nerves are attuned, accordingly, to the breath of her voice; and, through life, the chords of the heart respond most readily to her touch.

3. Yet how often is this result impeded by the processes of artificial culture; by the over-excitement of mind and nerve, attending excessive application; by that unwise neglect of health and healthful action, which dims the eye and deadens the ear to beauty, and robs

life of the joyous and sympathetic spirit which is native to childhood; and which, otherwise, would ever be gushing forth in notes of gladness and endearment, the physical not less than the moral charm of human utterance!

4. There are beautiful exceptions, undoubtedly, to this general fact of ungainly habit. But the ground of just complaint is, that there is no provision made in our systems of education for the cultivation of one of woman's peculiar endowments—an attractive voice. Our girls do not come home to us, after their period of school life, qualified to read with effect in their own language. There is wanting in their voices that adaptation of tone to feeling, which is the music of the heart in reading; there is wanting that clear, impressive style which belongs to the utterance of cultivated taste and judgment, and which enhances every sentiment by appropriate emphasis and pause; there is even a want of that distinct articulation which alone can make sound the intelligible medium of thought.   Prof. William Russell.

4. THE ART OF READING.

1. The art of reading well is an accomplishment that all desire to possess, many think they have already, and that a few set about to acquire. These, believing their power is altogether in their genius, are, after a few lessons from an elocutionist, disappointed at not becoming themselves at once masters of the art; and with the restless vanity of their belief, abandon the study for some new subject of trial and failure. Such cases of infirmity result in part from the wavering character of the human tribe; but they chiefly arise from defects in the usual course of instruction.

2. Go to some of our colleges and universities, and observe how the art of speaking *is not* taught there.

See a boy of but fifteen years, with no want of youthful diffidence, and not without a craving desire to learn, sent upon a stage, pale and choking with apprehension; being forced into an attempt to do that, without instruction, which he came purposely to learn; and furnishing amusement to his classmates, by a pardonable awkwardness, that should be punished, in the person of his pretending but neglectful preceptor, with little less than scourging.

3. Then visit a conservatorio of music; observe there the elementary outset, the orderly task, the masterly discipline, the unwearied superintendence, and the incessant toil to reach the utmost accomplishment in the Singing-Voice; and afterwards do not be surprised that the pulpit, the senate, the bar, and the chair of medical professorship, are filled with such abominable drawlers, mouthers, mumblers, clutterers, squeakers, chanters, and mongers in monotony; nor that the Schools of Singing are constantly sending abroad those great instances of vocal wonder who triumph along the crowded resorts of the world; who contribute to the halls of fashion and wealth their most refined source of gratification; who sometimes quell the pride of rank by a momentary sensation of envy; and who draw forth the admiration and receive the crowning applause of the prince and sage.

4. The high accomplishments in elocution are supposed to be universally the unacquired gifts of genius, and to consist of powers and graces beyond the reach of art. So seem the plainest services of arithmetic to a savage; and so, to the slave, seem all the ways of music which modern art has so accurately penned, as to time, and tune, and momentary grace. Ignorance knows not what *has* been done; indolence thinks nothing *can* be done; and both uniting, borrow from the abused eloquence of poetry an aphorism to justify supineness of inquiry.

Dr. Rush.

5. ON LEARNING BY HEART.

1. Till he has fairly tried it, I suspect a reader does not know how much he would gain from committing to memory passages of real excellence; precisely because he does not know how much he overlooks when merely reading. Learn one true poem by heart, and see if you do not find it so. Beauty after beauty will reveal itself, in chosen phrase, or happy music, or noble suggestion, otherwise undreamed of. It is like looking at one of Nature's wonders through a microscope.

2. Again: how much in such a poem that you really did feel admirable and lovely on a first reading, passes away, if you do not give it a further and much better reading!—passes away utterly, like a sweet sound, or an image on the lake, which the first breath of wind dispels. If you could only fix that image, as the photographers do theirs, so beautifully, so perfectly! And you can do so! Learn it by heart, and it is yours for ever!

3. I have said, a true poem; for naturally men will choose to learn poetry—from the beginning of time they have done so. To immortal verse the memory gives a willing, a joyous, and a lasting home. Some prose, however, is poetical, is poetry, and altogether worthy to be learned by heart; and the learning is not so very difficult. It is not difficult or toilsome to learn that which pleases us; and the labor, once given, is forgotten, while the result remains.

4. Poems, and noble extracts, whether of verse or of prose, once so reduced into possession and rendered truly our own, may be to us a daily pleasure;—better far than a whole library *unused*. They may come to us in our dull moments, to refresh us as with spring flowers; in our selfish musings, to win us by pure delight from the tyranny of foolish castle-building, self-gratulations,

and mean anxieties. They may be with us in the workshop, in the crowded street, by the fireside; sometimes, perhaps, on pleasant hill-sides, or by sounding shores;—noble friends and companions—our own! never intrusive, ever at hand, coming at our call.

5. For those, in particular, whose leisure time is short, I believe there could not be a better expenditure of time than deliberately giving an occasional hour—it requires no more—to committing to memory chosen passages from great authors. If the mind were thus daily nourished with a few choice words of the best English poets and writers; if the habit of learning by heart were to become so general, that, as a matter of course, any person presuming to be educated might be expected to be equipped with a few good pieces,—I believe that it would lead, much more than the mere sound of it suggests, to the diffusion of the best kind of literature and to the right appreciation of it; and that men would not long rest satisfied with knowing a few stock pieces.

6. The only objection I can conceive to what I have been saying is, that a relish for higher literature may be said to be the result of cultivation, and to belong only to the few. But I do not admit that even the higher literature must belong only to the few. Poetry is, in the main, essentially catholic—addressed to all men; and though some poetry requires knowledge and culture, much, and that the noblest, needs only natural feeling, and common experience. Such poetry, taken in moderation, followed with genuine good-will, shared in common, will be intelligible and delightful to most men who take the trouble to be students at all, and ever more and more so.

7. Perhaps, also, there may be a fragment of truth in what Charles Lamb has said—that any *spouting* "withers and blows upon a fine passage;" that there is no enjoy-

ing it after it has been "pawed about by declamatory boys and men." But surely there is a reasonable habit of recitation as well as an unreasonable one; there is no need of declamatory pawing. To abandon all recitation, is to give up a custom which has unquestionably given delight and instruction to all the races of mankind. If our faces are set against vain display, and set towards rational enjoyment of one another, we need not fear that our social evenings will be marred by an occasional recitation. And, moreover, it is not for reciting's sake that I chiefly recommend this most faithful form of reading—learning by heart.

8. I come back, therefore, to this, that learning by heart is a good thing, and that it is neglected among us. Why is it neglected? Partly because of our indolence; but partly, I believe, because we do not sufficiently consider that it *is* a good thing, and needs to be taken in hand. We need to be reminded of it. I here remind you. Like a town-crier, ringing my bell, I would say to you, "Oyez, oyez! Lost, stolen, or strayed, a good ancient practice—the good ancient practice of learning by heart. Every finder shall be handsomely rewarded."

9. If you ask, "What shall I learn?" the answer is, do as you do with tunes—begin with what you sincerely like best, what you would most wish to remember, what you would most enjoy saying to yourself or repeating to another. You will soon find the list inexhaustible. Then "keeping up" is easy. Every one has spare ten minutes: one of the problems of life is how to employ them usefully. You may well spend some in looking after and securing this good property you have won.

LUSHINGTON.

6. SCHOOL LIBRARIES.

1. The influence of well-selected books in a school is second only to that of the teacher; and in many instances the information, self-gleaned by the pupils, is the most valuable part of a common-school education.

2. A teacher may fail in the discharge of duty; but the golden grains of thought gleaned from good books will spring up in the youthful minds and yield their fruit, just as certainly as the fertile soil of our beautiful valleys rewards the toil of the husbandman with a bountiful harvest.

3. The object and aim of the public school should be to give children a thirst for information, a taste for reading; to make them *alive* to knowledge; to set them out on the path of self-education through life. Why teach them to read at all, if books be not afterwards furnished for them to read?

4. Not many years ago, in one of the obscure towns of Massachusetts, there lived a farmer's boy who "went to a common school" in the winter, and worked on the farm in summer. The books of a little town library fell into his hands; he devoured them, and hungered for more. He grew to be a man, and was acknowledged by all to be the most distinguished American educator of his time.

5. Every public school in our country is a debtor to Horace Mann. He thus graphically sums up the advantage of a school library: "Now no one thing will contribute more to intelligent reading in our schools than a well-selected library; and, through intelligence, the library will also contribute to rhetorical ease, grace, and expressiveness. Wake up a child to a consciousness of power and beauty, and you might as easily confine Hercules to a distaff, or bind Apollo to a tread-mill, as to confine his spirit within the mechanical round of a

school-room where such mechanism still exists. Let a child read and understand such stories as the friendship of Damon and Pythias, the integrity of Aristides, the fidelity of Regulus, the purity of Washington, the invincible perseverance of Franklin, and he will think differently and act differently all the days of his remaining life.

6. "Let boys or girls of sixteen years of age read an intelligible and popular treatise on astronomy and geology, and from that day new heavens will bend over their heads, and a new earth will spread out beneath their feet. A mind accustomed to go rejoicing over the splendid regions of the material universe, or to luxuriate in the richer worlds of thought, can never afterwards read like a wooden machine—a thing of cranks and pipes—to say nothing of the pleasures and the utility it will realize."

7. POEMS.

1. Now I tell you a poem must be kept *and used*, like a meerschaum or a violin. A poem is just as porous as the meerschaum—the more porous it is, the better. I mean to say that a genuine poem is capable of absorbing an indefinite amount of the essence of our own humanity—its tenderness, its heroism, its regrets, its aspirations—so as to be gradually stained through with a divine secondary color derived from ourselves. So, you see, it must take time to bring the sentiment of a poem into harmony with our nature by staining ourselves through every thought and image our being can penetrate.

2. Then, again, as to the mere music of a new poem; why, who can expect anything more from that than from the music of a violin fresh from the maker's hands? Now you know very well that there are no less than fifty-eight different pieces in a violin. These

pieces are strangers to each other, and it takes a century, more or less, to make them thoroughly acquainted. At last they learn to vibrate in harmony, and the instrument becomes an organic whole, as it were a great seed capsule, which had grown from a garden-bed in Cremona, or elsewhere. Besides, the wood is juicy and full of sap for fifty years or so, but at the end of fifty or a hundred more gets tolerably dry and comparatively resonant.

3. Don't you see that all this is just as true of a poem? Counting each word as a piece, there are more pieces in an average copy of verses than in a violin. The poet has forced all these words together, and fastened them, and they don't understand it at first. But let the poem be repeated aloud, and murmured over in the mind's muffled whisper often enough, and at length the parts become knit together in such absolute solidarity that you could not change a syllable without the whole world's crying out against you for meddling with the harmonious fabric.
HOLMES.

8. SCROOGE AND MARLEY.

1. Marley was dead, to begin with. There is no doubt whatever about that. The register of his burial was signed by the clergyman, the clerk, the undertaker, and the chief mourner. Scrooge signed it. And Scrooge's name was good upon 'Change, for anything he chose to put his hand to. Old Marley was as dead as a door-nail.

2. Mind! I don't mean to say that I know, of my own knowledge, what there is particularly dead about a door-nail. I might have been inclined myself, to regard a coffin-nail as the deadest piece of ironmongery in the trade. But the wisdom of our ancestors is in

the simile; and my unhallowed hands shall not disturb it, or the country's done for. You will therefore permit me to repeat, emphatically, that Marley was as dead as a door-nail.

3. Scrooge knew he was dead? Of course he did. How could it be otherwise? Scrooge and he were partners for I don't know how many years. Scrooge was his sole executor, his sole administrator, his sole assign, his sole residuary legatee, his sole friend, and sole mourner. And even Scrooge was not so dreadfully cut up by the sad event, but that he was an excellent man of business on the very day of the funeral, and solemnized it with an undoubted bargain.

4. Scrooge never painted out old Marley's name. There it stood, years afterwards, above the warehouse door: Scrooge and Marley. The firm was known as Scrooge and Marley. Sometimes people new to the business called Scrooge, Scrooge, and sometimes Marley, but he answered to both names. It was all the same to him.

5. Oh! but he was a tight-fisted hand at the grindstone, Scrooge! A squeezing, wrenching, grasping, scraping, clutching, covetous old sinner! Hard and sharp as flint from which no steel had ever struck out generous fire; secret, and self-contained, and solitary as an oyster. The cold within him froze his old features, nipped his pointed nose, shriveled his cheek, stiffened his gait; made his eyes red, his thin lips blue; and spoke out shrewdly in his grating voice. A frosty rime was on his head, and on his eyebrows, and his wiry chin. He carried his own low temperature always about with him; he iced his office in the dog-days; and didn't thaw it one degree at Christmas.

6. External heat and cold had little influence on Scrooge. No warmth could warm, no wintry weather chill him. No wind that blew was bitterer than he, no

falling snow was more intent upon its purpose, no pelting rain less open to entreaty. Foul weather did n't know where to have him. The heaviest rain, and snow, and hail, and sleet, could boast of the advantage over him in only one respect. They often "came down handsomely," and Scrooge never did.

7. Nobody ever stopped him in the street to say, with gladsome looks, "My dear Scrooge, how are you? When will you come to see me?" No beggars implored him to bestow a trifle, no children asked him what it was o'clock, no man or woman ever once in all his life inquired the way to such and such a place, of Scrooge. Even the blind men's dogs appeared to know him; and when they saw him coming on, would tug their owners into doorways and up courts; and then would wag their tails as though they said, "No eye at all is better than an evil eye, dark master!"

8. But what did Scrooge care! It was the very thing he liked. To edge his way along the crowded paths of life, warning all human sympathy to keep its distance, was what the knowing ones called "nuts" to Scrooge.

9. Once upon a time—of all the good days in the year, on Christmas eve—old Scrooge sat busy in his counting-house. It was cold, bleak, biting weather: foggy withal; and he could hear the people in the court outside go wheezing up and down, beating their hands upon their breasts, and stamping their feet upon the pavement stones to warm them. The city clocks had only just gone three, but it was quite dark already—it had not been light all day—and candles were flaring in the windows of the neighboring offices, like ruddy smears upon the palpable brown air. The fog came pouring in at every chink and key-hole, and was so dense without, that although the court was of the narrowest, the houses opposite were mere phantoms. To

see the dingy cloud come drooping down, obscuring everything, one might have thought that Nature lived hard by, and was brewing on a large scale.

10. The door of Scrooge's counting-house was open, that he might keep his eye upon his clerk, who in a dismal little cell beyond, a sort of tank, was copying letters. Scrooge had a very small fire, but the clerk's fire was so very much smaller that it looked like one coal. But he could not replenish it, for Scrooge kept the coal-box in his own room; and so surely as the clerk came in with the shovel, the master predicted that it would be necessary for them to part. Wherefore, the clerk put on his white comforter, and tried to warm himself at the candle; in which effort, not being a man of a strong imagination, he failed.

11. "A merry Christmas, uncle! God save you!" cried a cheerful voice. It was the voice of Scrooge's nephew, who came upon him so quickly that this was the first intimation Scrooge had of his approach.

"Bah!" said Scrooge; "humbug!"

"Christmas a humbug, uncle! You don't mean that, I am sure?"

12. "I do. Out upon merry Christmas! What's Christmas time to you but a time for paying bills without money; a time for finding yourself a year older, and not an hour richer; a time for balancing your books and having every item in 'em through a round dozen of months presented dead against you? If I had my will, every idiot who goes about with 'Merry Christmas' on his lips should be boiled with his own pudding, and buried with a stake of holly through his heart. He should!"

"Uncle!"

13. "Nephew, keep Christmas in your own way, and let me keep it in mine."

"Keep it! But you don't keep it."

"Let me leave it alone, then. Much good may it do you! Much good it has ever done you!"

14. "There are many things from which I might have derived good, by which I have not profited, I dare say, Christmas among the rest. But I am sure I have always thought of Christmas time, when it has come round—apart from the veneration due to its sacred origin, if anything belonging to it *can* be apart from that—as a good time; a kind, forgiving, charitable, pleasant time; the only time I know of, in the long calendar of the year, when men and women seem by one consent to open their shut-up hearts freely, and to think of people below them as if they really were fellow-travelers to the grave, and not another race of creatures bound on other journeys. And therefore, uncle, though it has never put a scrap of gold or silver in my pocket, I believe that it *has* done me good, and *will* do me good; and I say, God bless it!"

The clerk in the tank involuntarily applauded.

15. "Let me hear another sound from *you*," said Scrooge, "and you'll keep your Christmas by losing your situation! You're quite a powerful speaker, sir," he added, turning to his nephew. "I wonder you don't go into Parliament."

"Don't be angry, uncle. Come! Dine with us to-morrow."

16. Scrooge said that he would see him—yes, indeed he did. He went the whole length of the expression, and said that he would see him in that extremity first.

"But why?" cried Scrooge's nephew. "Why?"

"Why did you get married?"

"Because I fell in love."

17. "Because you fell in love!" growled Scrooge, as if that were the only one thing in the world more ridiculous than a merry Christmas. "Good-afternoon!"

"Nay, uncle, but you never came to see me before

that happened. Why give it as a reason for not coming now?"

"Good-afternoon!"

"I want nothing from you; I ask nothing of you; why cannot we be friends?"

"Good-afternoon!"

18. "I am sorry, with all my heart, to find you so resolute. We have never had any quarrel to which I have been a party. But I have made the trial in homage to Christmas, and I'll keep my Christmas humor to the last. So a merry Christmas, uncle!"

"Good-afternoon!"

"And a happy New Year!"

"Good-afternoon!" DICKENS'S "*Christmas Carol.*"

9. DEFENSE OF POETRY.

1. We believe that *póetry,* far from *injuring* society, is one of the great instruments of its refínement and exaltàtion. It lifts the mind *abòve* ordinary *lífe,* gives it a *rèspite* from *deprèssing cáres,* and awakens the consciousness of its affinity with what is *púre* and *nòble.* In its *legítimate* and *híghest* efforts, it has the same tendency and aim with *Christiánity;* that is, to *spíritualize* our nàture.

2. *Trúe, póetry* has been made the instrument of *více,* the pander of bad pássions; but when genius thus *stóops,* it dims its *fíres,* and párts with much of its *pòwer;* and even when Poetry is enslaved to *licéntiousness* and *misànthropy,* she can not *whŏlly* forget her *trúe vocàtion.* Strains of *púre féeling,* touches of *ténderness,* images of innocent *háppiness,* sympathies with what is *góod* in our náture, bursts of scorn or indignation at the hollowness of the *wòrld,* passages true to our *mòral* nature, often escape in an *immóral wòrk,* and

show us how hard it is for a *gĭfted* spirit to divorce itself wholly from what is *gŏod*.

3. Poetry has a natural alliance with our best *affèctions*. It delights in the beauty and sublimity of *ŏutward* nature and of the *sŏul*. It indeed portrays with terrible energy the *exc̆esses* of the *pássions*, but they are passions which show a *mĭghty nàture*, which are full of *pŏwer*, which command *áwe*, and excite a deep though shuddering *sỳmpathy*.

4. Its great *téndency* and *púrpose* is to carry the mind *beyónd* and *abóve* the béaten, dústy, wéary walks of *ŏrdinary* life; to lift it into a *pùrer* élement, and to breathe into it more profound and *génerous emòtion*. It reveals to us the *lóveliness* of *nàture*, brings back the freshness of youthful *fèeling*, revives the relish of simple *plèasures*, keeps unquenched the enthusiasm which warmed the *spring-time* of our *bèing*, refines youthful· *lòve*, strengthens our interest in human *nàture* by vivid delineations of its tenderest and loftiest *fèelings*, spreads our sympathies over all classes of *socìety*, knits us by new ties with *univérsal bèing*, and, through the brightness of its prophetic *vìsions*, helps *fàith* to lay hold on the *future lĭfe*.

5. We are aware that it is *objécted* to póetry that it gives *wróng vièws* and excites *fălse expectàtions of life*, peoples the mind with *shădows* and *illùsions*, and builds up *imaginátion* on the ruins of *wĭsdom*. That there *ĭs* a wisdom against which poetry wárs—the wisdom of the *sĕnses*, which makes *phýsical* comfort and gratification the supreme *gŏod*, and *wéalth* the chief *ínterest* of life— we do not *denỳ;* nor do we deem it the *lĕast* sérvice which poetry renders to mankínd, that it *redèems* them from the thralldom of this earth-born prúdence.

6. But, passing over *thĭs* topic, we would observe that the complaint against *póetry*, as abounding in *illúsion* and *decéption*, is, in the main, *gròundless*. In many *pŏems* there is more of *trŭth* than in many *hístories* and

philosophic *thèories.* The *fictions* of *génius* are often the *véhicles* of the *sublimest vèrities,* and its *fláshes* often open *new règions* of thought, and throw *new light* on the *mysteries of our bèing.* In *pòetry,* when the letter is *fálsehood,* the *spírit* is often *profoundest wísdom.*

7. And if *trúth* thus dwells in the boldest *fictions* of the póet. much more may it be expected in his *delineations of life;* for the *prèsent* life, which is the *first stáge* of the immortal mínd, *abóunds* in the materials of pòetry, and it is the high office of the bard to detect this divine element among the grosser labors and pleasures of our earthly being. The *prĕsent* life is *nôt* wholly prosáic, precíse, táme, and fínite. To the *gĭfted* eye it abounds in the *poètic.*

8. The *affèctions,* which spread beyond ourselves and stretch far into *futúrity;* the workings of *mighty pássions,* which seem to arm the soul with an almost *superhuman énergy;* the innocent and irrepressible joy of *infancy;* the blóom, and búoyancy, and dazzling hópes of *youth;* the throbbings of the heart, when it first wakes to *lóve,* and dreams of a happiness *too vast for éarth; wóman,* with her beaúty, and gráce, and géntleness, and fullness of féeling, and depth of afféction, and blushes of púrity, and the tónes and lóoks which only a *mŏther's* heart can inspíre—*thĕse* are *ăll* poetical.

9. It is *not trúe* that the poet paints a life which does not *exíst.* He only extrácts and concèntrates, as it were, life's ethereal *èssence,* arrésts and condénses its volatile *frágrance,* brings together its scattered *bèauties,* and prolongs its more refined but evanescent *jòys.* And in *thĭs* he does *wĕll;* for it is *gòod* to feel that life is not *whŏlly* usurped by cares for *subsístence* and *physical gratificátions,* but admits, in measures which may be indefinitely *enlárged, sentiments* and *delights* worthy of a *hígher bèing.* CHANNING.

10. FALSTAFF.

[This extract affords an example of "humorous style," with prevailing circumflex inflections.]

1. There is something cordial in a *făt* mán. Everybody likes *hĭm*, and *hĕ* likes *évcrybody*. *Fôod* does a *făt* man *gôod;* it *clĭngs* to him; it *frùctifies* upon him; he swells *nóbly ôut*, and fills a *génerous spàce* in lífe. A *făt* man, therefore, almost in virtue of *béing* a fat mán, is, *per sé*, a *pôpular* màn; and he commonly *desérves* his popularity.

2. A *făt* man feels his position *sólid* in the world; he knows that his being is *cògnizable;* he knows that he has a *márked plàce* in the úniverse, and that he need take no extraordinary pains to advertise mankind that *hĕ* is *amòng* them; he knows that he is in no danger of being *overlôoked*.

3. A *făt* man is the nearest to that most perfect of figures, a *mathemátical sphêre;* a *thĭn* man, to that most limited of conceivable dimensions, a *símple líne*. A *făt* man is a being of *harmónious vòlume*, and holds relations to the material universe in *évery* direction; a *thĭn* man has nothing but *léngth;* a *thĭn* man, in fact, is but the *continuátion of a pôint*.

4. Well then might Falstaff exult in his *sìze;* well might he mock at the *prĭnce*, and his other *léan contèmporaries;* and, accordingly, when he would address the prince in terms the most *degráding*, he heaps *èpithet* upon *èpithet*, each expressive of the *útmost lèanness*. "*Awây*, you *stârveling*," he exclaims; " you *éel-skin;* you dried *néat's*-tongue; you *stóck*-fish. O for *bréath* to utter what is *lĭke* thee !"

5. Falstaff was an *èpicure*, but no *glútton*. He was not a great *ĕater*, for his bill contained a halfpennyworth of *brĕad* to an intolerable quantity of *sáck*. And although Falstaff was a large *drĭnker*, he was no *inébriate*.

And here we conceive a *consúmmate árt* in Shákespeare, who sustains Falstaff throughout in our *intelléctual respèct*. . . .

6. As to *lĭes*, they were in the way of his *vocátion*. The highest stretch of *imaginátion* could not even *sŭspect* him of *verăcity;* and if he had any *dúpes*, they were strongly in love with *decèption*. His lies, too, were the lies of a professed and known *wĭt;* they were designed only for *lúdicrous èffect*, and generally were little more than *cómic exaggerátions*. In the events at Gad's hill, and those that immediately follow them, there is an epitome of the *whóle chăracter* of Fàlstaff; but there ís, at the same tíme, an evident design on the part of the poet, to bring out his peculiarities with *grotésque extrăvagance*, and to produce the broadest and the most *cómic resùlt*. . . .

7. Falstaff has both *wĭt* and *hùmor;* but more of *wĭt*, I think, than *hŭmor*. Between wit and humor there is an evident *distínction*, but to submit the distinction to minute criticism would require more time than we can spàre; and, after all, it is more easy to *fĕel* than to *expláin* it. *Wĭt* implies *thóught;* *hŭmor*, *sensibílity*. *Wĭt* deals with *idéas;* *hŭmor*, with *áctions* and with *mánners*. *Wĭt* may be a thing of pure *imaginátion;* *hŭmor* involves *séntiment* and *chăracter*. *Wĭt* is an *éssence;* *hŭmor*, an *incarnátion*.

8. Wit and humor, however, have *sŏme* qualities in còmmon. Both develop unexpected *análogies;* both include the principles of *cóntrast* and *assimilàtion;* both detect inward *resĕmblances* amidst *éxternal dĭfferences*, and the result of both is *pléasurable surprĭse;* the surprise from *wĭt* excites *admirátion*, the surprise from *hŭmor* stimulates *mérriment*, and produces *làughter*.

9. Falstaff's *wĭt* is rich as his *imaginátion;* as *prolífic* as it is *felĭcitous*. It is *pùngent, còpious*, brilliant in *expréssion*, and decisive in *effèct*. It never *falls shŏrt* of

its aim, and never *misses* it. And this *rare wit* is wholly devoted to the *ludicrous*.

HENRY GILES.

11. WEALTH.

1. As soon as a stranger is introduced into any company, one of the first questions which all wish to have answered, is, How does that man get his living? And with reason. He is no whole man until he knows how to earn a blameless livelihood. Society is barbarous, until every industrious man can get his living without dishonest customs.

2. Every man is a consumer, and ought to be a producer. He fails to make his place good in the world, unless he not only pays his debt, but also adds something to the common wealth. Nor can he do justice to his genius, without making some larger demand on the world than a bare subsistence. He is by constitution expensive, and needs to be rich.

3. Wealth has its source in applications of the mind to nature, from the rudest strokes of spade and ax, up to the last secrets of art. Intimate ties subsist between thought and all production; because a better order is equivalent to vast amounts of brute labor. The forces and the resistances are Nature's, but the mind acts in bringing things from where they abound to where they are wanted; in wise combining; in directing the practice of the useful arts, and in the creation of finer values, by fine art, by eloquence, by song, or the reproductions of memory.

4. Wealth is in applications of mind to nature; and the art of getting rich consists not in industry, much less in saving, but in a better order, in timeliness, in being at the right spot. One man has stronger arms, or longer legs; another sees by the course of streams,

and growth of markets, where land will be wanted, makes a clearing to the river, goes to sleep, and wakes up rich. Steam is no stronger now, than it was a hundred years ago; but is put to better use. A clever fellow was acquainted with the expansive force of steam; he also saw the wealth of wheat and grass rotting in Michigan. Then he cunningly screws on the steam-pipe to the wheat crop. Puff now, O Steam! The steam puffs and expands as before, but this time it is dragging all Michigan at its back to hungry New York and hungry England.

5. Coal lay in ledges under the ground since the flood, until a laborer with pick and windlass brings it to the surface. We may well call it black diamonds. Every basket is power and civilization. For coal is a portable climate. It carries the heat of the tropics to Labrador and the polar circle: and it is the means of transporting itself whithersoever it is wanted. Watt and Stephenson whispered in the ear of mankind their secret, that *a half ounce of coal will draw two tons a mile,* and coal carries coal, by rail and by boat, to make Canada as warm as Calcutta, and with its comfort brings its industrial power.

6. When the farmer's peaches are taken from under the tree, and carried into town, they have a new look, and a hundredfold value over the fruit which grew on the same bough, and lies fulsomely on the ground. The craft of the merchant is this bringing a thing from where it abounds, to where it is costly.

7. Wealth begins in a tight roof that keeps the rain and wind out; in a good pump that yields you plenty of sweet water; in two suits of clothes, so to change your dress when you are wet; in dry sticks to burn; in a good double-wick lamp; and three meals; in a horse, or a locomotive, to cross the land; in a boat to cross the sea; in tools to work with; in books to read;

and so, in giving, on all sides, by tools and auxiliaries, the greatest possible extension to our powers, as if it added feet, and hands, and eyes, and blood, length to the day, and knowledge, and good-will.

8. Wealth begins with these articles of necessity. And here we must recite the iron law which Nature thunders in these northern climates. First, she requires that each man should feed himself. If, happily, his fathers have left him no inheritance, he must go to work, and by making his wants less, or his gains more, he must draw himself out of that state of pain and insult in which she forces the beggar to lie. She gives him no rest until this is done. She starves, taunts, and torments him, takes away warmth, laughter, sleep, friends, and daylight, until he has fought his way to his own loaf. Then, less peremptorily, but still with sting enough, she urges him to the acquisition of such things as belong to him. Every warehouse and shop-window, every fruit-tree, every thought of every hour, opens a new want to him, which it concerns his power and dignity to gratify.
Emerson's Essays.

12. THE ASTRONOMER'S VISION.

[*This extract, translated and paraphrased by Professor Mitchell, is characterized by solemnity and sublimity, awe and wonder. It should be read with subdued force, median stress, orotund quality, low pitch.*]

1. Gòd called up from dreams a man into the *vestibule of hèaven,* saying, "Come thou hither and see the glory of my hòuse." And to the servants that stood around his throne he sáid, "Take him, and undress him from his robes of flèsh: cleanse his vísion, and put a new breath into his nòstrils: only touch not with any change his human *heàrt*—the *heárt* that *wèeps* and *trèmbles.*"

2. It was dòne: and, with a *mighty àngel* for his

guíde, the man stood ready for his *ínfinite vòyage;* and from the terraces of *héaven*, without sound or farewell, at once they wheeled away into *éndless spàce*. Sometimes with the solemn flight of *angel wing* they fled through infinite realms of *dárkness*, through wildernesses of *déath*, that divided the *wórlds* of *lìfe;* sometimes they swept over *fróntiers* that were quickening under *prophetic mótions* from *Gòd.*

3. *Thén* from a distance that is counted only in *héaven*, *lìght* dawned for a time through a sleepy *fìlm;* by unutterable *páce*, the light swept to *thĕm, thĕy*, by unutterable páce, to the *lìght*. In a moment, the *rúshing* of *plànets* was upòn them: in a *móment*, the *blázing* of *sùns* was around them.

4. Then came *etérnities of twìlight*, that *revéaled*, but were *nòt* revealed. On the *rìght* hand and on the *lèft* toward *míghty constellátions*, that by self-repetitions and answers from afár, that by counter-posítions, built up *triúmphal gátes*, whose *árchitraves*, whose *árchways—* horizóntal, uprìght—résted, rose at altitude, by *spans* that seemed *ghóstly* from *infìnitude*. Without *méasure* were the *árchitraves*, *past númber* were the *árchways*, *beyond mémory* the *gátes.*

5. *Wíthin* were stairs that scaled the *etérnities* belòw; *abóve* was *belòw—belów* was *abòve*, to the man stripped of gravitating *bòdy: dépth* was swallowed up in *height insurmòuntable, height* was swallowed up in *dépth unfàthomable*. *Súddenly*, as thus they rode from *ínfinite* to *ínfinite*, *súddenly*, as thus they tilted over abysmal *wórlds*, a *míghty crỳ* aròse—that systems *more mystérious*, that *worlds* more *bíllowy*,—other *héights* and other *dépths*,—were *cóming*, were *néaring*, were at *hànd*.

6. Then the man *sighed*, and *stóoped*, *shúddered*, and *wèpt*. His overladen *héart* uttered itself in *téars*, and he sáid: "Angel', I will go nò *fàrther*. For the spirit of man *ácheth* with this *infìnity*. *Insùfferable* is the

glory of *Gŏd.* Let me lie down in the *gráve* and hide me from the prosecution of the *ĭnfinite;* for *énd,* I see, there is *nòne.*"

7. And from all the listening *stárs* that shone around issued a choral *vóice:* "The man speaks *trŭly: énd* there is *nŏne,* that ever yet we *hèard* of." "*End'* is there nóne?" the angel solemnly demánded. "Is there indeed *no* énd?—and is *thĭs* the sorrow that *kĭlls* you?" But no *vóice ănswered,* that he might answer *himsèlf.* Then the *ángel* threw up his glorious hands to the heaven of heavens, sáying, "End' is there *nŏne* to the universe of *Gŏd.* Ló! álso, there is *no begĭnning.*"

13. EDUCATION.

1. Suppose it were perfectly certain that the life and fortune of every one of us would, one day or other, depend upon his winning or losing a game at chess. Don't you think that we should all consider it to be a primary duty to learn at least the names and the moves of the pieces; to have a notion of a gambit, and a keen eye for all the means of giving and getting out of check? Do you not think that we should look with a disapprobation amounting to scorn, upon the father who allowed his son, or the state which allowed its members, to grow up without knowing a pawn from a knight?

2. Yet it is a very plain and elementary truth, that the life, the fortune, and the happiness of every one of us, and, more or less, of those who are connected with us, do depend upon our knowing something of the rules of a game infinitely more difficult and complicated than chess. It is a game which has been played for untold ages, every man and woman of us being one of the two players in a game of his or her own. The chess-board is the world, the pieces are the phenomena of the

universe, the rules of the game are what we call the laws of Nature.

3. The player on the other side is hidden from us. We know that his play is always fair, just, and patient. But also we know, to our cost, that he never overlooks a mistake, or makes the smallest allowance for ignorance. To the man who plays well, the highest stakes are paid, with that sort of overflowing generosity with which the strong shows delight in strength. And one who plays ill is checkmated—without haste, but without remorse.

4. Well, what I mean by Education is learning the rules of this mighty game. In other words, education is the instruction of the intellect in the laws of Nature, under which name I include not merely things and their forces, but men and their ways; and the fashioning of the affections and of the will into an earnest and loving desire to move in harmony with those laws. For me, education means neither more nor less than this. Anything which professes to call itself education must be tried by this standard, and if it fails to stand the test, I will not call it education, whatever may be the force of authority, or of numbers, upon the other side.

5. It is important to remember that, in strictness, there is no such thing as an uneducated man. Take an extreme case. Suppose that an adult man, in the full vigor of his faculties, could be suddenly placed in the world, as Adam is said to have been, and then left to do as he best might. How long would he be left uneducated? Not five minutes. Nature would begin to teach him, through the eye, the ear, the touch, the properties of objects. Pain and pleasure would be at his elbow telling him to do this and avoid that; and by slow degrees the man would receive an education, which, if narrow, would be thorough, real, and adequate to his circumstances, though there would be no extras and very few accomplishments.

6. Those who take honors in Nature's university, who learn the laws which govern men and things and obey them, are the really great and successful men in this world. Those who won't learn at all are plucked; and then you can't come up again. Nature's pluck means extermination.

7. Thus the question of compulsory education is settled so far as Nature is concerned. Her bill on that question was framed and passed long ago. But, like all compulsory legislation, that of Nature is harsh and wasteful in its operation. Ignorance is visited as sharply as willful disobedience—incapacity meets with the same punishment as crime. Nature's discipline is not even a word and a blow, and the blow first; but the blow without the word. It is left to you to find out why your ears are boxed.

HUXLEY.

14. MATHEMATICS AND PHYSICS.

1. For all the higher arts of construction, some acquaintance with mathematics is indispensable. The village carpenter, who, lacking rational instruction, lays out his work by empirical rules learnt in his apprenticeship, equally with the builder of a Britannia Bridge, makes hourly reference to the laws of quantitative relations. The surveyor on whose survey the land is purchased, the architect in designing a mansion to be built on it, the builder in preparing his estimates, his foreman in laying out the foundations, the masons in cutting the stones, and the various artisans who put up the fittings, are all guided by geometrical truths. Railway-making is regulated from beginning to end by mathematics: alike in the preparation of plans and sections, in staking out the line, in the mensuration of cuttings and embankments, in the designing, estimating,

and building of bridges, culverts, viaducts, tunnels, stations. And similarly with the harbors, docks, piers, and various engineering and architectural works that fringe the coasts and overspread the face of the country, as well as the mines that run underneath it.

2. Out of geometry, too, as applied to astronomy, the art of navigation has grown; and so, by this science, has been made possible that enormous foreign commerce which supports a large part of our population, and supplies us with many necessaries and most of our luxuries.

3. And nowadays even the farmer, for the correct laying out of his drains, has recourse to the level—that is, to geometrical principles. When from those divisions of mathematics which deal with *space*, and *number*, some small smattering of which is given in schools, we turn to that other division which deals with *force*—of which even a smattering is scarcely ever given—we meet with another large class of activities which this science presides over.

4. On the application of rational mechanics depends the success of nearly all modern manufacture. The properties of the lever, the wheel and axle, etc., are involved in every machine; every machine is a solidified mechanical theorem; and to machinery in these times we owe nearly all production.

5. Trace the history of the breakfast-roll. The soil out of which it came was drained with machine-made tiles; the surface was turned over by a machine; the seed was put in by a machine; the wheat was reaped, thrashed, and winnowed by machines; by machinery it was ground and bolted; and had the flour been sent to Gosport, it might have been made into biscuits by a machine.

6. Look round the room in which you sit. If modern, probably the bricks in its walls were machine-made;

by machinery the flooring was sawn and planed, the mantel-shelf sawn and polished, the paper-hangings made and printed; the veneer on the table, the turned legs of the chairs, the carpet, the curtains, are all products of machinery.

7. And your clothing—plain, figured, or printed—is it not wholly woven, nay, perhaps even sewed, by machinery? And the volume you are reading—are not its leaves fabricated by one machine and covered with these words by another? Add to which, that, for the means of distribution over both land and sea, we are similarly indebted.

8. And then let it be remembered that according as the principles of mechanics are well or ill used to these ends, comes success or failure—individual and national. The engineer who misapplies his formulæ for the strength of materials, builds a bridge that breaks down. The manufacturer whose apparatus is badly devised, can not compete with another whose apparatus wastes less in friction and inertia.

9. The ship-builder adhering to the old model is out-sailed by one who builds on the mechanically justified wave-line principle. And as the ability of a nation to hold its own against other nations depends on the skilled activity of its units, we see that on such knowledge may turn the national fate. Judge, then, the worth of mathematics.

10. Pass next to physics. Joined with mathematics, it has given us the steam-engine, which does the work of millions of laborers. That section of physics which deals with the laws of heat, has taught us how to economize fuel in our various industries; how to increase the produce of our smelting furnaces by substituting the hot for the cold blast; how to ventilate our mines; how to prevent explosions by using the safety-lamp; and, through the thermometer, how to regulate innumer-

able processes. That division which has the phenomena of light for its subject, gives eyes to the old and the myopic; aids through the microscope in detecting diseases and adulterations; and by improved lighthouses prevents shipwrecks.

11. Researches in electricity and magnetism have saved incalculable life and property by the compass; have subserved sundry arts by the electrotype; and now, in the telegraph, have supplied us with the agency by which, for the future, all mercantile transactions will be regulated, political intercourse carried on, and perhaps national quarrels often avoided. While in the details of indoor life, from the improved kitchen range up to the stereoscope on the drawing-room table, the applications of advanced physics underlie our comforts and gratifications.
HERBERT SPENCER.

SECTION II.

PROSE DECLAMATIONS.

1. CHARACTER OF TRUE ELOQUENCE.

[*This speech is characterized by full declamatory force, long pauses, strong emphasis, prevailing downward inflection, orotund quality, and radical stress. Require pupils to give reasons for the marking of rhetorical pauses and inflections.*]

1. When public *bódies* | are to be addressed | on momentous *occásions,* when great *ínterests* | are at stake, and strong *pássions* | *excíted,* *nòthing* | is valuable | in spéech, further than it is connected | with high *intelléctual* | and *mòral* endowments. *Cleàrness, fòrce,* and *eàrnestness* | are the *quálities* | which produce *convìction.* True *éloquence,* indeed, does not consìst in *spéech.* It *cánnot* be brought from *făr.* Labor and learning may

tóil for it, but they will toil in *vàin*. *Wórds* and *phráses* | may be marshaled in *èvery* wáy, but they can not *còmpass* it. It must exist in the *màn*, in the *sùbject*, and in the *occàsion*.

2. Affected *pássion*, intense *expréssion*, the pomp of *declamátion*, *àll* | may *aspíre* after it; they *cannot rèach* it. It *cómes*, if it come *at áll*, like the outbreaking of a *fòuntain* from the *èarth*, or the *bursting fòrth* of volcanic *fìres*, with *spontàneous*, *oríginal*, *nátive fòrce*.

3. The *gráces* | taught in the schóols, the costly *órnaments* | and studied *contrívances* of speech, *shóck* and *disgùst* men, when their *own líves*, and the fate of their *wíves*, their *chíldren*, and their *coúntry*, hang on the *decísion* of the *hòur*. Then, *wórds* have lost their *pòwer*, *rhĕtoric* is *văin*, and all *clàborate óratory* | *contèmptible*. Even *genius itsèlf* | then feels *rebùked* and *subdùed*, as in the presence of *hígher* qualities. *Thĕn*, *pàtriotism* | is èloquent; *thĕn*, *self-devòtion* | is èloquent.

4. The *cléar concèption*, outrunning the deductions of *lògic*, the *hígh pùrpose*, the *fírm resòlve*, the *dáuntless spìrit*, *spéaking* on the *tòngue*, *béaming* from the *eỳe*, informing *évery fèature*, and urging the *whole mán* | *ònward, ríght ònward*, to his *òbject*—*thĭs, thĭs* | is *éloquence;* or, rather, it is something *gréater* and *hígher* than *áll* eloquence—it is *àction*, nòble, *sublìme*, *gòdlike* àction.

2. NATIONAL GREATNESS.

1. I believe there is no permanent *gréatness* to a nation except it be based upon *morálity*. I do not care for *mílitary* greatness or military *renówn*. I care for the condition of the *pèople* among whom I live. There is no man in England who is less likely to speak irreverently of the crown and monarchy of England than I am; but crówns, córonets, míters, military displáy, the pomp of wár, wide cólonies, and a *huge émpire* are, in

my view, all trifles light as *àir*, and not worth considering, unless with them you can have a fair share of cómfort, conténtment, and háppiness among the great body of the pèople.

2. Pálaces, baronial cástles, great hálls, stately mánsions, do not make a *nátion*. The nátion, in every country, dwells in the *còttage;* and unless the light of your constitution can shine *thère*, unless the beauty of your legislation and excellence of your statesmanship are impressed *théré* in the feelings and condition of the péople, rely upon it you have yet to learn the duties of gòvernment. JOHN BRIGHT.

3. THE PASSING OF THE RUBICON.

[*An example of impassioned argumentative declamation.*]

1. A gentleman, Mr. President, speaking of Cæsar's *benevolent disposition*, and of the *reluctance* with which he entered into the civil wár, obsérves, "*How long* did he *pàuse* upon the brink of the *Rùbicon?*" How càme he to the brink of that river? How dàred he cròss it? Shall *prívate* men respect the boundaries of *prívate* property, and shall a man pay no respect to the boundaries of his *country's ríghts?* How dàred he cross that river? O, but he *páused* upon the brink! He should have *pérished* upon the brink ere he had crossed it!

2. *Whỳ* did he pause? Why does a man's heart *pàlpitate* when he is on the point of committing an *unláwful dèed?* Why does the very *múrderer*, his victim sleeping before him, and his glaring eye taking the measure of the blow, strike *wìde* of the mortal part? Because of *cônscience!* 'T was *thât* made Cæsar pause upon the brink of the Rubicon.

3. *Compássion! Whàt* compassion! The compassion of an *assàssin*, that feels a *mòmentary shúdder* as his

weapon begins to *cùt!* Cæsar paused upon the brink of the Rubicon? What *wàs* the Rubicon? The boundary of Cæsar's *pròvince.* From what did it *sèparate* his province? From his *còuntry.* Was that country a *désert? Nò:* it was *cúltivated* and *fèrtile; rích* and *pòpulous!* Its sons were men of *génius, spírit,* and *gèn-erosity!* Its daughters were *lóvely, suscéptible,* and *chàste!* *Frìendship* was its inhabitant! *Lòve* was its inhabitant! *Domestic affèction* was its inhabitant! *Lìberty* was its inhabitant! All bounded by the stream of the *Rùbicon!*

4. What was *Cæsar,* that stood upon the brink of that river? A *tráitor,* bringing war and pestilence into the *hèart* of that country! No *wónder* that he paused—no *wónder* if, his imagination wrought upon by his cón-science, he had beheld *blóod* instead of *wàter;* and heard *gròans* instead of *mùrmurs!* No *wónder* if some gorgon horror had *turned him into stóne upon the spòt!* But, *nò!*—he cried, "*The die is cast!*" He *plùnged!*—he *cròssed!*—and *Rome was free no mòre!*   KNOWLES.

4. OUR DUTIES TO OUR COUNTRY.

[*An example of oratorical declamation. Movement, slow; quality, orotund; prevailing inflections, falling.*]

1. This lovely *lánd,* this glorious *líberty,* these benign *institútions,* the dear purchase of our *fáthers,* are *òurs;* ours to *enjóy,* ours to *presérve,* ours to *transmìt.* Generations *pást,* and generations to *còme,* hold us responsible for this sacred *trùst.* Our *fáthers,* from behínd, admonish us, with their anxious paternal *vòices;* posterity calls out to us, from the bosom of the *fùture;* the world turns hither its solicitous *eỳes*—àll, *àll* conjure us to act wisely, and faithfully, in the relations which we sustàin.

2. We can never, indeed, pay the debt which is *upòn* us; but by *vírtue,* by *morálity,* by *relígion,* by the culti-

vation of every good prínciple and every good *hábit*, we may hope to enjoy the blessing through ŏur day, and to leave it unimpaired to our *chíldren*. Let us feel deeply how much of what we *áre*, and what we *posséss*, we owe to this *líberty*, and these *institutions of gòvernment*.

3. Nature has, indeed, given us a soil which yields bounteously to the hands of ìndustry; the mighty and fruitful ocean is *befóre* us, and the skies over our heads shed health and vìgor. But what are *lànds*, and *sèas*, and *skìes*, to civilized mán, without *socìety*, without *knòwledge*, without *mòrals*, without religious *cùlture?* and how can these be enjóyed, in all their exténts, and all their éxcellence, but under the protection of wise institutions and a *free gòvernment?*

4. Fellow-cítizens, there is not one of us here présent who does not, at *thís* moment, and at *évery* moment, experience in his own condítion, and in the condition of those most near and déar to him, the influence and the benefits of this *líberty*, and these *institùtions*. Let us then acknowledge the *blèssing;* let us feel it *deeply* and *pòwerfully;* let us cherish a strong *affèction* for it, and resolve to *maintáin* and *perpètuate* it. The *blood of our fáthers*, let it not have been shed in vàin; the *great hope of posterity*, let it not be *blàsted*. WEBSTER.

5. THE AMERICAN WAR.

1. These *abominable prínciples*, and this *mòre* abominable *avówal* of them, demand the most decisive *indignàtion!* I call upon that Right Reverend *Bènch*, those holy ministers of the *Gòspel*, and pious pastors of our *Chùrch;* I *conjùre* them to join in the *holy wórk*, and to vindicate the religion of their *Gòd!* I appeal | to the *wísdom* | and the *láw* | of this learned *Bènch*, to de-

fend and support the *jústice* of their *còuntry!* I call upon the *Bĭshops* | to interpose the unsullied *sánctity* | of their *làwn*, upon the *jŭdges* | to interpose the *púrity* | of their *èrmine*, to save us from *this pollùtion!*

2. I call upon the *hŏnor* of your *Lȯrdships*, to reverence the dignity of your *áncestors*, and to maintain your *òwn!* I call upon the *spirit* and *humánity* of my *còuntry*, to vindicate the *nátional cháracter!* I invoke the *génius* of the *Constitùtion!* From the tapestry | that adorns these *wálls*, the immortal ancestor of the noble Lórd | frowns with *indignàtion* at the *disgráce* of his *còuntry!*

3. Turn forth into our *séttlements*, among our ancient *connéctions, friénds*, and *relátions*, the *merciless cánnibal*, thirsting for the blood of *mán, wóman*, and *chĭld?* Send forth the *infidel săvage?* Against *whòm?* Against your *bréthren!* To lay waste their *còuntry*, to desolate their *dwèllings*, and *extirpate* their *ráce* and *náme*, with these horrible *hóunds* of savage *wàr!*

4. *Spáin* | armed herself with *blòod-hounds* to extirpate the wretched natives of *Amèrica;* and *wĕ* | improve on the *inhuman exámple* | of even *Spánish* crúelty;—we turn loose these *sávages*, these fiendish *hóunds*, against our *bréthren* and *còuntrymen* in Amèrica, of the same *lànguage, làws, líberties*, and *relĭgion*—endéared to us by every *tíe* that should sanctify *humànity!* Pitt.

6. FREEDOM.

I will speak the words of Freedom; I will listen to her *mùsic;* I will acknowledge her *ĭmpulses;* I will stand beneath her *flàg;* I will fight in her *rànks;* and, when I *dŏ* só, I shall find myself surrounded by the *greát*, the *wíse*, the *góod*, the *bráve*, the *nóble* of *évery lànd*. If I could stand for a moment upon one of your high *moúntain*-tops, far above all the kingdoms of the civilized *wórld*, and there might *sée*, coming up, one after another, the bravest and wisest of the ancient *wárriors*, and *státesmen*, and *kíngs*, and *mónarchs*, and *príests;* and if, as they came úp, I might be permitted to ask from them an expression of opinion upon such a case as *thĭs*, with a *common vòice* and in *thúnder tònes*, reverberating through a *thòusand vàlleys*, and *èchoing dòwn the àges*, they would crȳ : "*Lĭberty, Frèedom,* the *Universal Brotherhood of Mȧn !*" *I* join that *shòut ;* I swell that *ánthem ;* I echo that *práise* FOREVER, and FOR EVERMORE.

Col. E. D. Baker.

7. THE VOICES OF THE DEAD.

1. The *wórld* | is filled | with the voices of the *dèad*. They *spéak* | not from the public records of the great *wórld* only, but from the private history | of our own *expèrience*. They speak to us | in a thousand *remémbrances*, in a thousand *íncidents, évents,* and *assocìátions.* They *spéak* to us, not only from their silent *gráves*, but from the throng of *lĭfe.* Though they are *invĭsible, yet* life | is *fĭlled* | with their prèsence. They are *wĭth* us by the silent *fíreside* | and in the secluded *chàmber.* They are *wĭth* us | in the paths of *socíety,* and in the crowded assemblies of *mèn*.

2. They speak to us | from the lonely *wáy-side;* and they speak to us | from the venerable *wàlls* | that echo to the steps of a múltitude | and to the voice of *pràyer.* Go where we will, the *déad* | are *wĭth* us. We *lĭve,* we *convèrse* with *thóse* | who once lived | and conversed | with *ŭs.* Their well-remembered tone | mingles with the whispering brèeze, with the sound of the falling léaf, with the jubilee shout | of the *sprĭng*-time.—The *éarth* | is *fĭlled* | with their shadowy tràin.

3. But there are more *substăntial* expressions | of the presence of the *dĕad* | with the *lĭving*. The earth | is filled with the *lăbors*, the *wŏrks*, of the dĕad. Almost all the *lĭterature* in the wórld, the *discoveries* of *science*, the *glories* of *árt*, the ever-enduring *témples*, the *dwelling-places* of *generátions*, the comforts and improvements of *lĭfe*, the *lánguages*, the *máxims*, the *ópinions* of the *lĭving*, the very *frame-work of society*, the institutions of *nátions*, the fabrics of *émpires*—*àll* | are the works of the *dèad*. By *thĕse*, they | who are dead | yet *spèak*.   Orville Dewey.

8. GRATTAN'S REPLY TO MR. CORRY.

[*An example of impassioned sarcasm and invective.*]

1. Has the gentleman *dŏne?* Has he *completely* dóne? He was *unparliaméntary* from the *begínning* to the *ĕnd* of his speech. There was scarce a *word he ŭttered* that was not a *violátion* of the privileges of the *Hòuse*. But I did not call him to *ŏrder*,—whý? because the limited talents of *sŏme* men render it impossible for them to be *sevĕre withôut* being unparliamèntary. But before I sit down, I shall show him how to be *sevĕre ănd* parliamentary at the same time.

2. The right honorable gentlemen has called me "an *unimpĕached trăitor.*" I ask why not "*trăitor*," unqualified by any *èpithet?* I will tell him: it was because he *dŭrst* not. It was the act of a *côward*, who raises his arm to *strĭke*, but has not courage to give the *blôw*. I will not call him *vĭllain*, because it would be *unparliaméntary*, and he is a privy counselor. I will not call him *fŏol*, because he happens to be *chăncellor* of the *exchèquer*. But I say, he is one who has abused the privilege of Párliament and the freedom of debáte, by uttering lánguage which, if spoken out of the Hóuse, I should answer only with a *blôw*. I care not how *hĭgh*

his *situátion*, how *lów* his *cháracter*, how *contémptible* his *spéech;* whether a *privy cóunselor* or a *párasite,* my answer would be a *blów.*

3. I have *retúrned,*—not as the right honorable member has said, to raise another *stŏrm,*—I have returned to discharge an honorable debt of *grátitude* to my còuntry, that conferred a great reward for *păst* services, which, I am proud to say, was not greater than my desèrt. I have *retúrned* to protect that *Constitùtion* of which I was thé parent and fóunder, from the *assassinàtion* of such men as the right honorable *géntleman* and his unworthy *assòciates.* They are *corrûpt,* they are *sedítious,* and they, at this *very mòment,* are in a *conspíracy* against their còuntry. I have returned to refute a *líbel,* as *fálse* as it is *malícious,* given to the public under the appellation of a report of the committee of the Lòrds. Here I *stánd,* ready for *impéachment* or *tríal.* I *dáre* accusàtion. I *defý* the honorable gèntleman; I defy the *góvernment;* I defy their *whóle phálanx;* let them come fòrth. I tell the *mínisters,* I will neither *gíve* quarter nor *táke* it. I am here to lay the shattered remains of my constitution on the floor of *this Hóuse,* in defense of the *líberties* of my còuntry.

9. SUPPOSED SPEECH OF JOHN ADAMS IN SUPPORT OF AMERICAN INDEPENDENCE.

1. *Sínk* or *swìm, líve* or *díe, survíve* or *pèrish,* I give my *hánd* and my *hèart* to this vòte. It is true, indeed, that in the beginning we aimed not at *Indepèndence.* But there's a Divinity which shapes our ènds. The injustice of England has driven us to *árms;* and, blinded to her own interest for our góod, she has obstinately persísted, till Independence is now within our gràsp. We have but to reach fórth to it, and it is oùrs.

2. Why, then, should we defer the *Declarǎtion?* Is any man so weak as now to hope for a *reconciliátion* with Éngland? Do we mean to submit to the measures of Parliament, Boston port-bill and áll? I know we do nǒt mean to submìt. We never shǎll submìt.

3. Sir, the Declaration will inspire the people with increased coùrage. Instead of a long and bloody war for restoration of prívileges, for redress of griévances, for chartered immúnities, held under a British kíng, set before them the glorious object of *entǐre Indepèndence,* and it will breathe into them anew the breath of lífe.

4. Read this Declaration at the head of the *ǎrmy:* every sword will be drawn from its scábbard, and the solemn vow úttered, to maintain it, or to perish on the field of hònor. Publish it from the *pùlpit;* religion will appróve it, and the love of religious liberty will *cling róund* it, resolved to *stǎnd* with it, or *fǎll* with it.

5. Send it to the *public hǎlls;* proclaim it *thère.* Let *thém* hear it who heard the first roar of the *enemy's cǎnnon;* let *thém* see it who saw their brothers and their sons fall on the field of Bunker Hìll, and in the streets of Lexington and Còncord, and the *very wǎlls* will cry out in its suppòrt.

6. Sir, before God, I believe the hour is *còme.* My júdgment approves this méasure, and my *whole heǎrt* is *ǐn* it. All that I *hǎve,* and all that I *ǎm,* and all that I *hòpe,* in *thís* life, I am now ready here to *stǎke* upon it; and I leave off as I begàn, that *líve or díe, survíve* or *pèrish, I* am for the *Declarǎtion.* It is my *líving* séntiment, and, by the blessing of Gód, it shall be my *dýing* sèntiment: Independence *nǒw;* and *Independence forèver.*

DANIEL WEBSTER.

10. THE CONSTITUTION AND THE UNION.

[*In this speech the movement is slow; the utterance deliberate, the pauses long; and the inflections strongly marked.*]

1. For *mysélf*, I propose, Sír, to abide by the *prínciples* | and the *púrposes* | which I have *avòwed*. I shall stànd bỳ the Únion, and by all | who stand bỳ it. I shall do justice to the *whole coùntry*, according to the best of my abílity, in all I *sày*, and act for the *gòod* of the whole *coúntry* | in all I *dò*. I mean to stánd upon the *Constitùtion*. I need no *óther plàtform*. I shall know but *óne coùntry*.

2. The ends I aim at | shall be my *coùntry's*, my *Gód's*, and *Trùth's*. I was *bórn* | an Amèrican; I will *líve* an Amèrican; I shall *díe* an Amèrican; and I intend to perform the duties incumbent upon me | in that cháracter | to the end of my *carèer*. I mean to *dó* this, with the absolute *disregàrd* of *pérsonal cònsequences*.

3. What *àre* | pérsonal cònsequences? What is the *individual mán*, with all the good or evil that may *betíde* him, in comparison with the good or evil | which may befall a *great coúntry* | in a crisis like *thìs*, and in the midst of great *transàctions* | which concern that *coúntry's fàte?* Let the *cònsequences* | be what they *will*. *I* am *càreless*. No man can suffer too *múch*, and no man can fall too *sòon*, if he súffer | or if he fàll | in defense of the *líberties* | and *Constitútion* | of his *coùntry*.

WEBSTER.

11. THE CONSTITUTION.

1. Never did there devolve on any generation of men higher trusts than now devolve upon us, for the preservation of this Constitution, and the harmony and peace of all who are destined to live under it. Let us make our generation one of the strongest and brightest links in that golden chain which is destined, I fondly

believe, to grapple the people of all the States to this Constitution for ages to come.

2. We have a great, popular, constitutional government, guarded by law and by judicature, and defended by the affections of the people. No monarchical throne presses these States together. They live and stand upon a government popular in its form, representative in its character, founded upon principles of equality, and so constructed, we hope, as to last forever.

3. In all its history it has been beneficent. It has trodden down no man's liberty, it has crushed no State. Its daily respiration is liberty and patriotism. Its youthful veins are full of enterprise, courage, and honorable love of glory and renown. Large before, the country has now, by recent events, become vastly larger. This republic now extends, with a vast breadth, across the whole continent. The two great seas of the world wash the one and the other shore. We realize on a mighty scale the beautiful description of the ornamental edging of the bucklers of Achilles:

> "Now the broad shield complete, the artist crowned
> With his last hand, and poured the ocean round.
> In living silver seemed the waves to roll,
> And beat the buckler's verge and bound the whole."

DANIEL WEBSTER.

12. DUTIES OF AMERICAN CITIZENS.

1. We have indulged in gratifying recollections of the past, in the prosperity and pleasures of the present, and in high hopes for the future. But let us remember that we have duties and obligations to perform, corresponding to the blessings which we enjoy.

2. Let us remember the trust, the sacred trust, attaching to the rich inheritance which we have received from our fathers. Let us feel our personal responsibility, to

the full extent of our power and influence, for the preservation of the principles of civil and religious liberty. And let us remember that it is only religion, and morals, and knowledge, that can make men respectable and happy, under any form of government.

3. Let us hold fast the great truth, that communities are responsible, as well as individuals; that no government is respectable, which is not just; that without unspotted purity of public faith, without sacred public principle, fidelity, and honor, no mere forms of government, no machinery of laws, can give dignity to political society. In our day and generation let us seek to raise and improve the moral sentiment, so that we may look, not for a degraded, but for an elevated and improved future.

4. And when both we and our children shall have been consigned to the house appointed for all living, may love of country and pride of country glow with equal fervor among those to whom our names and our blood shall have descended.

5. And then, when honored and decrepit age shall lean against the base of this monument, and troops of ingenuous youth shall be gathered round it, and when the one shall speak to the other of its objects, the purposes of its construction, and the great and glorious events with which it is connected, there shall rise from every youthful breast the ejaculation, "*Thank God, I— I also—am an American!*"   DANIEL WEBSTER.

13. LABOR.

1. *Làbor* is heaven's great ordinance for human *impròvement*. Let not the great ordinance be broken *dòwn*. *Whát* do I sáy? It *is* broken dòwn; and *hàs* been broken down for àges. Let it, then, be *bùilt* again; hère, if ánywhere, on the shores of a *new wòrld*—of a *new civilizàtion*.

2. But hów, it may be ásked, is it *broken dòwn?* Do not men *tóil?* it may be sáid. They do, indeed, tòil; but they too génerally dó, because they *mùst*. Many submit to it, as to, in some sórt, a *degrading necèssity;* and they desire nothing so much on éarth as an *escàpe* from it. This way of thinking is the heritage of the absurd and unjust feudal sýstem, under which *serfs* lábored, and *gĕntlemen* spent their lives in *fíghting* and *fèasting*. It is time that this opprobrium of toil were *done awáy*.

3. *Ashamed to tŏil!* Ashamed of thy dingy *wórkshop* and dusty *lábor*-field; of thy hard *hánd*, scarred with service more honorable than that of *wár;* of thy soiled and weather-stained *gárments*, on which mother Nature has embroidered *míst, sún* and *ráin, fíre* and *stéam*— her own heraldic *hŏnors!*

4. *Ashămed* of those *tókens* and *títles*, and envious of the flaunting robes of imbecile *ĭdleness* and *vănity!* It is treason to *Nàture;* it is impiety to *Hèaven:* it is breaking Heaven's *greát òrdinance. Tóil—tóil*—either of the *bráin*, of the *heárt*, or of the *hánd*—is the only *trúe mànhood*, the only *trúe nobĭlity!*   ORVILLE DEWEY.

14. THE FUTURE OF AMERICA.

1. It cannot be denied, but by those who would dispute against the *sún*, that *with* America, and *ín* America, a *néw èra* commences in human affàirs. *This éra* is distinguished by free representative *góvernments*, by entire *relígious líberty*, by improved systems of national *íntercourse*, by a newly awakened and an unconquerable spirit of *free inquíry*, and by a diffusion of knowledge through the *commúnity*, such as has been before altogether *unknówn* and *unhèard of*.

2. América, *América*, our *coúntry*, our own dear and

nátive lánd, is inseparably connécted, fast bóund up, in fórtune and by fáte, with these *gréat ìnterests.* If they *fáll, wé* fall *wìth* them; if they *stănd,* it will be because we have *uphéld* them.

3. Let us contémplate, then, this connection which binds the prosperity of *ŏthers* to our *ôwn;* and let us manfully discharge all the *dúties* which it *impòses.* If we cherish the *vírtues* and the *prínciples* of our fáthers, *Héaven* will assist us to carry on the work of *humăn líberty* and *human háppiness.*

4. Auspicious *ómens chèer* us. Great *exámples* are *befòre* us. Our *ôwn* fírmament now shines brightly upon our *pàth. Wáshington* is in the clear upper *skỳ.* Those *ŏther* stars have now joined the American *constellàtion;* they circle round their cénter, and the heavens beam with *new lìght. Benéath* this illuminátion, let us walk the course of lífe, and at its clóse devoutly commend our beloved coúntry, the common parent of us áll, to the *Divine Benìgnity.*   DANIEL WEBSTER.

15. PATRIOTISM.

1. Bereft of patriotism, the heart of a nation will be cold and cramped and sordid; the arts will have no enduring impulse, and commerce no invigorating soul; society will degenerate, and the mean and vicious will triumph. Patriotism is not a wild and glittering passion, but a glorious reality. The virtue that gave to Paganism its dazzling luster, to Barbarism its redeeming trait, to Christianity its heroic form, is not dead. It still lives to console, to sanctify humanity. It has its altar in every clime; its worship and festivities.

2. On the heathered hills of Scotland, the sword of Wallace is yet a bright tradition. The genius of France, in the brilliant literature of the day, pays its high

homage to the piety and heroism of the young Maid of Orleans. In her new Senate-hall, England bids her sculptor place, among the effigies of her greatest sons, the images of Hampden and of Russell. In the gay and graceful capital of Belgium, the daring hand of Geefs has reared a monument full of glorious meaning to the three hundred martyrs of the revolution.

3. By the soft blue waters of Lake Lucerne stands the chapel of William Tell. On the anniversary of his revolt and victory, across those waters, as they glitter in the July sun, skim the light boats of the allied cantons, from the prows hang the banners of the republic, and as they near the sacred spot, the daughters of Lucerne chant the hymns of their old poetic land. Then bursts forth the glad Te Deum, and Heaven again hears the voice of that wild chivalry of the mountains, which five centuries since pierced the white eagle of Vienna, and flung it bleeding on the rocks of Uri.

T. F. MEAGHER.

16. THE FOURTH OF JULY.

1. On the Fourth of July, 1776, the representatives of the United States of America, in Congress assembled, declared that these United Colonies are, and of right ought to be, free and independent States. This declaration, made by most patriotic and resolute men, trusting in the justice of their cause, and the protection of Providence—and yet not without deep solicitude and anxiety—has stood for seventy-five years, and still stands.

2. It was sealed in blood. It has met dangers and overcome them; it has had enemies, and it has conquered them; it has had detractors, and it has abashed them all; it has had doubting friends, but it has cleared all doubts away; and now, to-day, raising its august form higher than the clouds, twenty millions of people

contemplate it with hallowed love; and the world beholds it, and the consequences which have followed, with profound admiration.

3. This anniversary animates, and gladdens, and unites all American hearts. On other days of the year we may be party men, indulging in controversies more or less important to the public good; we may have likes and dislikes, and we may maintain our political differences often with warm, and sometimes with angry feelings. But to-day we are Americans all in all, nothing but Americans.

4. As the great luminary over our heads, dissipating mists and fogs, cheers the whole hemisphere, so do the associations connected with this day disperse all cloudy and sullen weather, and all noxious exhalations in the minds and feelings of true Americans. Every man's heart swells within him;—every man's port and bearing become somewhat more proud and lofty, as he remembers that seventy-five years have rolled away, and that the great inheritance of liberty is still his; his, undiminished and unimpaired; his, in all its original glory; his to enjoy, his to protect, and his to transmit to future generations. DANIEL WEBSTER.

17. TRUE GREATNESS.

1. The poet tells us, in pathetic cadence, that
"The paths of glory lead but to the grave."
But this is true only in the *superfĭcial* sense. It is true that the *fámous* and the *obscúre*, the *devóted* and the *ignóble*, "alike await the *inevitable hòur*." But the path of *trŭe* glory does not *énd* in the *gràve*. It passes *thrŏugh* it to larger opportunities of *sèrvice*.

2. A *great náture* is a *sèed*. "It is sown a *nátural* body; it is raised a *spĭritual* body." It germinates thus

in *thĭs* world as well as in the *ŏther*. Was Warren *bŭried* when he fell on the field of a *defĕat*, pierced through the *bráin*, at the commencement of the Revolútion, by a *búllet* that put the land in *móurning?*

3. *Nŏ;* the monument that has been raised where his blood reddened the *sŏd*—*grănite* though it be in a *hundred cóurses*—is a feeble witness of the permanence and influence of *hĭs spĭrit* among the *Amĕrican pèople.* He mounted into *lĭterature* from the moment that he *fĕll;* he began to move the soul of a *great commùnity;* and part of the *prínciple* and *enthúsiasm* of Massachusetts to-dáy is due to *his sácrifice,* to the presence of *his spĭrit* as a *pówer* in the life of the *Stàte.*

4. Did *Montgómery* lose his influence as a force in the *Revolútion,* because he died without *víctory* on its *thréshold,* pierced with three *wŏunds,* before *Quebĕc?* Philadelphia was in *téars* for him; his eulogies were uttered by the most eloquent tongues of Amĕrica and Brítain, and a thrill of his power beats in the volumes of our hístory, and runs yet through the onset of every Irish brigade beneath the American bánner, which he planted on *Montreàl.*

5. Did *Lăwrence* díe when his breath expired in the defeat on the *séa,* after his exclamátion, "Don't give up the *shĭp!*" What victorious captain in that naval war shed forth such *pòwer?* His spirit soared and touched *every flăg* on *every frìgate,* to make its red more *commánding* and its stars *flame brìghter;* it went abroad in *sŏngs,* and *every sailor* felt him and feels him now as an *inspirátion.*

6. The soul is *nŏt* a *shădow.* The body *ĭs. Génius* is not a *shădow;* it is *sŭbstance. Pátriotism* is not a *shădow;* it is *lĭght.* Great purposes, and the spirit that counts *déath* nothing in contrast with *hónor* and the welfare of our *cóuntry—thĕse* are the witnesses that man is not a *passing vápor,* but an *immórtal spĭrit.*   Thomas Starr King.

18. THE NORMANS.

1. In 1066, the Normans invaded England, and the battle of Hastings broke, forever, the Saxon and Danish power. But years passed, and several monarchs filled and vacated the English throne before these Norman pioneers had accomplished their work, and molded the nation to their will.

2. They were warriors—not reformers. They were greedy of power, but impatient of its exercise upon themselves; greedy of wealth, but lavish in its expenditure. They were reckless alike of their own and the life of others. Turbulent, unruly—equally dangerous to the people whom they subdued, and to the princes who led them to conquest. Gallant men, full of deeds of knightly courtesy, yet reddening their hands with the blood of civil broil, and ever ready to maintain their right with their swords.

3. Men of clear intellect and giant will, they acknowledged an uncertain allegiance to their king, and only bowed their necks to the yoke of God, when at the close of life they deemed it necessary to assume the monastic habit, or to do penance of their goods for the salvation of their souls.

4. From these stern and bloody men, "who came in with the Conqueror," or followed in the train of his successors, the noblest families of England are proud to derive their descent; and even we republicans, upon this distant coast, and at this late period of time, do not refuse our admiration to these Norman pioneers, who, through the mists of the past, loom up like giants before us.

5. Yet our admiration of these old warriors, the admiration of the world for them, is not because they shed blood, or amassed or squandered wealth, or swore fealty to their kings, or broke their oaths in rebellion,

or committed or abstained from the crimes that were common to their age. The Norman pioneers are enrolled in history among the most illustrious of men, because in the dark and troublous times in which they lived, in the midst of confusion and blood, with strong hands and undaunted hearts, they laid deep the first foundations of English liberty, and became the fathers of that system of common law which, at the end of eight hundred years, is the protection and the glory of all who speak the English tongue.
F. P. Tracy.

19. WASHINGTON'S BIRTHDAY.

1. Inspiring auspices, this day, surround us and cheer us. It is the anniversary of the birth of Washington. We should know this, even if we had lost our calendars, for we should be reminded of it by the shouts of joy and gladness. The whole atmosphere is redolent of his name; hills and forests, rocks and rivers, echo and re-echo his praises.

2. All the good, whether learned or unlearned, high or low, rich or poor, feel, this day, that there is one treasure common to them all, and that is the fame and character of Washington. They recount his deeds, ponder over his principles and teachings, and resolve to be more and more guided by them in the future.

3. To the old and the young, to all born in the land, and to all whose love of liberty has brought them from foreign shores to make this the home of their adoption, the name of Washington is this day an exhilarating theme. Americans by birth are proud of his character, and exiles from foreign shores are eager to participate in admiration of him; and it is true that he is this day, here, everywhere, all the world over, more an object of love and regard than on any day since his birth.

4. On Washington's principles, and under the guidance of his example, will we and our children uphold the Constitution. Under his military leadership our fathers conquered; and under the outspread banner of his political and constitutional principles will we also conquer.

5. To that standard we shall adhere, and uphold it through evil report and through good report. We will meet danger, we will meet death, if they come, in its protection; and we will struggle on, in daylight and in darkness, ay, in the thickest darkness, with all the storms which it may bring with it, till

"Danger's troubled night is o'er,
And the star of Peace return." WEBSTER.

20. NATIONS AND HUMANITY.

1. It was *nót* his olive valleys and orange groves which made the *Gréece* of the *Gréek*. It was *nót* for his apple orchards or potato fields that the farmer of New England and New York left his plow in the furrow and marched to Bunker Hill, to Bénnington, to *Saratóga*. A man's *coŭntry* is not a certain area of *lănd*, but it is a *prĭnciple;* and *pătriotism* is *lòyalty* to that prĭnciple. The secret sanctification of the soil and symbol of a country is the *idéa* which they *represènt;* and *thĭs* idea the patriot *wórships* through the name and the *sўmbol*.

2. So with passionate *héroism*, of which tradition is never weary of tenderly télling, *Arnold von Winkelreid* gathers into his bosom the sheaf of *foreign spèars*. So, *Nathan Hàle*, disdaining no service that duty demánds, perishes untimely with no *ŏther* friend than Gód and the satisfied sense of *dùty*. So, through all history from the beginning, a noble *army of mártyrs* has fought

fiercely, and fallen *brávely,* for that unseen mistress, their coùntry. So, through all history to the énd, *thát* army must still *márch,* and *fight,* and *fàll.*

3. But *coúntries* and *fámilies* are but *núrseries* and *ìnfluences.* A man is a *fáther,* a *bróther,* a *Gérman,* a *Róman,* an *Américan;* but beneath all *thĕse* relations, he is a *màn.* The end of his human destiny is not to be the best Gérman, or the best Róman, or the best fáther; but the *best màn* he can be. George W. Curtis.

21. CHARACTER OF WASHINGTON.

1. Sir, it matters very little what immediate *spót* may be the birthplace of such a man as *Wàshington.* No people can *cláim,* no *coúntry* can *appròpriate* him. The boon of Providence to the *human ráce,* his fame is *etérnity,* and his residence *creàtion.* Though it was the defeat of our *árms,* and the disgrace of our *pólicy,* I almost *blèss* the *convúlsion* in which he had his *òrigin.* If the heavens *thúndered,* and the earth *rócked,* yet, when the storm *pássed,* how *púre* was the climate that it *clèared;* how *bríght,* in the brow of the firmament, was the *plánet* which it *revèaled* to us!

2. In the production of *Wáshington,* it does really appear as if Nature was endeavoring to *impròve* upon herself, and that all the virtues of the *ăncient* world were but so many studies preparatory to the patriot of the *néw.* Individual *ínstances* no doubt there wére— splendid exemplifications of some *síngle qualificàtion.* Cæsar was *mèrciful;* Scipio was *cóntinent;* Hannibal was *pàtient;* but it was reserved for *Wăshington* to blend them *all in óne,* and, like the lovely masterpiece of the Grecian artist, to exhíbit, in one glow of associated beaúty, the pride of *every módel,* and the perfection of *every màster.*

3. As a *géneral*, he marshalled the *péasant* into a *vèteran*, and supplied by *díscipline* the absence of *expérience;* as a *státesman*, he enlarged the policy of the cabinet into the most comprehensive system of general advàntage; and such was the wisdom of his *víews*, and the philosophy of his *cóunsels*, that to the *sóldier* and the státesman, he almost added the character of the *ságe!* A *cónqueror*, he was untainted with the crime of *blòod;* a *revolútionist*, he was free from any stain of *tréason;* for *aggréssion commènced* the contest, and his country called him to the *commánd*.

4. Liberty *unshéathed* his sword, necessity *stáined*, victory *retùrned* it. If he had paused *hĕre*, history might have doubted what station to *assĭgn* him; whether at the head of her *cítizens* or her *sòldiers*, her *héroes* or her *pàtriòts*. But the last glorious act crowns his caréer, and banishes all *hesitátion*. *Whó*, like Wáshington, after having emancipated a *hémisphere*, resigned its *crówn*, and preferred the retirement of *domestic lífe* to the adoration of a *lánd* he might be almost said to have *creáted?*   PHILLIPS.

22. BUNKER-HILL MONUMENT.

1. The Bunker-Hill *mónument* is *fĭnished*. *Here* it *stánds*. Fortunate in the natural eminence on which it is pláced—higher, *ĭnfinitely* hígher, in its objects and púrpose, it rises over the lánd, and over the séa; and vísible, at their hómes, to three hundred thousand citizens of Massachúsetts—it stánds, a memorial of the *pást*, and a monitor to the *présent*, and all succeeding *generátions*.

2. I have spoken of the loftiness of its pùrpose. If it had been without any *ŏther* design than the creation of a work of *árt*, the granite of which it is composed

would have slept in its native bĕd. It *hăs* a purpose; and *thăt* purpose gives it *chàracter*. *Thát* púrpose enrobes it with dignity and *móral gràndeur*. That *wéllknown purpose* it ís, which causes us to look up to it with a feeling of àwe. It is *itsélf* the *órator* of this *occàsion*.

3. It is not from *mў* lips, it is not from any *hŭman* lips, that that strain of eloquence is this day to flów, most competent to move and excite the vast multitudes aròund. The potent speaker stands motionless *befòre* them. It is a *plain shăft*. It bears no inscríptions, fronting to the rising sún, from which the future antiquarian shall wipe the dúst. Nor does the rising sun cause tones of *mùsic* to issue from its *sùmmit*. But at the *rìsing* of the sun, and at the *sètting* of the sun, in the blaze of *nóon*-day, and beneath the milder effulgence of *lùnar* light, it *lòoks*, it *spèaks*, it *àcts*, to the full comprehension of every American mínd, and the awakening of glowing enthusiasm in every American heàrt.

4. Its silent, but awful útterance; its deep páthos, as it brings to our contemplation the 17th of June, 1775, and the consequences which have resulted to us, to our cóuntry, and to the wórld, from the events of that dáy, and which we know must continue to rain influence on the destinies of mankínd to the end of tíme; the elevation with which it raises us high above the *ŏrdinary* feelings of lífe—surpass all that the study of the clóset, or even the inspiration of *gènius* can prodùce.

5. *To-dáy*, it speaks to *ùs*. Its *fùture* auditories will be through successive generations of mén, as they rise up *befóre* it, and gather rònd it. Its speech will be of *pátriotism* and *còurage;* of civil and religious *lìberty;* of free *gòvernment;* of the moral improvement and elevation of *mankìnd;* and of the *immortal mèmory* of those whó, with heroic devótion, have sacrificed their *líves* for their *còuntry*.

DANIEL WEBSTER.

23. THE BIRTHDAY OF WASHINGTON.

1. The birthday of the "Father of his Country"! May it ever be freshly remembered by American hearts! May it ever re-awaken in them a filial veneration for his memory; ever rekindle the fires of patriotic regard for the country which he loved so well, to which he gave his youthful vigor and his youthful energy, during the perilous period of the early Indian warfare; to which he devoted his life in the maturity of his powers, in the field; to which again he offered the counsels of his wisdom and his experience, as president of the convention that framed our Constitution; which he guided and directed while in the chair of state, and for which the last prayer of his earthly supplication was offered up, when it came the moment for him so well, and so grandly, and so calmly, to die.

2. He was the first man of the time in which he grew. His memory is first and most sacred in our love, and ever hereafter, till the last drop of blood shall freeze in the last American heart, his name shall be a spell of power and of might.

3. Yes, gentlemen, there is one personal, one vast felicity, which no man can share with him. It was the daily beauty, and towering and matchless glory of his life which enabled him to create his country, and at the same time secure an undying love and regard from the whole American people. "The first in the hearts of his countrymen!" Yes, first! He has our first and most fervent love.

4. Undoubtedly there were brave and wise and good men, before his day, in every colony. But the American nation, as a nation, I do not reckon to have begun before 1774. And the first love of that Young America was Washington. The first word she lisped was his name. Her earliest breath spoke it. It still is her

proud ejaculation; and it will be the last gasp of her expiring life!

5. Yes; others of our great men have been appreciated—many admired by all; but him we love; him we all love.. About and around him we call up no dissentient and discordant and dissatisfied elements—no sectional prejudice nor bias—no party, no creed, no dogma of politics. None of these shall assail him. Yes; when the storm of battle blows darkest and rages highest, the memory of Washington shall nerve every American arm, and cheer every American heart. RUFUS CHOATE.

24. THE NATIONAL CLOCK.

1. Every nation is like a *clòck*, the forces at work within carrying forward some purpose or plan of Providence with patient *cònstancy;* but when the season comes that the *sixtieth mĭnute* is dúe, and a *new hóur* must be sóunded, perhaps not for the *nătion* alóne, but for the *wŏrld*, thén—*thĕn* the clock *strìkes*, and it may be with a force and *résonance* that startles and inspires the ràce.

2. The first American *revolútion* was such a *pèriod*—*thăt* was the *glòry* of it. The English *Góvernment* had oppressed our *fàthers*. It tried to break their *spìrit*. For several yéars it was a *dark tĭme*, like the hours before the striking of the *dàwn*.

3. But the Colonial time-piece kept *tĭcking, tĭcking* to the pressure of the English Góvernment, the giant wheels playing calmly till about 1775', when there was a *strange stĭr* and *bŭzz* within the càse. The *péople* could not bear any *mòre* of it. But the *sixtieth mĭnute* cáme, and the clock *strŭck*.

4. The *wŏrld hèard*—the battle of *Léxington—òne;* the Declaration of *Indepéndence—twò;* the surrender of *Bur-*

góyne—thrèe; the siege of *Yórktown—fòur;* the Treaty of *Páris—fĭve;* the inauguration of *Wáshington—sĭx.*

5. And then it was *súnrise* of the *néw dày,* of which we have seen yet only the *glórious forenòon.*

THOMAS STARR KING.

25. FREE SCHOOLS.

1. It is impossible for us adequately to conceive the boldness of the measure which aimed at universal education through the establishment of Free Schools. As a fact, it had no precedent in the world's history; and, as a theory, it could have been refuted and silenced by a more formidable array of argument and experience than was ever marshaled against any other institution of human origin.

2. But time has ratified its soundness. Two centuries of successful operation now proclaim it to be as wise as it was courageous, and as beneficent as it was disinterested. Every community in the civilized world awards it the meed of praise, and States at home, and nations abroad, in the order of their intelligence, are copying the bright example.

3. What we call the enlightened nations of Christendom are approaching, by slow degrees, to the moral elevation which our ancestors reached at a single bound; and the tardy convictions of the one have been assimilating, through a period of two centuries, to the intuitions of the other.

4. The establishment of Free Schools was one of those grand mental and moral experiments whose effects could not be developed and made manifest in a single generation. But now, according to the manner in which human life is computed, we are the sixth generation from its founders; and have we not reason to be grateful, both to God and man, for its unnumbered blessings? The

sincerity of our gratitude must be tested by our efforts to perpetuate and to improve what they established. The gratitude of the lips only is an unholy offering.

Horace Mann.

26. THE BALLOT.

1. Consider, for a moment, what it is to *cást* a *vòte*. It is the token of *inestimable privileges*, and involves the responsibilities of an *heréditary trùst*. It has passed into your hands as a *rìght*, reaped from fields of suffering and blòod.

2. The *grándeur of hìstory* is represented in your àct. Men have wrought with *pen* and *tóngue*, and pined in *dúngeons*, and died on *scáffolds*, that you might obtain this symbol of *fréedom*, and enjoy this consciousness of a *sácred individuálity*. To the ballot have been transmitted, as it wére, the dignity of the *scéptre* and the potency of the *swòrd*.

3. And that which is so potent as a *rìght*, is also pregnant as a *dùty;* a duty for the *présent* and for the *fùture*. If you *will*, that folded *léaf* becomes a *tóngue* of *jùstice*, a voice of *òrder*, a force of *impérial láw—* securing *ríghts*, abolishing *abúses*, erecting new institutions of *trúth* and *lòve*. And, however you *will*, it is the expression of a *sólemn responsibìlity*, the *éxercise* of an immeasurable *pòwer* for góod or for évil, *nów* and *hereáfter*.

4. It is the medium through which you act upon your còuntry—the *organic nérve* which incorporates *yóu* with its *lífe* and *wèlfare*. There is no agent with which the possibilities of the republic are more *intimately invólved*, none upon which we can fall back with more *cònfidence* than the *bállot*-box.

E. H. Chapin.

27. EDUCATIONAL POWER.

1. The true teacher must have the faith of martyrs. In the limited horizon of the school-room, the teacher can dimly see only the beginning of the effects of his training upon his pupils. The solid and lasting results, the building up of character, the creative power of motives, are made evident only in the wider circle of the world, and at the end of a life-time. Hence the power of the teacher, like that of the silent and invisible forces of nature, is only feebly realized.

2. I once visited, in the Sierra, a quartz mine of fabulous richness. Deep in the bowels of the earth, swarthy miners were blasting out the gold-bearing rock; above, the powerful mill was crushing the quartz with its iron teeth. In the office, piles of yellow bars, ready to be sent to the mint to be poured into the channels of trade, showed the immediate returns of well-directed labor and wisely invested capital. An hour later, I stepped into a public school-house not half a mile distant, where fifty children were conning their lessons. What does the school yield, I asked myself, on the investment of money by the State? The returns of the mine were made in solid bullion; the school returns were all far in the unknown future.

3. I crossed the continent from the Pacific to the Atlantic on the grandest commercial highway ever built, and all along, towns, villages, cities, mines, farms, machine shops, manufactories, and converging roads bore evidence of the mighty physical forces of the nation; and when I entered a meeting of the National Educational Association in a Boston school-house, where two hundred thoughtful men and women were assembled, it seemed, after witnessing the gigantic play of industrial and commercial forces, that the school-masters and school-mistresses were lookers-on and idlers in the bustling life around.

4. But when, in the mild summer evening, I walked under the elms of Boston Common and reflected that independence was once only a dim idea in the minds of a few leading patriots; that the engine which had whirled me over the iron track, three thousand miles in seven days, was once only an idea in the brain of an enthusiast; that the telegraph wires, radiating like nerves from the centers of civilization, were created by the inventive genius of an educated thinker, I realized that there is a silent power, mightier than all mechanical forces, which preserves, directs, and controls the material prosperity of a great nation.

5. I go out into the streets of the great commercial center of our country. I hear everywhere the hum of industry, and see around the stir of business. I see the steamships plying like gigantic shuttles to weave a network of commercial relations between the new world and the old. I see the smoke of manufactories where skillful artisans are constructing the marvelous productions of inventive genius. The banks are open; keen capitalists are on 'Change; and the full tide of humanity is pulsating through every artery of the town. The results of business are solid and tangible. I step into the New York Normal College where a thousand young women are fitting for the profession of teaching, and if asked for the tangible results of the educational investment, the evidences are not at hand.

6. But when I pause to consider that intelligence is the motive power of trade; that the city with its banks, warehouses, churches, residences, and manufactories, is the product of skilled labor; that the steamship is navigated by means of science, and is built as a triumph of art: that science surveyed the railroad lines, and that skill runs the trains freighted with the products of industry and art; then I begin to perceive some connection between educational forces and the material results of civilization.

28. SCHOOLS AND TEACHERS.

1. Looking into the near future, I see the aisles of the school-room widen into the broad streets of the city. The boys are business men. One commands the steamship, one operates the telegraph, and another runs an engine; one is a railroad director, and another rides over the road to take his seat in the senate of the United States. One works a gold mine, another an iron mine, and another a coal mine; one is a merchant, one a banker, one a Wall-street speculator; one is a farmer in the west, another a manufacturer in the east; one is a merchant, another a mechanic, and a third is an inventor.

2. The girls have become women. Some preside as queens in home circles, some are teachers, some are writers, some are artists, and others are skilled in household work. I realize that the life of a nation is made up of mothers that guard the homes of the men who drive the plow, build the ships, run the mills, work the mines, construct machinery, print the papers, shoulder the musket, and cast the ballots; and it is for all these that the public schools have done and are now doing their beneficent work.

3. When I ponder over the far-reaching influence of the teacher and the school, I comprehend, in some measure, the relation to our national well-being, of our American system of free public schools—the best, notwithstanding its defects and shortcomings, that the world has ever known. It is the duty of every teacher to strive with all his heart, and with all his soul, and with all his might, to perfect a system of education which shall train a race of men and women in the next generation, that shall inherit, with the boundless resources of our favored land, something of the energy, enterprise, talent, and character of the sturdy pioneers who settled and subdued the wilderness.

4. Only timid and despairing souls are frightened into the belief that the foundations of society are breaking up on account of over-education in the common schools. Neither representatives of the Caste of Capital nor the Caste of Culture can convince the American people that vice, crime, idleness, poverty, and social discontent are the necessary result of an elementary education among the workers of society. No demagogue, with specious statements, can lead any considerable number of citizens to regard the school-master as a public enemy.

5. The free common school is the Plymouth Rock of American liberty. If the system of free schools, as now conducted and organized, fails to meet the needs of social progress, not the extent, but the *kind* and *quality*, of education must be changed. Neither high school nor university must be lopped off from our free-school system.

6. It is only through skilled labor, wisely and intelligently directed, that a people can become or remain permanently prosperous and happy; it is only by means of intelligent and educated voters that liberty can be preserved; and it is only by means of a more complete education among all classes that humanity can rise to a higher type of social evolution. There is no slavery so oppressive as that of ignorance.

29. ELEMENTS OF THE AMERICAN GOVERNMENT.

1. The English colonists in America, generally speaking, were men who were seeking new homes in a new world. They brought with them their families and all that was most dear to them. Many of them were educated men, and all possessed their full share, according to their social condition, of knowledge and attainments of that age.

2. The distinctive characteristic of their settlement is the introduction of the civilization of Europe into a wilderness, without bringing with it the political institutions of Europe. The arts, sciences, and literature of England came over with the settlers. That great portion of the common law which regulates the social and personal relations and conduct of men, came also.

3. The jury came; the *habeas corpus* came; the testamentary power came; and the law of inheritance and descent came also, except that part of it which recognizes the rights of primogeniture, which either did not come at all, or soon gave way to the rule of equal partition of estates among children.

4. But the monarchy did not come, nor the aristocracy, nor the Church, as an estate of the realm. Political institutions were to be framed anew, such as should be adapted to the state of things. But it could not be doubtful what should be the nature and character of these institutions. A general social equality prevailed among the settlers, and an equality of political rights seemed the natural, if not the necessary consequence.

Daniel Webster.

SECTION III.

RECITATIONS AND READINGS: POETRY.

1. THE CROWDED STREET.

1. Let me move slowly | through the stréet,
   Filled | with an ever-shifting *tráin,*
   Amid the sound | of steps that beat |
   The murmuring *wálks* | like *áutumn ràin.*

2. How fast | the flitting *fìgures* | come!
   The míld, the fiérce, the *stòny* fàce;
   Sóme | bright with thoughtless *smíles,* and *sóme* |
   Where secret *tèars* | have left their tràce.

3. They páss—to toil, to strife, to *rèst;*
   To *hálls* | in which the *fèast* | is spréad;
   To chámbers | where the funeral guést |
   In silence | sits | beside the dèad!

4. And *sóme* | to happy *hòmes* repàir,
   Where *chíldren* pressing cheek to cheek,
   With mute *carésses* | shall decláre |
   The *ténderness* | they cannot spèak.

5. And *sóme,* who walk in *cálmness* hére,
   Shall *shùdder* when they reach the dóor |
   Where óne | who made their dwelling déar,
   Its flówer, its líght, is seen no mòre.

6. Yóuth, with pale cheek | and slender fráme,
   And dreams of greátness | in thine eȳe!
   Goest thou to build an early náme,
   Or early | in the tásk | to dìe?

7. Keen son of tráde, with eager brów!
   Who | is now fluttering | in thy snàre?
   Thy golden fórtunes, *tówer* they nów,
   Or *mélt* | the glittering spires | in àir?

8. *Whó* | of this crowd | to-night | shall tread |
   The dance | till daylight gleam agàin ?
   Whó | sorrow o'er the untimely *déad?*
   Whó | writhe | in throes | of *mórtal páin ?*

9. *Sóme* | famine-struck, shall think how long |
   The cold | dark hóurs, how slow | the líght;
   And *sóme*, who flaunt amid the thróng,
   Shall hide | in dens of *shàme* | to-nìght.

10. Each, where his tasks or pleasures cáll,
    They páss, and heed each other nòt.
    There *is* | who heeds, who holds them áll,
    In His large *lóve* | and boundless *thòught*.

11. These struggling tides | of life | that seem |
    In wayward, aimless course to ténd,
    Are éddies | of the *mighty stréam* |
    That *rólls* | to its appointed *ènd*.   BRYANT.

2. THE BUILDERS.

1. *All* | are architects of *Fàte,*
     Working | in these walls of Time;
   Sóme | with *mássive* deeds | and *gréat,*
     Sŏme | with ornaments | of rhȳme.

2. Nothing | *ùseless* is | or *lòw;*
     Each thing | in its place | is *bèst;*
   And what *sĕems* | but idle *shów* |
     Strengthens | and supports the rèst.

3. For the *strúcture* | that we ráise,
     Tíme | is with materials | filled;
   Our to-days | and yesterdays |
     Are the *blócks* | with which we *bùild*.

4. Truly shape | and fashion *thèse;*
     Leave no yawning *găps* | between;

    Think not, because no man *sées,*
      Sŭch things | will remain *unsèen.*

5. In the elder days | of árt,
    Builders wrought | with greatest cáre |
  Each minute | and unseen pùrt;
    For the *góds* are *èverywhere.*

6. Let us do *ŏur* work | as *wèll,*
    Both the *únseen* | and the *sèen;*
  Make the house, where *góds* | may dwell,
    Beaútiful, entíre, and clèan.

7. Else our lives | are incomplète,
    Standing | in these walls of Tíme;
  Broken *stàirways,* where the feet |
    Stùmble | as they seek to clímb.

8. Build to-day, then, *stróng* and *sùre,*
    With a firm | and ample *báse,*
  And | ascending and secúre |
    Shall *to-mórrow* | find its plàce.

9. Thus alone | can we attain |
    To those túrrets, where the eye |
  Sees the wórld | as one vast pláin,
    And one boundless réach | of skȳ.

3. PSALM OF LIFE.

1. Tell me *not* | in mournful númbers,
    Lífe | is but an empty *dréam;*
  For the soul | is *dèad* | that slúmbers,
    And things | *are* not | what they *sèem.*

2. Life | is *rèal!* Life | is *èarnest!*
    And the grave | is *nòt* its goal;
  Dust | thou árt, to dust retúrnest,
    Was not spoken | of the sòul.

3. Not *enjóyment*, and not *sòrrow*,
    Is our destined end or wáy;
  But to *àct* that each to-morrow |
    Finds us farther | than to-dày.

4. Art | is lóng, and Time | is flèeting,
    And our héarts, though stout and bráve,
  Still, like muffled drums, are beáting |
    Funeral marches | to the gràve.

5. In the world's broad field of báttle,
    In the bivouac of Lífe,
  Be not like dumb, driven *cáttle;* —
    Be a *hèro* | in the strife!

6. Trust no Fúture, howe'er *plèasant!*
    Let the dead Past | *bùry* its dead!
  Act—act in the *living Prèsent!*
    Heart *withín*, and Gód | *o'erhèad*.

7. Lives of great men | all remínd us |
    We can make *oùr* lives | sublíme,
  And, depárting, leave behínd us |
    Foot-prints | on the sands of tíme.

8. Foot-prints, that perhaps anóther,
    Sailing o'er life's solemn máin—
  A forlorn | and shipwrecked bróther—
    Seeing, shall take *hèart* again.

9. Let us, then, be *úp* and *dòing,*
    With a heart | for *àny* fate;
  Still *achiéving,* still *pursúing,*
    Learn to *lábor* | and to *wàit.*   LONGFELLOW.

4. APOSTROPHE TO THE OCEAN.

[*This poem is to be read with slow movement, median stress, expulsive orotund quality, and strong force.*]

1.

There is a *pléasure* | in the pathless *wòods*,
There is a *rápture* | on the lonely *shòre*,
There is *sócicty*, where none *intrùdes*,
By the *deep sèa*, and *mùsic* in its *ròar*.
I love not man the *léss* | but nature | *mòre*,
From these our ínterviews, in which I steal |
From all I *may* be, or *have* been befóre,
To mingle with the *ùniverse*, and feel |
What I can ne'er *expréss*, yet can not all *concèal*.

2.

Rōll on, thou dēep and dārk blūe ōcean, *ròll!*
Ten thousand fleets | sweep over thee in *vàin*.
Mán | marks the *éarth* with *rùin*—his control |
Stops with the *shòre;*—upon the watery *pláin* |
The *wrécks* | are all *thý* deed, nor doth remain |
A *shàdow* of *màn's rávage*, save his *ŏwn*,
When, for a moment, like a drop of *ráin*,
He sinks into thy dépths | with bubbling gróan—
Without a *gráve*, unknōlled, uncōffined, and unknòwn.

3.

The *ármaments* | which thunderstrike the walls |
Of *rock-built cíties*, bidding *nàtions* quáke, |
And *mónarchs* | tremble in their cápitals;
The oak *levíathan*, whose *huge ríbs* make |
Their clay creator | the vain *títle* take |
Of lord of thee, and arbiter of *wár*—
Thése | are thy *tòys*, and, as the snowy *flàke*,
They melt into thy yeast of *wáves*, which mar
Alike | the Armada's *príde*, or spoíls of *Trafalgàr*.

4.

Thy shores are *èmpires*, changed in all save *thèc;*—
Assýria, Gréece, Róme, Cárthage, *whàt* are *thèy?*
Thy waters | washed them power | while they were *frée*,
And many a *týrant* | *sìnce;* their shores obey |
    The *stránger, sláve,* or *sávage;* their decay |
Has dried up *réalms* to *dèserts:* not so | thôu;
    Unchángeable | save to thy wild waves' pláy,
Tíme | writes *nó wrìnkle* | on thine azure bròw:
    Such as *creation's dáwn behéld,* thou rollest *nòw.*

5.

Thou glorious *mìrror*, where the Almighty's form |
Glasses itself in *tèmpests;* in all *tìme,*
    Cálm or *convùlsed*—in bréeze, or gále, or stórm—
Icing the *póle,* or in the *tòrrid* clime |
    Dark héaving; bōundless, ēndless, and sublīme!
The image of *etèrnity*—the *thróne* |
    Of the *Invìsible;* even from out thy *slìme* |
The monsters of the *dèep* | are *màde;* each zóne |
    Obeỳs thee; thou goest forth, drēad, fāthomless, *alòne.*

6.

And I have *lòved* thee, ócean! and my joy |
Of youthful spórts | was on thy *brèast* to be
    Bórne, like thy búbbles, *ònward;* from a *bòy* |
I wantoned with thy brèakers—they | to me |
    Were a *delìght;* and, if the freshening séa |
Made them a térror, 't was a *pléasing* féar;
    For I was, as it were, a child of *thèc,*
And trusted to thy bíllows | *fár* and *nèar,*
    And laid my hand upon thy *máne*—as do I *hère.*

BYRON.

5. BATTLE OF WATERLOO.

1.

There was a sound of *rèvelry* by nĭght,
 And Belgium's *cápital* had gathered then
Her *beaúty* and her *chĭvalry*, and bright
 The lamps shone o'er fair *wómen* and *bráve mèn;*
A *thoúsand heárts* beat hăppily; and when
 Músic arose with its *voluptuous swéll,*
Soft *cýes* looked *lòve* to eyes which *spàkc* again,
 And all went *mérry* as a *màrriage*-bell;—
But *hùsh! hàrk!* a *deep sóund* strikes like a rising *knèll!*

2.

Did ye not *héar* it?—*Nò;* 't was but the *wĭnd,*
 Or the *càr* rattling o'er the stony strèet:
On with the *dànce!* let joy be unconfĭned;
 No sleep till *mòrn,* when youth and pleasure meet
To chase the glowing hours with flying féet——
 But *hàrk!*—that heavy sound breaks in *once mòre,*
As if the *clòuds* its *ècho* would repèat;
 And *nèarer, clèarer, dèadlier* than befòre!
Arm! ARM! it is—it is—the *cànnon's* opening roar!

3.

Ah! then and there was hurrying to and fró,
 And gathering téars, and tremblings of dístress,
And cheeks all pále, which but an hour agó
 Blùshed at the praise of their own *lòveliness;*
And there were *sudden pàrtings,* such as press
 The *lĭfe* from out *yŏung* hearts, and choking *sĭghs*
Which ne'er might be *repèated; who* could guess
 If ever more should meet those mutual *eýes,*
Since upon *night* so *swéet* such *awful mòrn* could rise?

4.

And there was mounting in hot hàste; the *stéed,*
 The mustering *squádron,* and the clattering *càr,*

Went pouring forward with impetuous speed,
  And swiftly forming in the ranks of wàr;
And the *deep thúnder peal* on *peal* afár;
  And *néar*, the beat of the *alárming drùm*
Roused up the *sóldier* ere the morning *stàr;*
  While thronged the *cítizens* with terror dumb,
Or whispering with white lips: "*The fòe! They còme! they còme!*"

5.

And Ardennes waves above them her green léaves,
  Dewy with nature's téar-drops, as they páss,
Griéving, if aught inanimate e'er griéves,
  Over the *unretúrning bràve*—alás!—
Ere evening to be trodden like the *gràss*,
  Which now *benĕath* them, but *abŏve* shall grow
In its *nĕxt* verdure, when this fiery mass
  Of *living válor, rolling* on the *fóe*,
And *burning with high hópe*, shall mōulder cōld and lòw

6.

Last *nóon* beheld them full of *lústy lìfe;*
  Last *éve* in *Beaùty's* circle *proudly gày;*
The *mídnight* brought the signal-sound of *strìfe;*
  The *mórn*, the marshaling in *àrms*—the *dáy*,
Battle's *magnificently stern arrày!*
  The thunder-clouds close *ò'er* it, which, when *rént*,
The earth is covered thick with *óther* clay—
  Which her *òwn* clay shall cóver, héaped and pént,
Ríder and hòrse—friénd, fòe—in ōne rēd būrial blēnt.

BYRON's *Childe Harold.*

6. SANTA FILOMENA.

This poem was written in honor of Florence Nightingale, an English lady, distinguished for her philanthropy, and for her devotion to the sick and wounded soldiers in the Crimean war. "Filomena" is the Latin for "Nightingale." There is a Saint Filomena, who is represented as floating down from heaven attended by two angels bearing the lily, palm, and javelin, and beneath, in the foreground, the sick and maimed, who are healed by her intercession.

1. Whene'er a noble deed | is wróught,
Whene'er is spoke | a noble thóught,
   Our heárts, in glad surprise,
   To higher *lèvels* | rise.

2. The tidal wave | of deeper souls |
Into our inmost being | rólls,
   And lifts us | unawáres |
   Out of all meaner càres.

3. Honor to those | whose words and deeds |
Thus help us | in our daily néeds.
   And | by their óverflow |
   Raise us | from what is lòw!

4. Thus thought I, as by night I réad |
Of the great army | of the déad,
   The trenches | cold and dámp,
   The starved | and frozen càmp;

5. The wounded | from the battle pláin,
In dreary hospitals of páin—
   The cheerless corridórs,
   The cold | and stony flòors.

6. Ló! in that house of misery |
A lady | with a lamp | I see |
   Pass through the glimmering glóom,
   And flit | from room to ròom.

7. And slow | as in a dream of bliss,
The speechless sufferer | turns to kiss |
   Her shádow, as it falls |
   Upon the darkening wàlls.

8. As if a door in heaven | should be |
 Opened | and then closed súddenly,
  The vision | came and wént,
  The light shone | and was spènt.

9. On England's annals, the long
 Hereafter | of her speech and sóng,
  That light | its rays | shall cast |
  From portals | of the pàst.

10. A Lady with a Lamp | shall stand |
 In the great history of the lánd,
  A noble type of góod,
  Heroic wòmanhood.

11. Nor even shall be wanting here |
 The pálm, the líly, and the spèar,
  The symbols | that of yore |
  Santa Filomèna bòre.   LONGFELLOW.

7. THE DEATH STRUGGLE.

[*An example of animated and impassioned description, characterized by fast movement and radical stress.*]

"Now *yièld* thee, or, by Him who made
The world, thy *heàrt's* blood dyes my blade!"
"Thy threats, thy mercy I *defŷ!*
Let recreant *yiéld*, who fears to *dîe.*"
—Like *adder* darting from his cóil,
Like *wolf* that dashes through the tóil,
Like *mountain-cat* who guards her yóung,
Full at Fitz-James's throat he sprùng;
Recóived, but recked not of a wóund,
And locked his arms his foeman ròund.—
Now, gallant Saxon, hold thine òwn!
No *maiden's* arm is round thee thrówn!

That desperate grasp thy frame might feél
Through bars of brass and triple steél!—
They túg, they stráin! dówn, dówn, they gò,
The Gael abóve, Fitz-James belòw.
The Chieftain's *gripe* his throat comprèssed;
His *knee* was planted in his brèast;
His clotted locks he backward thréw,
Across his brow his hand he dréw,
From blood and mist to clear his síght,
Then gleamed aloft his dagger bríght!
—But hate and fury ill supplied
The stream of life's exhausted tíde;
And all too late the advantage came,
To turn the odds of deadly gàme;
For, while the dagger gleamed on hígh,
Reeled *sóul* and *sénse*, reeled *brain* and *èye*.
Down came the blòw! but in the heath
The erring *bláde* found bloodless *shèath*.
The struggling foe may now unclasp
The fainting Chief's relaxing gràsp;
Unwounded from the dreadful clóse,
But breathless áll, Fitz-James aròse.

Scott.

8. SANDALPHON.

1. Have you read in the Talmud of óld,
   In the Legends the Rabbins have tóld
     Of the limitless realms of the áir;
   Have you *réad* it—the marvelous stóry
   Of Sandalphon, the Angel of Glóry,
     Sandálphon, the Angel of Práyer?

2. How, erect, at the outermost gates
   Of the City Celestial he wáits,
     With his feet on the ladder of líght,

That, crowded with angels unnúmbered,
By Jacob was seen, as he slúmbered
   Alone in the desert at night?

3. The Angels of Wind and of Fíre
Chant only one hymn, and expíre
   With the song's irresistible strèss—
Expíre in their rapture and wónder,
As harp-strings are broken asúnder
   By music they throb to expréss.

4. But serene in the rapturous thróng,
Unmoved by the rush of the sóng,
   With eyes unimpassioned and slów,
Among the dead ángels, the deathless
Sandálphon stands listening, bréathless,
   To sounds that ascend from belów;—

5. From the spirits on earth that adóre,
From the souls that entreat and implóre
   In the fervor and passion of práyer;
From the hearts that are broken with lósses,
And weary with dragging the crósses
   Too heavy for mortals to beàr.

6. And he gathers the prayers as he stánds,
And they change into flowers in his hánds,
   Into garlands of purple and rèd;
And beneath the great arch of the pórtal,
Through the streets of the City Immórtal
   Is wafted the *frágrance* they shed.

7. It is but a legend I knów,
A fáble, a phántom, a shów,
   Of the ancient Rabbinical lóre;
Yet the old mediæval tradítion,
The beautiful, strange superstítion,
   But haunts me and holds me the mòre.

8. When I look from my window at nĭght,
   And the welkin above is all whĭte,
     All throbbing and panting with stărs,
     Amŏng them, majĕstic, is stănding
     Sandălphon, the ăngel, expănding
       His pĭnions in nebulous bàrs.

9. And the lĕgend, I fĕel, is a părt
   Of the hunger and thirst of the heărt—
     The frĕnzy and fire of the brăin,
     That grasps at the fruitage forbĭdden,
     The golden pomegranates of Ĕden,
       To quiet its fever and pàin. LONGFELLOW.

9. THE OLD CONTINENTALS.

[*This piece may be rendered with a considerable degree of imitative reading. It is characterized by declamatory force, radical stress, and orotund quality. Let the class mark for rhetorical pauses, emphasis, and inflections.*]

1. In their ragged *regiméntals*,
     Stood the old *Continéntals*,
       Yielding *nót*,
     When the Grenadiers were *lúnging*,
     And like hail fell the *plúnging*
       Cànnon-shot;
       When the files
       Of the ísles,
   From the smoky night encámpment bore the banner of the rampant
       Únicorn,
   And *grummer, grummer, grummer, rolled the roll of the drummer,*
       Through the mòrn!

2. Then with eyes to the *frónt* all,
     And with guns *horizóntal,*
       Stood our sìres;

And the balls whistled *déadly*,
And in streams flashing *rédly*
    Blazed the *fìres;*
    As the rōar
    On the shōre,
Swept the strong battle-breákers o'er the green-sodded ácres
    Of the plàin;
And *louder, louder, louder, cracked the black gunpowder,*
    Cracked amàin!

3. Now like smiths at their fórges
Worked the red St. Geórge's
    Cannonièrs;
And the villainous "saltpéter"
Rang a fierce, discordant méter
    Round their èars;
    As the swift
    Stórm-drift,
With hot, sweeping ánger, came the horse-guards' clangor
    On our flànks.
Then *higher, higher, higher, burned the old-fashioned fire*
    Through the rànks!

4. Then the old-fashioned Cólonel
Galloped through the white infernal
    Pòwder-cloud;
And his broadsword was *swínging,*
And his brazen throat was *rínging*
    Trùmpet-loud.
    Then the blue
    Bullets fléw,
And the *tróoper*-jackets rédden at the touch of the leáden
    Rìfle-breath.
And *rounder, rounder, rounder, roared the iron six-pounder,*
    Hurling dèath!   McMASTERS.

10. THE WINDS.

[Read this poem line by line, and let the class repeat, in concert, after you. Then require each pupil, in turn, to go upon the platform and read one stanza, subject to the criticism of the class and teacher.]

1.

Ye winds, ye unseen currents of the áir,
   Softly ye played, a few brief hours agó;
Ye bore the murmuring bèe; ye tossed the hair
   O'er maiden cheeks that took a *frèsher* glow;
Ye rolled the round white cloud through depths of blùe,
Ye shook from shaded flowers the lingering dèw;
Before you the *catàlpa's* blossom fléw,
   Lìght blossoms, dropping on the grass like snòw.

2.

What *chànge* is this? Ye take the *càtaract's* sound;
   Ye take the *whìrlpool's* fury and its mìght;
The mountain *shùdders* as ye sweep the gròund;
   The valley *wòods* lie *próne* beneath your flìght;
The clouds before you shoot like *èagles* past;
The homes of men are rócking in your blàst;
Ye lift the roofs like *autumn lèaves*, and cást,
   Skyward, the whirling fragments out of sìght.

3.

The weary fowls of heaven make wing in vain,
   To 'scape your wràth; ye seize and dash them dèad;
Against the earth ye drive the *roaring ràin;*
   The harvest field becomes a *rìver's* bed;
And *tòrrents* tumble from the hills aròund;
Plains turn to lákes, and villages are dròwned;
And wailing *vòices*, midst the tempest's sóund,
   Rìse, as the rushing waters *swéll* and *sprèad*.

4.

Ye dart upon the *dèep;* and straight is heard
   A *wìlder* roar; and men grow pále and pràv;

Ye fling its floods around you, as a bird
  Flings o'er his shivering plumes the fountain's spray.
See! to the breaking mast the *sailor* clings;
Ye scoop the *ocean* to its briny springs,
And take the *mountain billow* on your wings,
  And pile the wreck of *navies* round the bay.

5.

Why rage ye thus?—no strife for liberty
  Has made you mad; no tyrant, strong through fear,
Has chained your pinions till ye wrenched them free,
  And rushed into the unmeasured atmosphere;
For ye were born in *freedom* where ye blow;
Free o'er the mighty deep to come and go;
Earth's solemn *woods* were yours, her wastes of snow,
  Her isles where summer blossoms all the year.

6.

O ye wild winds; a *mightier* power than yours
  In chains upon the shore of *Europe* lies;
The sceptered throng, whose fetters he endures,
  Watch his mute throes with *terror* in their eyes;
And armed *warriors* all around him stand,
And, as he struggles, tighten every band,
And lift the heavy spear, with threatening hand,
  To *pierce* the victim, should he strive to rise.

7.

Yet oh! when that wronged Spirit of our race
  Shall break, as soon he must, his long-worn chains,
And leap in freedom from his *prison*-place,
  Lord of his ancient hills and fruitful plains,
Let him not rise, like these mad winds of air,
To waste the loveliness that time could spare,
To fill the earth with woe, and blot the fair
  Unconscious breast with blood from *human* veins.

8.

But may he like the *Spring*-tìme come abròad,
   Who crumbles *Wìnter's* gyves with gentle mìght,
When in the genial brĕeze, the breath of Gód,
   Come spouting up the unsealed *sprìngs* to light;
Flowers start from their dark prisons at his fèet,
The *wóods*, long dúmb, awake to hymnings swèet;
And morn and eve, whose glimmerings almost mèet,
   Crowd back to narrow bounds the ancient nìght.

BRYANT.

11. THE DAY IS DONE.

1. The day is *dòne*, and the dárkness
    Falls from the wings of Níght,
As a *fèather* is wafted dównward
    From an *èagle* in his flìght.

2. I see the lights of the village
    Gleam through the rain and the mìst,
And a feeling of sadness comes o'er me
    That my soul cannot resìst.

3. A feeling of sadness and longing,
    That is not akín to páin,
And resembles sorrow only,
    As the *mìst* resembles the *ràin*.

4. Come, read to me some *pòem*,
    Some simple and heartfelt láy,
That shall soothe this restless fèeling,
    And banish the thoughts of dày.

5. *Nót* from the grand old másters,
    Nót from the bards sublíme,
Whose distant footsteps echo
    Through the corridors of Tíme.

6. For, like strains of *mártial mùsic*,
    Their mighty thoughts suggést
   Life's endless *tóil* and *endèavor;*
    And to-níght I long for rèst.

7. Read from some *hûmbler* poet,
    Whose songs gushed from his heárt,
   As *shówers* from the clouds of *sùmmer*,
    Or *téars* from the *èyclids* stàrt;

8. Whó, through long days of lábor,
    And nights devoid of éase,
   Still heard in his soul the music
    Of wonderful mèlodies.

9. Such songs have power to quiet
    The restless pulse of cáre,
   And come like the benediction
    That follows after pràyer.

10. Then read from the treasured volume
     The poem of thy chóice,
    And lend to the rhyme of the póet
     The beauty of thy vòice.

11. And the *níght* shall be filled with *mùsic*,
     And the cares that infest the dáy,
    Shall fold their tents like the Arabs,
     And as silently steal awày.
     LONGFELLOW.

12. THE BATTLE-FIELD.

1. Once this soft *túrf*, this rivulet's *sánds,*
    Were trampled | by a hurrying *crówd,*
   And fiery *heárts* | and armód *hánds* |
    Encountered in the *bàttle*-cloud.

2. Ah′! never shall the land forget |
    How gushed the *life-blood* | of her bráve—
  Gúshed, warm with hope and courage yét,
    Upon the *sóil* | they fought to sàve.

3. Now all is cálm, and frésh and stíll;
    Alone the chirp of flitting bírd,
  And talk of children on the híll,
    And bell of wandering *kìne* | are hèard.

4. No solemn host goes trailing by
    The black-mouthed *gún* | and staggering *wáin*;
  Men start not at the *báttle*-cry;
    Óh, be it never *héard agàin!*

5. Soon rested | those who fóught; but thóu,
    Who minglest in the *hărder* strife |
  For truths | which men receive not nów,
    Thў warfare | only ends with *lìfe*.

6. A friendless wàrfare! lingering long |
    Through weary dáy | and weary yèar.
  A wild and many-weaponed thróng |
    Hang on thy frónt, and flánk, and rèar.

7. Yet nerve thy spirit | to the próof,
    And blench not at thy chosen lót;
  The timid good may stand alóof,
    The sage may frówn—yet faint thou *nòt*.

8. Nor heed the sháft | too surely cást,
    The foul | and hissing bolt of scórn;
  For with thy side | shall dwell, at lást,
    The víctory | of *endùrance* | born.

9. *Trúth* | crushed to éarth | shall *rìse* again;
    The *etérnal yéars* | of *Gòd* are hèrs;
  But *Érror* | wounded, writhes in páin,
    And *díes* | among his *wòrshipers*.

SCHOOL ELOCUTION.   359

10. Yeá, though thou lie upon the dúst,
    When they who helped thee flee in féar,
 Díe | full of hope and manly trúst,
    Like those who fell in *battle hère*.

11. An*ŏ́ther* hand | the sword shall wiéld,
    An*ŏ́ther* hand | the standard wáve,
 Till from the trumpet's mouth | is péaled
    The blast of *trìumph* | o'er thy gráve.
                                    BRYANT.

13. HYMN TO MONT BLANC.

[*This is a difficult piece of reading. It should be first analyzed grammatically and rhetorically, to enable the pupil to comprehend the full meaning. The reading, in general, will be characterized by median stress, orotund quality, strong force, and slow movement.*]

Hast thou a *chàrm* to stay the morning-star
In his steep cóurse ? So *lòng* he seems to pause
On thy bald, awful héad, *O sovereign Blànc!*
The Arve and Arveiron at thy base
Rave *cèaselessly;* but thou, most awful fórm,
Risest from forth thy silent sea of pines,
How *sìlently!* Around thee and above,
Dèep is the air and *dàrk;* substantial black;
An *ébon màss:* methinks thou *pìercest* it
As with a *wèdge!* But when I look agáin,
It is thine own *cálm hòme*, thy *crýstal shrìne*,
Thy *hábitation* from *èternity.*
O dread and silent *Mòunt!* I gazed upon thee,
Till thóu, still present to the *bŏdily* sense,
Didst *vànish* from my thòught: entranced in *pràyer*,
I worshiped the *Invìsible* alone.
    Yet, like some sweet, beguiling *mélody*—
So sweet, we know not we are *lìstening* to it—
Thou, the meanwhile, wast blending with my *thòught*,
Yea, with my *lìfe* and life's own secret *jòy;*

Till the dilating sóul—enrápt, transfúsed
Into the mighty vision pássing—thére,
As in her natural fórm, *swelled vast* to *Hèaven!*
 Awàke, my *sòul!* not only *pássive* praise
Thou ówest; not alone these swelling *téars,*
Mute *thánks,* and secret *écstasy.* Awàke,
Voice of sweet sòng! Awàke, my heart, *awàke!*
Green *váles* and icy *clìffs, àll* join my hỳmn.
 Thòu first and *chíef,* sole sovereign of the vàle!
O, struggling with the darkness all the *níght,*
And visited all night by troops of *stárs,*
Or when they *clímb* the sky or when they *sìnk;*
Companion of the morning-star at dáwn,
Thýself Earth's rosy *stár,* and of the dáwn
Co-hérald; wàke, O *wàke,* and utter *pràise!*
 Whò sank thy *sunless pìllars* deep in èarth?
 Whò filled thy *coùntenance* with rosy light?
 Whò made thee parent of *perpetual strèams?*
 And *yòu,* ye five wild torrents, fiercely glàd!
Who called *yóu* forth from night and utter *dèath,*
From dark and *icy càverns* called you forth,
Down those precìpitous, blàck, jàgged ròcks,
For ever *sháttered* and the same for èver?
Whò gave you your *invúlnerable lífe,*
Your strèngth, your spèed, your fúry, and your jòy,
Uncéasing thùnder and etérnal fòam?
And who *commánded* (and the silence cáme),
"Here let the billows stiffen, and have rèst?"
 Ye *ìce*-falls! ye that from the mountain's brow
Adòwn *enormous ràvines* slope amàin—
Tórrents, methinks, that heard a *mighty vóice,*
And stopped at ònce amid their maddest plùnge!
Mòtionless tòrrents! sìlent càtaracts!—
Who made you *glòrious* as the gates of *Hèaven*
Beneath the keen full mòon? Who bade the *sùn*
Clothe you with *ràinbows?* Who, with living *flòwers*

Of loveliest blúe, spread *gàrlands* at your féet? —
Gôd! let the torrents, like a shout of *nàtions*
Ànswer! and let the *ìce*-plains echo, *Gôd!*
Gôd! sing ye meadow-streams with gladsome voice!
Ye *pìne*-groves, with your soft and soul-like sòunds!
And *thèy*, too, have a voice, you piles of snòw,
And in their perilous fall shall thunder, *Gôd!*
Ye living *flòwers* that skirt the eternal fròst!
Ye *wild gòats* sporting round the *èagle's* nest!
Ye *èagles*, playmates of the *mountain-stòrm!*
Ye *lìghtnings*, the dread arrows of the clòuds!
Ye signs and wonders of the *èlements!*
Utter forth "*Gôd!*" and fill the *hìlls* with *pràise.*

Once *mòre*, hoar mòunt! with thy sky-pointing péak,
Oft from whose feet the ávalanche, unhéard,
Shoots dównward, glittering through the pure seréne,
Into the depth of clouds that veil thy bréast—
Thòu, too, again, *stupéndous mòuntain!* thóu,
That, as I raise my héad, awhile bowed low
In adóration, upward from thy base
Slow-traveling with dim eyes suffused with téars,
Solemnly séemest, like a vapory *clòud,*
To rise befóre me—*rìse*, oh, *èver* rise;
Rìse, like a *cloud* of *ìncense*, from the èarth!
Thou *kìngly spìrit* throned among the hìlls,
Thou *dréad ambàssador* from earth to hèaven,
Gréat hìerarch! tell thou the *silent skỳ,*
And tell the *stàrs*, and tell yon *rising sùn,*
Eárth, with her thousand vòices, *pràises Gòd!*

COLERIDGE.

14. MORNING HYMN.

[*This piece is characterized by slow movement, median stress, and orotund quality.*]

These are *thỳ glórious wòrks*, Parent of gòod,
Almíghty! *Thíne* this *univérsal fràme*,
Thus wondrous fàir; *Thýself hòw* wondrous thèn!
Unspéakable, who sit'st above these heavens
To us invísible, or *dímly* seen
In these thy lowest wòrks; yet *thése* declare
Thy *góodness* beyond *thòught*, and power divìne.
Spèak, ye who best can téll, ye *sons of líght*,
Angels; for ye behóld him, and with songs
And choral sýmphonies, dáy without níght,
Circle his throne *rejòicing;* ye, in *Héaven*,
On *èarth*, join *àll* ye creatures, to extol
Him *fírst*, him *lást*, him *mídst*, and *without ènd*.
Fairest of *stàrs*, last in the train of níght,
If better thou belong not to the *dáwn*,
Sure pledge of dáy, that crown'st the smiling morn
With thy bright círclet, *práise* him in thy sphére,
While *dày* arises, that sweet hour of príme.
Thou *Sùn*, of this great world both *eýe* and *sóul*,
Acknowledge him thy *grèater;* sound his praise
In thy *éternal còurse*, both when thou *clímb'st*,
And when high *nóon* hast gained, and when thou *fàll'st*.
Mòon, that now meet'st the *orient Sún*, now fly'st,
With the *fixed stàrs*, fixed in their orb that flíes;
And ye five *òther* wandering fíres, that move
In mystic dánce not without sóng, resound
His praise, who out of *dárkness* called up *líght*.
Air, and ye *èlements*, the eldest birth
Of Nature's wòmb, that in quaternion run,
Perpétual círcle, múltiform; and mix
And nourish *áll* things; let your ceaseless chánge
Vary to our *great Máker* still *new práise*.

Ye *mists* and *exhalàtions*, that now rise
From hill or steaming láke, dúsky or gráy,
Till the sun paint your fleecy skirts with góld,
In honor to the *world's great Aúthor rìse;*
Whether to deck with clouds the uncolored skỳ,
Or wet the thirsty earth with falling shòwers,
Rìsing or fàlling, still *advance his pràise.*
His praise, ye *wìnds*, that from four quárters blow,
Breathe *sóft* or *lòud;* and wave your tops, ye *pìnes,*
With every plant, in *sign of wòrship,* wàve.
Foùntains, and ye that warble as ye flow,
Melódious mùrmurs, warbling, *tune his pràise.*
Join voices àll, ye *lìving sòuls:* ye *bìrds,*
That singing, up to *hèaven's* gate *ascénd,*
Bear on your *wìngs* and in your *nótes his pràise.*

MILTON.

15. THANATOPSIS.

[*As a preliminary exercise, let pupils name all the phrases and clauses, and tell what each modifies; also, call on them to parse the more difficult words. The reading of this poem is characterized by slow movement, median stress, and orotund quality.*]

To him | who | in the love of *Náture* | holds
Communion | with her *visible fórms*, she speaks |
A *várious lànguage;* for his *gáyer* hours |
She has a voice of *glàdness,* and a smile
And eloquence of bèauty, and she glides |
Into his *dárker* musings with a mild |
And healing *sýmpathy,* that steals awày
Their sharpness | ere he is aware. When thoughts |
Of the last bitter hour | come like a blight |
Over thy spírit, and sad images |
Of the stern *ágony,* and *shróud,* and *páll,*
And breathless *dárkness,* and the narrow *hóuse,*
Make thee to *shúdder* | and grow sick at *héart,*

Go fórth | under the *open skỳ*, and list
To *Nàture's* teachings; while from all aróund—
Éarth and her *wáters*, and the depths of *áir*—
Comes | a still vòice:—Yet a few dáys | and *theè* |
The all-beholding *sún* | shall see no more |
In all his *còurse;* nor yet | in the cold *gróund*,
Where thy pale form | was laid with many *téars*,
Nor in the embrace of *òcean*, shall exist |
Thý ìmage. Éarth, that *nóurished* theè, shall *clàim*
Thy growth, to be resolved to *èarth* again;
And, lost each *hùman* tráce, sùrrendering up
Thine *indivìdual* béing, shalt thou go |
To mix forever with the *èlements*,
To be a brother | to the insensible *ròck* |
And to the sluggish *clòd*, which the rude swain |
Turns with his *sháre*, and *trèads* upon. The *òak*
Shall send his roots abroad, and pierce thy mòld.

  Yet not to thine eternal resting-place |
Shalt thou retire *alŏne*—nor could'st thou *wìsh* |
Couch *móre magnìficent*. Thou shalt lie down |
With patriarchs | of the *ínfant wòrld*—with *kìngs*,
The *pówerful* of the *èarth*—the *wìse*, the *gòod*,
Fair *fórms*, and hoary *séers* of ages *pást*,
All | in one *mighty sèpulcher*. The *hìlls*,
Rock-ribbed and ancient as the *sún;* the *vàles*,
Stretching in pensive qùietness betwèen;
The venerable *wòods; rívers*, that move
In *májesty;* and the complaining *bròoks*,
That make the meadows *grèen;* and, poured round *áll*
Old *òcean's* gray and melancholy *wáste*—
Are but the solemn *decoràtions* | *áll* |
Of the great *tómb* of *màn!* The golden *sùn*,
The *plànets*, all the *infìnite host* of *hèaven*,
Are shining on the sad abodes of *déath*,
Through the still lapse of àges. All that *trèad*
The globe | are but a *hàndful* | to the tribes

That slumber in its *bòsom*. Take the wings
Of *mòrning*, and the Barcan desert pièrce,
Or lose thyself | in the continuous woods |
Where rolls the Òregon, and hears no sound |
Save his own dàshings—yet | the dēad | āre thère;
And *mìllions* | in those solitudes, since first
The flight of years begán, have laid them down |
In their last slēep: the dēad | rēign thēre | alònc!
So shalt *thóu* rest; and what if thou withdraw |
Unheeded by the *lìving*, and no *frièud* |
Take note of thy depàrture! All that *brèathe* |
Will share thy dèstiny. The *gáy* | will laugh
When thou art góne, the solemn brood of care |
Plód ón, and each one, as *befòre*, will chase
His favorite *phàntom;* yet *all thése* | shall lèave
Their mirth and their emplóyments, and shall come |
And make their bed | with *thèe.* As the long train
Of ages glides awáy, the sons of mén—
The *yóuth* | in life's green *sprìng*, and he who goes |
In the full strength of *yèars, mátron* and *máid,*
The bowed with *àge,* the *ìnfant* | in the smiles |
And beauty of its innocent age | cut óff—
Shall | one by one | be gathered to thy síde |
By thóse | who in *thèir* túrn | shall fóllow *thèm.*

So *lìve,* that when *thȳ* summons | comes to join |
The innumerable caravan | that moves |
To that mysterious realm where each shall take
His chamber | in the silent halls of déath,
Thou gó, not like the quarry-slave at night,
Scoùrged to his dúngeon; but, sustained and soothed |
By an unfaltering trúst, approach thy gráve |
Like one who wraps the drapery of his couch
Abóut him, and lies down | to pleasant drèams.

BRYANT.

16. ELEGY WRITTEN IN A COUNTRY CHURCHYARD.

1.

The *cúrfew* | tolls the knell | of parting dày;
　The lowing *hérd* | winds slowly | o'er the lèa;
The *plówman* | homeward | plods his weary wáy,
　And leaves the *wórld* | to dárkness | and to mè.

2.

Now fades ⌋ the glimmering *lándscape* | on the sìght,
　And all the *áir* | a solemn *stìllness* | holds,
Save where the *béetle* | wheels his droning *flíght*,
　And drowsy *tínklings* | lull the distant *fòlds;*

3.

Save | that from yonder | ivy-mantled tówer,
　The moping owl | does to the moon | compláin |
Of such as, wand'ring near her secret bówer,
　Molest her áncient, solitary rèign.

4.

Beneath those rugged élms, that yew-tree's sháde,
　Where heaves the turf | in many a moldering héap,
Each | in his narrow cell | forever láid,
　The rude *fórefathers* | of the *hàmlet* | sleep.

5.

The breezy *cáll* | of incense-breathing mórn,
　The *swállow* | twittering | from the straw-built shéd,
The cock's shrill *clárion*, or the echoing *hórn*,
　No móre | shall rouse thém | from their lowly bèd.

6.

For them | no móre the blazing *héarth* | shall búrn,
　Or busy *hóusewife* | ply her evening càre;
No *chíldren* | run | to lisp their sire's retúrn,
　Or climb his *knées* | the envied *kìss* | to share.

7.

Oft did the *hárvest* | to their *sìckle* | yield,
   Their *fúrrow* | oft | the stubborn *glèbe* | has broke;
How *jocund* | did they drive their team a-fièld!
   How bowed | the *wóods* | beneath their sturdy *stròke!*

8.

Let not Ambítion | mock their useful tóil,
   Their homely jóys, and destiny | obscúre;
Nor Gràndeur | hear | with a disdainful smíle |
   The short | and simple annals | of the pòor.

9.

The boast of *héraldry*, the pomp of *pówer*,
   And all that *beaúty*, all that *weálth* | e'er gáve,
Await | alike | the *inévitable hòur:*
   The paths of *glŏry* | lead | but to the *gràve.*

10.

Nor yóu, ye proúd, impute to these the fáult,
   If Memory | o'er their tomb | no *tróphies* raise,
Where, through the long-drawn aisle | and fretted váult,
   The pealing *ánthem* | swells the note | of *pràise.*

11.

Can storied *úrn*, or animated *búst*,
   Back to its mansion | call the fleeting *bréath?*
Can *Hónor's* voice | provoke the silent *dúst*,
   Or *Fláttery* soothe | the dull, cold ear | of *Déath?*

12.

Perhaps in this neglected spot | is | laid |
   Some *héart* | once pregnant | with celestial *fìre—*
Hánds | that the rod of *èmpire* | might have swàyed,
   Or waked to *écstasy* | the living lyre:

13.

But *Knówledge* | to their eyes | her ample páge,
    Rich with the spoils of time, did ne'er unròll;
Chill *Pénury* | repressed their noble ráge,
    And froze the genial *cúrrent* | of the sòul.

14.

Full many a *gém* | of purest ray serene |
    The dark, unfathomed caves of *òcean* | bear;
Full many a *flòwer* | is born to blush unséen,
    And waste | its *swéetness* | on the *désert àir.*

15.

Some village *Hàmpden*, that, with dauntless bréast,
    The little tyrant | of his fields | withstóod;
Some mute, inglorious *Mìlton* | here may rest—
    Some *Cròmwell*, guiltless of his country's blòod.

16.

The applause | of listening *sénates* | to commánd,
    The threats | of pain and ruin | to despíse,
To scatter *plénty* | o'er a smiling láud,
    And read their *history* | in a nation's *éyes*,

17.

Their *lót* | *forbàde;* nor circumscribed | alóne |
    Their growing *vìrtues*, but their *crìmes* confined;
Forbade to wade | through slaughter | to a thróne,
    And shut the gates | of *mércy* | on *mankìnd;*

18.

The struggling pangs | of conscious *trùth* | to hide,
    To quench the blushes of ingenuous *shàme*,
Or heap the shrine of Luxury and Príde |
    With *incense* | kindled at the *Mùse's* flame.

19.

Far from the madding crowd's | ignoble strífe,
   Their sober *wishes* | never learned to *strày;*
Along the cool, sequestered vale | of lífe |
   They kept the noiseless ténor | of their wày.

20.

Yet e'en these *bònes* | from insult to protéct,
   Some frail *memórial* | still erected nígh,
With uncouth *rhýmes* | and shapeless *scúlpture* | decked,
   Implores the passing *tríbute* | of a sìgh.

21.

Their náme, their yéars, spelt by the unlettered Múse,
   The place of *fáme* | and *èlegy* | supply;
And many a holy *téxt* | around she stréws,
   That teach the rustic *móralist* | to dìe.

22.

For whó, to dumb forgetfulness | a préy,
   This pleasing, anxious *béing* | e'er resígned,
Left the warm précincts | of the cheerful dáy,
   Nor cast | one *lónging, lingering lóok* | behìnd?

23.

On some fond *bréast* | the parting *sòul* | relìes,
   Some pious *dróps* | the closing *eye* requìres;
E'en from the *tòmb* | the voice of Nature | crìes,
   E'en in our *àshes* | live | their wonted fìres.

24.

For thée, whó, mindful of the unhonored déad,
   Dost | in these línes | their artless tale | reláte,
If chánce, by lonely contemplation léd,
   Some kindred *spírit* | shall inquire *thў* fáte—

25.

Háply | some hoary-headed swain | may sáy:
"Oft have we seen him, at the peep of dáwn,
Brushing with hasty steps | the dews awáy,
To meet the *sún* | upon the upland *làwn.*

26.

"There, at the foot | of yonder nodding béech,
That wreathes its old, fantastic roots so high,
His listless léngth | at nóontide | would he strétch,
And pore upon the bróok | that babbles bỳ.

27.

"Hard by yon *wóod*, now smiling | as in scórn,
Muttering his wayward fáncies, he would róve;
Now drooping, woful-wan, like one forlórn,
Or crazed with *cáre*, or crossed in hopeless *lòve.*

28.

"One morn | I missed him | on the 'customed hill,
Along the héath, and near his favorite trée;
Anòther | came, nor yet beside the rill,
Nor up the *láwn*, nor at the *wòod* | was he;

29.

"The néxt, with dirges dúe, in sad arráy,
Slow | through the church-way path | we saw him bòrne:
Approach and réad | (for *thou* canst réad) | the láy |
Graved on the stóne | beneath yon aged thòrn."

THE EPITAPH.

Hére | rests his *héad* | upon the lap of *éarth,*
A *youth* | to *Fórtune* | and to *Fáme* | *unknòwn;*
Fair *Science* | frowned not | on his humble *birth,*
And *Mèlancholy* | marked him | for her *òwn.*

31.

Lárge | was his bóunty, and his sóul | sincère;
　Héaven | did a récompense | as largely sènd:
He gave to *mísery*—all he hád—a tèar;
　He gained from *Héaven*—'t was all he wíshed—a *frièud*.

32.

No further seek | his mĕríts | to disclóse,
　Or dráw his *fráilties* | from their dread abóde
(There | they alike | in trembling hópe | repóse)—
　The *bósom* | of his *Fáther* | and his Gòd.

　　　　　　　　　　　　　　　Thomas Gray.

17. DANIEL WEBSTER.

1. When life hath run its largest round |
　　Of toil and tríumph, joy and wóe,
　How brief | a storied page is found |
　　To compass all its outward shòw!

2. The world-tried sailor tíres and dròops;
　　His flag is rént, his keel forgòt;
　His farthest voyages | seem but lóops |
　　That float | from life's entangled knòt.

3. But when within the narrow space |
　　Some *larger* soul hath lived and wróught,
　Whose sight | was open to embrace |
　　The boundless realms | of deed and thóught,—

4. When, stricken by the freezing blast,
　　A nation's living pillars fáll,
　How rich | the storied pàge, how vàst,
　　A wórd, a whísper, can recàll!

5. No medal | lifts its fretted fáce,
　　Nor speaking márble | cheats your eýe,

Yet, while these pictured lines I tráce,
A *living ìmage* | passes bỳ:

6. A róof | beneath the mountain pínes;
  The clóisters | of a hill-girt pláin;
  The front of life's embattled línes;
  A mound | beside the heaving máin.

7. Thése | are the scènes: a *bòy* appèars;
  Set life's round dial | in the sún,
  Count the swift arc | of seventy yéars,
  His fráme | is dùst; his tásk | is dòne.

8. Yet pause upon the noontide hóur,
  Ere the declining sún | has laid |
  His bleaching rays | on manhood's pówer,
  And look upon the mighty shàde.

9. No gloom | that stately shape can híde,
  No change | uncrown its bŕow; behóld!
  Dárk, cálm, lárge-fronted, líghtning-eyed,
  Earth has no double | from its mòld.

10. Ere from the fields | by valor won |
  The battle-smoke | had rolled awáy,
  And bared the blood-red setting sún,
  His eýes | were opened on the dày.

11. His lánd | was but a shelving stríp |
  Black | with the strife | that made it frée;
  He líved | to see its banners dip |
  Their frinψes | in the western sèa.

12. The boundless *pràiries* | learned his nàme,
  His wórds | the mountain *èchoes* knèw,
  The northern bréezes | swept his fame |
  From icy lake | to warm bayoù.

13. In tóil | he líved; in péace | he díed;
	When life's full cycle was compléte,
Put off his robes of power and príde,
	And laid them | at his Master's fèet.

14. His rest | is by the storm-swept wáves |
	Whom life's wild tempests | roughly tríed,
Whose heárt | was like the streaming cáves |
	Of ocean, throbbing at his sìde.

15. Death's cold white hand | is like the snów |
	Laid softly | on the furrowed híll—
It hides the broken seams belów,
	And leaves the summit | brighter stìll.

16. In vain the envious tongue upbráids;
	His name | a nation's heart shall kéep |
Till morning's latest sunlight fádes |
	On the blue tablet | of the dèep! HOLMES.

18. ST. AUGUSTINE'S LADDER.

1. Saint Augustine! well hast thou said,
	That | of our vices | we can frame |
A ladder, if we will but tread |
	Beneath our feet | each deed of shàme!

2. All common thíngs, each day's evénts,
	That | with the hour | begin and énd,
Our pleasures | and our disconténts,
	Are róunds | by which | we may ascènd.

3. The low desíre, the base desígn,
	That makes another's virtues | léss;
The revel | of the ruddy wíne,
	And all occasions | of excéss;

4. The lónging | for ignoble thíngs
   The strífe | for triumph | more than trúth;
The hardening of the heart, that brings |
   Irreverence | for the dreams of yóuth;

5. All thoughts of íll; all evil déeds,
   That have their *root* | in thoughts of íll;
Whatever hinders | or impedes |
   The action | of the noble wíll;—

6. All these | must first | be trampled down |
   Beneath our feet, if we would gain |
In the bright fields | of fair renown |
   The right | of eminent domáin.

7. We have not wíngs, we can not sóar;
   But we have feet | to scale and clímb,
By slow degrees, by more and móre,
   The cloudy summits | of our tìme.

8. The distant mountains, that uprear |
   Their solid bastions | to the skíes,
Are crossed | by pathways, that appear |
   As we | to higher *lèvels* | rise.

9. The heights | by great men | reached and kept |
   Were not attained | by sudden flíght,
But they, while their companions slépt,
   Were toiling upward | in the nìght.

10. Standing | on what | too long | we bore |
    With shoulders bent | and downcast eyes,
We may discérn—unseen befóre—
    A path | to higher dèstinies;

11. Nor deem the irrevocable Past |
    As wholly wasted, wholly váin,
If, rising on its wrécks, at lást |
    To something nobler | we attàin.   LONGFELLOW.

19. RING OUT, WILD BELLS.

[*This extract should be read with radical and median stress, strong force, and strongly contrasted inflections. Let the class mark for emphasis and inflection.*]

1. Ring out, wild bells, to the wild sky,
    The flying cloud, the frosty light;
    The year is dying in the night;
  Ring out, wild bells, and let him die.

2. Ring out the old, ring in the new,
    Ring, happy bells, across the snow;
    The year is going; let him go;
  Ring out the false, ring in the true.

3. Ring out the grief that saps the mind,
    For those that here we see no more;
    Ring out the feud of rich and poor,
  Ring in redress to all mankind.

4. Ring out a slowly dying cause,
    And ancient forms of party strife,
    Ring in the nobler modes of life,
  With sweeter manners, purer laws.

5. Ring out the want, the care, the sin,
    The faithless coldness of the times;
    Ring out, ring out my mournful rhymes,
  But ring the fuller minstrel in.

6. Ring out false pride, in place and blood,
    The civic slander and the spite;
    Ring in the love of truth and right,
  Ring in the common love of good.

7. Ring out old shapes of foul disease,
    Ring out the narrowing lust of gold,
    Ring out the thousand woes of old,
  Ring in the thousand years of peace.

8. Ring in the valiant man and free,
   The larger heart, the kindlier hand;
   Ring out the darkness of the land,
   Ring in the Christ that is to be.   TENNYSON.

20. SUMMER RAIN.

[*This extract should be read with varying degrees of force, and with the radical stress, ranging from unimpassioned to emotional. The last two stanzas afford scope for "imitative expression."*]

1. Now on the hills I hear the thunder mutter;
     The wind is gathering in the west;
   The upturned leaves first whiten and flutter,
     Then droop to a fitful rest;
   Up from the stream with sluggish flap
     Struggles the gull, and floats away;
   Nearer and nearer rolls the thunder-clap;
     We shall not see the sun go down to-day.
   Now leaps the wind on the sleepy marsh,
     And tramples the grass with terrified feet;
   The startled river turns leaden and harsh—
     You can hear the quick heart of the tempest beat.

2. Look! look!—that livid flash!
   And instantly follows the rattling thunder,
   As if some cloud-crag, split asunder,
     Fell, splintering with a ruinous crash,
   On the earth, which crouches in silence under;
     And now a solid gray wall of rain
   Shuts off the landscape, mile by mile.
     For a breath's space I see the blue wood again,
   And, ere the next heart-beat, the wind-hurled pile,
     That seemed but now a league aloof,
     Bursts rattling over the sun-parched roof.

3. Against the windows the storm comes dashing;
Through tattered foliage the hail tears crashing;
   The blue lightning flashes;
   The rapid hail clashes;
    The white waves are tumbling;
And, in one baffled roar,
   Like the toothless sea mumbling
A rock-bristled shore,
   The thunder is rumbling,
   And crashing, and crumbling—
Will silence return never more ?   LOWELL.

21. HYMN TO THE NORTH STAR.

[*The reading of this poem will be characterized by slow movement, median stress, orotund quality, and middle key.*]

1.

The sad and solemn níght
Hath yet her multitude | of cheerful *fìres;*
   The glorious host of líght |
Walk the dark atmosphere | till she *retìres;*
All through her silent *wátches,* gliding slów,
Her constellations *cóme,* and climb the *héavens,* and *gò.*

2.

Dáy, too, hath many a *stár* |
To grace his gorgeous réign, as bright as *thèy:*
   Through the blue fields afár,
Unséen, they follow in his flaming wày:
Many a bright língerer, as the eve grows *dím,*
Tells what a radiant tróop | arose and set with *hìm.*

3.

And *thŏu* | dost see them *ríse,*
Star of the Póle! and *thŏu* | dost see them *sèt.*
   Alóne, in thy cold skíes,
Thou keep'st thy old unmoving station yét,

Nor join'st the dances | of that glittering tráin,
Nor dipp'st thy virgin órb | in the blue western màin.

4.

Thére, at morn's rosy bírth,
Thou lookest meekly through the kindling àir,
And *eve*, that round the Eárth |
Chases the dáy, beholds thee | *wàtching thère;*
Thére | *nóontide* finds thée, and the hour that cálls |
The shapes of polar fláme | to scale heaven's azure wàlls.

5.

Alíke, beneath thine eỹe,
The deeds of *dárkness* | and of *líght* | are dòne;
High toward the starlit ský |
Towns bláze, the smoke of battle blots the Sún;
The night-storm on a thousand hills | is lóud,
And the strong wind of dáy | doth mingle sea and clòud.

6.

On thy unaltering bláze |
The half-wrecked máriner, his compass lóst,
Fixes his steady gáze,
And stéers, undóubting, to the friendly còast;
And they who stray in perilous wástes, by *nìght*,
Are *glàd* when thou dost shíne | to guide their footsteps ríght.

7.

And therefóre | bards of óld,
Ságes and hérmits of the solemn wóod,
Did | in thy beams | behóld |
A beauteous týpe | of that unchanging góod,
That bright | eternal béacon, by whose ráy |
The voyager of tíme | should shape his heedful wày.

BRYANT

22. THE AMERICAN FLAG.

[*To be read with declamatory and dramatic force, radical and thorough stress, and orotund quality.*]

1. When Freedom from her mountain height
    Unfurled her standard to the air,
   She tore the azure robe of night,
    And set the stars of glory there;
   She mingled with its gorgeous dyes
   The milky baldric of the skies,
   And striped its pure celestial white
   With streakings of the morning light;
   Then, from his mansion in the sun,
   She called her eagle-bearer down,
   And gave into his mighty hand
   The symbol of her chosen land.

2. Majestic monarch of the cloud!
    Who rear'st aloft thy regal form,
   To hear the tempest-trumpings loud
    And see the lightning lances driven,
   When strive the warriors of the storm,
    And rolls the thunder-drum of heaven,—
   Child of the Sun! to thee 'tis given
    To guard the banner of the free;
   To hover in the sulphur-smoke,
   To ward away the battle-stroke,
   And bid its blendings shine afar,
   Like rainbows on the cloud of war—
    The harbingers of victory!

3. Flag of the brave! thy folds shall fly,
   The sign of hope and triumph high,
   When speaks the signal trumpet tone,
   And the long line comes gleaming on.
   Ere yet the life-blood, warm and wet,
   Has dimmed the glistening bayonet,

Each soldier's eye shall brightly turn
To where thy sky-born glories burn;
And, as his springing steps advance,
Catch war and vengeance from the glance;
And, when the cannon-mouthings loud
Heave in wild wreaths the battle-shroud,
And gory sabres rise and fall
Like shoots of flame on midnight's pall,
Then shall thy meteor glances glow,
   And cowering foes shall fall beneath
Each gallant arm that strikes below
   That lovely messenger of death.

4. Flag of the seas! on ocean's wave
Thy stars shall glitter o'er the brave.
When Death, careering on the gale,
Sweeps darkly round the bellied sail,
And frighted waves rush wildly back,
Before the broadside's reeling rack,
Each dying wanderer of the sea
Shall look at once to heaven and thee,
And smile to see thy splendors fly,
In triumph, o'er his closing eye.

5. Flag of the free heart's only home,
   By angel hands to valor given,
Thy stars have lit the welkin dome,
   And all thy hues were born in heaven.
Forever float that standard sheet!
   Where breathes the foe but falls before us,
With Freedom's soil beneath our feet,
   And Freedom's banner waving o'er us!

DRAKE.

23. THE CHAMBERED NAUTILUS.

[*The reading of this poem should be characterized by slow movement, median stress, pure tone, and orotund quality. To be marked by the class for emphasis, inflection, and pauses.*]

1.

This is the ship of pearl, which, poets feign,
    Sails the unshadowed main,—
    The venturous bark that flings
On the sweet summer wind its purpled wings
In gulfs enchanted, where the siren sings,
    And coral reefs lie bare,
Where the cold sea-maids rise to sun their streaming hair.

2.

Its webs of living gauze no more unfurl;
    Wrecked is the ship of pearl!
    And every chambered cell,
Where its dim dreaming life was wont to dwell,
As the frail tenant shaped his growing shell,
    Before thee lies revealed—
Its irised ceiling rent, its sunless crypt unsealed!

3.

Year after year beheld the silent toil
    That spread his lustrous coil;
    Still, as the spiral grew,
He left the past year's dwelling for the new,
Stole with soft step its shining archway through,
    Built up its idle door,
Stretched in his last found home, and knew the old no more.

4.

Thanks for the heavenly message brought by thee,
    Child of the wandering sea,
    Cast from her lap forlorn!

From thy dead lips a clearer note is born
Than ever Triton blew from wreathéd horn!
    While on my ear it rings,
Through the deep caves of thought I hear a voice that sings,—

5.

Build thee more stately mansions, O my soul,
    As the swift seasons roll!
    Leave thy low-vaulted past!
Let each new temple, nobler than the last,
Shut thee from heaven with a dome more vast,
    Till thou at length art free,
Leaving thine outgrown shell by life's unresting sea!

HOLMES.

24. KENTUCKY BELLE.

1.

Summer of 'sixty-three, sir, and Conrad was gone away,
Gone to the county-town, sir, to sell our first load of hay;
We lived in the log-house yonder, poor as ever you've seen;
Röschen there was a baby, and I was only nineteen.

2.

Conrad, he took the oxen, but he left Kentucky Belle.
How much we thought of Kentuck, I could n't begin to tell—
Came from the Blue-Grass country; my father gave her to me
When I rode north with Conrad, away from the Tennessee.

3.

Conrad lived in Ohio, a German he is, you know;
The house stood in broad cornfields, stretching on, row after row.

The old folks made me welcome; they were kind as
    kind could be;
But I kept longing, longing, for the hills of the Ten-
    nessee.

4.

Oh! for a sight of water, the shadowed slope of a hill!
Clouds that hang on the summit, a wind that never is
    still!
But the level land went stretching away to meet the
    sky,
Never a rise, from north to south, to rest the weary eye!

5.

From east to west, no river to shine out under the moon,
Nothing to make a shadow in the yellow afternoon:
Only the breathless sunshine, as I looked out, all forlorn;
Only the "rustle, rustle," as I walked among the corn.

6.

When I fell sick with pining, we did n't wait any more,
But moved away from the corn-lands, out to this river-
    shore—
The Tuscarawas it's called, sir; off there's a hill, you
    see;
And now I've grown to like it next best to the Ten-
    nessee.

7.

I was at work that morning. Some one came riding
    like mad
Over the bridge and up the road—Farmer Rouf's little
    lad.
Bareback he rode; he had no hat; he hardly stopped
    to say,
"Morgan's men are coming, Frau; they're galloping on
    this way.

8.

"I'm sent to warn the neighbors. He isn't a mile
  behind;
He sweeps up all the horses—every horse that he can
  find.
Morgan, Morgan the raider, and Morgan's terrible men,
With bowie-knives and pistols, are galloping up the
  glen!"

9.

The lad rode down the valley, and I stood still at the
  door;
The baby laughed and prattled, played with spools on
  the floor;
Kentuck was out in the pasture; Conrad, my man, was
  gone.
Near, nearer, Morgan's men were galloping, galloping on!

10.

Sudden I picked up baby, and ran to the pasture-bar;
"Kentuck!" I called—"Kentucky!" She knew me ever
  so far!
I led her down the gully that turns off there to the right,
And tied her to the bushes, her head just out of sight.

11.

As I ran back to the log house, at once there came a
  sound—
The ring of hoofs, galloping hoofs, trembling over the
  ground—
Coming into the turnpike out from the White-Woman
  Glen,
Morgan, Morgan the raider, and Morgan's terrible men.

12.

As near they drew and nearer, my heart beat fast in
  alarm;

But still I stood in the door-way, with baby on my arm.
They came; they passed; with spur and whip in haste they sped along—
Morgan, Morgan the raider, and his band, six hundred strong.

13.

Weary they looked and jaded, riding through night and through day;
Pushing on east to the river, many long miles away,
To the border-strip where Virginia runs up into the west,
And fording the Upper Ohio before they could stop to rest.

14.

On like the wind they hurried, and Morgan rode in advance;
Bright were his eyes like live coals, as he gave me a sideways glance;
And I was just breathing freely, after my choking pain,
When the last one of the troopers suddenly drew his rein.

15.

Frightened I was to death, sir; I scarce dared look in his face,
As he asked for a drink of water, and glanced around the place.
I gave him a cup, and he smiled—'t was only a boy, you see;
Faint and worn, with dim-blue eyes; and he'd sailed on the Tennessee.

16.

Only sixteen he was, sir—a fond mother's only son—
Off and away with Morgan before his life had begun!
The damp drops stood on his temples; drawn was the boyish mouth;
And I thought me of the mother waiting down in the South.

17.

Oh! pluck was he to the backbone, and clear grit through
  and through;
Boasted and bragged like a trooper; but the big words
  would n't do;—
The boy was dying, sir, dying, as plain as plain could be,
Worn out by his ride with Morgan up from the Tennessee.

18.

But when I told the laddie that I too was from the
  South,
Water came in his dim eyes, and quivers around his
  mouth.
"Do you know the Blue-Grass country?" he wistful
  began to say;
Then swayed like a willow-sapling, and fainted dead
  away.

19.

I had him into the log house, and worked and brought
  him to;
I fed him, and I coaxed him, as I thought his mother'd
  do;
And when the lad got better, and the noise in his head
  was gone,
Morgan's men were miles away, galloping, galloping on.

20.

"Oh, I must go," he muttered; "I must be up and away!
Morgan—Morgan is waiting for me! Oh, what will
  Morgan say?"
But I heard a sound of tramping and kept him back
  from the door—
The ringing sound of horses' hoofs that I had heard
  before.

21.

And on, on, came the soldiers—the Michigan cavalry—
And fast they rode, and black they looked, galloping rapidly,—
They had followed hard on Morgan's track; they had followed day and night;
But of Morgan and Morgan's raiders they never had caught a sight.

22.

And rich Ohio sat startled through all those summer days;
For, strange, wild men were galloping over her broad highways—
Now here, now there, now seen, now gone, now north, now east, now west,
Through river-valleys and corn-land farms, sweeping away her best.

23.

A bold ride and a long ride! But they were taken at last.
They almost reached the river by galloping hard and fast;
But the boys in blue were upon them ere ever they gained the ford,
And Morgan, Morgan the raider, laid down his terrible sword.

24.

Well, I kept the boy till evening—kept him against his will—
But he was too weak to follow, and sat there pale and still.
When it was cool and dusky—you'll wonder to hear me tell—
But I stole down to that gully, and brought up Kentucky Belle.

25.

I kissed the star on her forehead—my pretty, gentle lass—
But I knew that she'd be happy back in the old Blue-Grass.
A suit of clothes of Conrad's with all the money I had,
And Kentuck, pretty Kentuck, I gave to the worn-out lad.

26.

I guided him to the southward as well as I knew how;
The boy rode off with many thanks, and many a backward bow;
And then the glow it faded, and my heart began to swell,
As down the glen away she went, my lost Kentucky Belle!

27.

When Conrad came in the evening, the moon was shining high;
Baby and I both were crying—I couldn't tell him why—
But a battered suit of rebel gray was hanging on the wall,
And a thin, old horse with drooping head, stood in Kentucky's stall.

28.

Well, he was kind, and never once said a hard word to me;
He knew I couldn't help it—'t was all for the Tennessee.
But, after the war was over, just think what came to pass—
A letter, sir; and the two were safe back in the old Blue-Grass.

The lad got over the border, riding Kentucky Belle;
And Kentuck she was thriving, and fat, and hearty, and well;
He cared for her and kept her, nor touched her with whip or spur.
Ah! we've had many horses since, but never a horse like her!

CONSTANCE F. WOOLSON.

25. THE CHARCOAL MAN.

1. Though rudely blows the wintry blast,
   And sifting snows fall white and fast,
   Mark Haley drives along the street,
   Perched high upon his wagon seat;
   His somber face the storm defies,
   And thus from morn till eve he cries,—
   "*Charco'! charco'!*"
   While echo faint and far replies,—
   "*Hark, O! Hark, O!*"
   "*Charco'!*"—"*Hark, O!*"—Such cheery sounds
   Attend him on his daily rounds.

2. The dust begrimes his ancient hat;
   His coat is darker far than that;
   'T is odd to see his sooty form
   All speckled with the feathery storm;
   Yet in his honest bosom lies
   Nor spot nor speck,—though still he cries,—
   "*Charco'! charco'!*"
   And many a roguish lad replies,—
   "*Ark, ho! ark, ho!*"
   "*Charco'!*"—"*Ark,-ho!*"—Such various sounds
   Announce Mark Haley's morning rounds.

3. Thus all the cold and wintry day
   He labors much for little pay;
   Yet feels no less of happiness
   Than many a richer man, I guess,
   When through the shades of eve he spies
   The light of his own home, and cries,—
       "*Charco'! charco'!*"
   And Martha from the door replies,—
       "*Mark, ho! Mark, ho!*"
   "*Charco'!*"—"*Mark, ho!*"—Such joy abounds
   When he has closed his daily rounds.

4. The hearth is warm, the fire is bright;
   And while his hand, washed clean and white,
   Holds Martha's tender hand once more,
   His glowing face bends fondly o'er
   The crib wherein his darling lies,
   And in a coaxing tone he cries,
       "*Charco'! charco'!*"
   And baby with a laugh replies,—
       "*Ah, go! ah, go!*"
   "*Charco'!*"—"*Ah, go!*"—while at the sounds
   The mother's heart with gladness bounds.

5. Then honored be the charcoal man!
   Though dusky as an African,
   'Tis not for you, that chance to be
   A little better clad than he,
   His honest manhood to despise,
   Although from morn till eve he cries,—
       "*Charco'! charco'!*"
   While mocking echo still replies,—
       "*Hark, O! hark, O!*"
   "*Charco'!*"—"*Hark, O!*"—Long may the sounds
   Proclaim Mark Haley's daily rounds.   <small>TROWBRIDGE.</small>

26. GRANDMOTHER'S STORY OF BUNKER HILL.

[*The spirited rendering of this graphic picture affords a wide scope for variety of expression. Care must be taken not to overdo it.*]

1.

'T is like stirring living embers when, at eighty, one remembers
All the achings and the quakings of "the times that tried men's souls";
When I talk of *Whig* and *Tory*, when I tell the *Rebel* story,
To you the words are ashes, but to me they're burning coals.

2.

I had heard the muskets' rattle of the April running battle;
Lord Percy's hunted soldiers, I can see their red coats still;
But a deadly chill comes o'er me, as the day looms up before me,
When a thousand men lay bleeding on the slopes of Bunker's Hill.

3.

'T was a peaceful summer's morning, when the first thing gave us warning
Was the booming of the cannon from the river and the shore:
"Child," says grandma, "what's the matter, what is all this noise and clatter?
Have those scalping Indian devils come to murder us once more?"

4.

Poor old soul! my sides were shaking in the midst of all my quaking,
To hear her talk of Indians when the guns began to roar:

She had seen the burning village, and the slaughter and the pillage,
When the Mohawks killed her father with their bullets through his door.

5.

Then I said, "Now, dear old granny, don't you fret and worry any,
For I'll soon come back and tell you whether this is work or play;
There can't be mischief in it, so I won't be gone a minute"—
For a minute then I started. I was gone the livelong day.

6.

No time for bodice-lacing or for looking-glass grimacing;
Down my hair went as I hurried, tumbling half-way to my heels;
God forbid your ever knowing, when there's blood around her flowing,
How the lonely, helpless daughter of a quiet household feels!

7.

In the street I heard a thumping; and I knew it was the stumping
Of the Corporal, our old neighbor, on that wooden leg he wore,
With a knot of women round him,—it was lucky I had found him,
So I followed with the others, and the Corporal marched before.

8.

They were making for the steeple,—the old soldier and his people;

The pigeons circled round us as we climbed the creaking stair,
Just across the narrow river—O, so close it made me shiver!—
Stood a fortress on the hill-top that but yesterday was bare.

9.

Not slow our eyes to find it; well we knew who stood behind it,
Though the earthwork hid them from us, and the stubborn walls were dumb:
Here were sister, wife, and mother, looking wild upon each other,
And their lips were white with terror as they said, THE HOUR HAS COME!

10.

The morning slowly wasted, not a morsel had we tasted,
And our heads were almost splitting with the cannons' deafening thrill,
When a figure tall and stately round the rampart strode sedately;
It was PRESCOTT, one since told me; he commanded on the hill.

11.

Every woman's heart grew bigger when we saw his manly figure,
With the banyan buckled round it, standing up so straight and tall;
Like a gentleman of leisure who is strolling out for pleasure,
Through the storm of shells and cannon-shot he walked around the wall.

12.

At eleven the streets were swarming, for the red-coats'
    ranks were forming;
At noon in marching order they were moving to the piers;
How the bayonets gleamed and glistened, as we looked
    far down and listened
To the tramping and the drum-beat of the belted gren-
    adiers!

13.

At length the men have started, with a cheer (it seemed
    faint-hearted),
In their scarlet regimentals, with their knapsacks on
    their backs,
And the reddening rippling water, as after a sea-fight's
    slaughter,
Round the barges gliding onward blushed like blood
    along their tracks.

14.

So they crossed to the other border, and again they
    formed in order;
And the boats came back for soldiers, came for soldiers,
    soldiers still:
The time seemed everlasting to us women faint and
    fasting,—
At last they're moving, marching, marching proudly up
    the hill.

15.

We can see the bright steel glancing all along the lines
    advancing—
Now the front rank fire a volley—they have thrown
    away their shot;
For behind their earthwork lying, all the balls above
    them flying,
Our people need not hurry; so they wait and answer not.

16.

Then the Corporal, our old cripple (he would swear sometimes and tipple),—
He had heard the bullets whistle (in the old French war) before,—
Calls out in words of jeering, just as if they all were hearing,—
And his wooden leg thumps fiercely on the dusty belfry floor :—

17.

"Oh! fire away, ye villains, and earn King George's shillin's,
But ye'll waste a ton of powder afore a 'rebel' falls;
You may bang the dirt and welcome, they're as safe as Dan'l Malcolm
Ten feet beneath the gravestone that you've splintered with your balls!"

18.

In the hush of expectation, in the awe and trepidation
Of the dread approaching moment, we are wellnigh breathless all;
Though the rotten bars are failing on the rickety belfry railing,
We are crowding up against them like the waves against a wall.

19.

Just a glimpse (the air is clearer), they are nearer,—nearer,—nearer,
When a flash—a curling smoke-wreath—then a crash—the steeple shakes—
The deadly truce is ended; the tempest's shroud is rended;
Like a morning mist it gathered, like a thunder-cloud it breaks!

20.

O the sight our eyes discover as the blue-black smoke
  blows over!
The red-coats stretched in windrows as a mower rakes
  his hay;
Here a scarlet heap is lying, there a headlong crowd is
  flying
Like a billow that has broken and is shivered into
  spray.

21.

Then we cried, "The troops are routed! they are beat—
  it can't be doubted!
God be thanked, the fight is over!"—Ah! the grim old
  soldier's smile!
"Tell us, tell us why you look so?" (we could hardly
  speak, we shook so),—
"Are they beaten? *Are* they beaten? ARE they beaten?"
  —"Wait a while."

22.

O the trembling and the terror! for too soon we saw
  our error:
They are baffled, not defeated; we have driven them
  back in vain,
And the columns that were scattered, round the colors
  that were tattered,
Toward the sullen silent fortress turn their belted breasts
  again.

23.

All at once, as we are gazing, lo the roofs of Charles-
  town blazing!
They have fired the harmless village; in an hour it will
  be down;
The Lord in heaven confound them, rain his fire and
  brimstone round them,—

The robbing, murdering red-coats that would burn a peaceful town!

24.

They are marching, stern and solemn; we can see each massive column
As they near the naked earth-mound with the slanting walls so steep.
Have our soldiers got faint-hearted, and in noiseless haste departed?
Are they panic-struck and helpless? Are they palsied or asleep?

25.

Now! the walls they're almost under! scarce a rod the foes asunder!
Not a firelock flashed against them! up the earthwork they will swarm!
But the words have scarce been spoken, when the ominous calm is broken,
And a bellowing crash has emptied all the vengeance of the storm!

26.

So again, with murderous slaughter, pelted backwards to the water,
Fly Pigot's running heroes and the frightened braves of Howe;
And we shout, "At last they're done for, it's their barges they have run for:
They are beaten, beaten, beaten; and the battle's over now!"

27.

And we looked, poor timid creatures, on the rough old soldier's features,
Our lips afraid to question, but he knew what we would ask:

"Not sure," he said; "keep quiet,—once more, I guess,
  they'll try it—
Here's damnation to the cut-throats!"—then he handed
  me his flask,

28.

Saying, "Gal, you're looking shaky; have a drop of
  old Jamaiky;
I'm afeard there'll be more trouble afore the job is
  done;"
So I took one scorching swallow; dreadful faint I felt
  and hollow,
Standing there from early morning when the firing was
  begun.

29.

All through those hours of trial I had watched a calm
  clock-dial,
As the hands kept creeping, creeping,—they were creep-
  ing round to four,
When the old man said, "They're forming with their
  bagonets fixed for storming:
It's the death-grip that's a coming,—they will try the
  works once more."

30.

With brazen trumpets blaring, the flames behind them
  glaring,
The deadly wall before them, in close array they come;
Still onward, upward toiling, like a dragon's fold un-
  coiling,—
Like the rattlesnake's shrill warning the reverberating
  drum!

31.

Over heaps all torn and gory—shall I tell the fearful
  story,

How they surged above the breastwork, as a sea breaks
o'er a deck;
How, driven, yet scarce defeated, our worn-out men re-
treated,
With their powder-horns all emptied, like the swimmers
from a wreck?

32.

It has all been told and painted; as for me, they say
I fainted,
And the wooden-legged old Corporal stumped with me
down the stair:
When I woke from dreams affrighted, the evening lamps
were lighted,—
On the floor a youth was lying; his bleeding breast
was bare.

33.

And I heard through all the flurry, "Send for WARREN!
hurry! hurry!
Tell him here's a soldier bleeding, and he'll come and
dress his wound!"
Ah, we knew not till the morrow told its tale of death
and sorrow,
How the starlight found him stiffened on the dark and
bloody ground.

34.

Who the youth was, what his name was, where the
place from which he came was,
Who had brought him from the battle, and had left
him at our door,
He could not speak to tell us; but 'twas one of our
brave fellows,
As the homespun plainly showed us which the dying
soldier wore.

35.

For they all thought he was dying, as they gathered
  round him crying,—
And they said, "O, how they'll miss him!" and, "What
  will his mother do?"
Then, his eyelids just unclosing like a child's that has
  been dozing,
He faintly murmured, "Mother!"—and—I saw his eyes
  were blue.

36.

—"Why, grandma, how you're winking!"—Ah, my child,
  it sets me thinking
Of a story not like this one. Well, he somehow lived
  along;
So we came to know each other, and I nursed him like
  a—mother,
Till at last he stood before me, tall, and rosy-cheeked,
  and strong.

37.

And we sometimes walked together in the pleasant sum-
  mer weather;
—"Please to tell us what his name was?"—Just your
  own, my little dear,
There's his picture Copley painted: we became so well
  acquainted,
That—in short, that's why I'm grandma, and you chil-
  dren all are here!

HOLMES.

www.ingramcontent.com/pod-product-compliance
Lightning Source LLC
Chambersburg PA
CBHW051247300426
44114CB00011B/929